Michael Zwz

POLITICS AND CLASS IN ZAIRE

Bureaucracy, Business, and Beer in Lisala

Michael G. Schatzberg

AFRICANA PUBLISHING COMPANY

A division of Holmes & Meier Publishers, Inc.

NEW YORK   LONDON

To the Memory of My Father

First published in the United States of America 1980 by
Africana Publishing Company,
a division of Holmes & Meier Publishers, Inc.
30 Irving Place
New York, N.Y. 10003

Great Britain:
Holmes & Meier Publishers, Ltd.
131 Trafalgar Road
Greenwich, London SE 10 9TX

Library of Congress Cataloging in Publication Data

Schatzberg, Michael G
    Politics and class in Zaire.

    Bibliography: p.
    Includes index.
    1. Zaire—Politics and government—1960–   —Case
studies.   2. Lisala, Zaire (Equateur)—Politics and
government.   3. Social classes—Zaire—Lisala (Equateur).
4. Social mobility—Zaire—Lisala (Equateur)   I. Title.
JQ3616.S32 1979   320'.9675'103   79-11852

ISBN 0-8419-0438-3

Manufactured in the United States of America

Contents

Page

Tables

Page

Acknowledgments

This book was begun over five years ago at the University of Wisconsin—Madison when I was first faced with the necessity of conceiving, researching, and writing a doctoral dissertation in political science. Throughout this lengthy gestation period I have been aided by many people and institutions, both at home and abroad. Since much of what I have to say may be seen—at least in some quarters—as politically sensitive, it must be stressed that ultimate responsibility for any misplaced facts or misguided interpretations is mine alone. Indeed, many of those who have graciously shared their knowledge of Zairian politics and society disagree with some of the points of view I have expressed.

I would nevertheless be remiss not to mention the boundless encouragement, enthusiasm, and optimistic good cheer of Crawford Young. He has generously shared his comprehensive knowledge of Zairian politics and has spent many hours, gently and patiently, trying to disabuse me of some of my more outrageous ideas. Jan Vansina offered detailed comments on all parts of the manuscript; his keen insights have saved me from more than one serious error. Fred Hayward, Dennis Dresang, David Henige, Bakonzi Agayo, Goran Hyden, and an anonymous reader for the Africana Publishing Company have also furnished valuable critiques and suggestions. Okello Oculi, Louis Picard, and the tavern-keepers of three continents have contributed—each in his own way. I am grateful for their assistance.

This study would not have been possible without the support and encouragement of many Zairian officials and ordinary citizens. Their hospitality is legendary and their respect for learning is genuine. I thank them for making my task easier by allowing me to share, for a short time, their lives and experiences. Although I would like to thank individually all those who aided me in Zaire, professional considerations require the preservation of their anonymity. To this end, interviews are listed by number and most documents are cited as administrative correspondence. Unless noted otherwise, all documents were consulted in the Archives of Mongala Subregion, Political Affairs Department, Lisala.

Funding for fieldwork in Zaire and Belgium was provided by a Fulbright-Hays Doctoral Dissertation Fellowship from the United States Office of Education. The task of writing was facilitated by a National Defense Foreign Language Title VI Fellowship. This generous support made the project possible. While I was in Zaire, research affiliation and institutional support were accorded by the Université Nationale du Zaire (UNAZA), the Faculté des Sciences Sociales at Lubumbashi, and the Centre d'Etudes Socio-politiques pour l'Afrique Centrale (CEPAC).

Finally, I would like to dedicate this work to the memory of my father, Jerome Schatzberg. Had he lived to see this book, I like to think that he would have been critical of its content yet proud of its author.

Michael G. Schatzberg
Madison, Wisconsin
July 1978

Abbreviations

ABAKO	Alliance des Bakongo
ANEZA	Association Nationale des Entreprises Zairoises
CEC	Centre Extra-Coutumier
CEPAC	Centre d'Etudes Socio-politiques pour l'Afrique Centrale
CND	Centre National de Documentation
CPM	Contribution Personnelle Minimum
CRISP	Centre de Recherches et d'Information Socio-politique
CVR	Corps des Voluntaires de la République
INEP	Institut National des Etudes Politiques
JMPR	Jeunesse du Mouvement Populaire de la Révolution
MPR	Mouvement Populaire de la Révolution
ONACER	Office National des Céréales
ONAFITEX	Office National des Fibres Textiles
ONATRA	Office National des Transports du Zaire
ONB	Office National du Bois
ONC	Office National du Café
PUNA	Parti de l'Unité Nationale
UNAZA	Université Nationale du Zaire
UNTZa	Union Nationale des Travailleurs Zairois

CHAPTER 1
Introduction

If the fact will not fit the theory—let the theory go.
—Hercule Poirot[1]

In some respects, this is a study I did not expect to write. The dependent variable, the political dynamics of class formation, is one I did not set out to examine. Initially I had been impressed with a body of literature that seemed to be emerging both in political science and in anthropology. Although in the early 1960s political scientists had paid primary attention to macropolitics, with little reference to local areas, and anthropologists had been interested in micropolitics, by the mid-1960s and early 1970s both disciplines appeared to be moving toward a synthesis of the macro- and micropolitical perspectives. I had read, and been influenced by, the work of Colin Leys on Acholi, Joel Samoff on Moshi, David Brokensha on Larteh, Maxwell Owusu on Swedru, and Nicholas Hopkins on Kita. Almost all these authors were concerned to some degree with the interactions and relationships between national and local politics.[2]

To cloak this interest in theoretical garb, I adopted the linkage framework of James Rosenau, who defines linkage as any "recurrent sequence of behavior that originates in one system and is reacted to in another." The aim was therefore to study linkages between the national poltical system and the local political system. Richard Stryker's work on the Ivory Coast had made the point that linkages must be conceived as a dual process. They may be initiated on either the national or the local level.[3] This, too, seemed to make sense.

Specifically I hoped to select a town in a predominantly rural area in which the central government had some administrative presence. The idea was to go to this town and determine who belonged to the local elite and in what policy areas they were interested. Based upon the research cited above, I believed that education, health, and agriculture would be likely areas of concentration. Once the policy-issue areas were isolated, I would interview members of the local elite as well as representatives of the national government in the town. I hoped to learn what the perceptions of each group were concerning the policy areas chosen. I would then proceed to the national capital, where I would consult ministry officials concerned with the policy areas and any well-placed representatives of the local elite in positions of influence and authority in the government. Once again, the aim was to see what the perspectives of these two groups of actors were. My intention was to include both the micro- and macropolitical perspectives.

This approach was firmly rooted in the theoretical writings of the

Committee on Comparative Politics of the Social Science Research Council. In the committee's collective volume, *Crises and Sequences in Political Development*, much attention is paid to what these scholars call the "penetration crisis"—a condition that is resolved when a polity can display "effective presence of a central government throughout a territory over which it pretends to exercise control." Once penetration has occurred, one of the necessary conditions for political development is present.[4]

Although the linkage framework was useful in launching my research and pointed me in the direction of some intriguing political phenomena, its applicability to the Zairian context soon proved highly limited. It could not cope with the extraordinary degree of governmental centralization. The degree of national-local interpenetration was so great that it was impossible even to isolate a local elite. It also failed to illuminate successfully questions of resource distribution. Finally, I soon discovered that attention to linkages could shed little or no light on the complex subject of class formation. Thus, like Hercule Poirot, I found that the facts did not fit the theory, and the theory was let go.

Chapter 2 presents my intellectual quest for a more appropriate and enlightening theoretical framework. The result, an unconventional contextual approach to class analysis, is one I believe will be useful in the study of politics in Zaire as well as in other African and Asian countries. Chapter 3 assesses the influence of the colonial system on the dynamics of class formation, with special emphasis on the question of social mobility over time. Local administration at the collectivity level, perhaps the most oppressive arm of government in Zaire, is treated in chapter 4. Collectivities directly administer the population and form the main point of contact between the Zairian state and its people. Here, stress is laid on the ways in which village farmers are systematically denied access to life and mobility chances, and on the ways in which they are prevented from rising in the social hierchy.

The degree of interpenetration between the political and commercial sectors is then evaluated. Chapter 5 is a case study of the political economy of beer. Chapter 6 is devoted to the development, role, and functions of the Mouvement Populaire de la Révolution (MPR). Chapter 7 discusses the economic reforms of 30 November 1973, when Zairians took over expatriate plantations and commercial houses. Throughout chapters 5, 6, and 7, care is taken to demonstrate the ways in which a numerically restricted, but politically powerful, minority has acted to promote its own economic interests at the expense of the majority of the population. Chapter 8 returns to the theoretical questions discussed in chapter 2 and pays particular attention to the thorny problem of class consciousness. In almost every chapter the themes of insecurity and scarcity are central. Some conclusions are drawn and the major contradictions of the Zairian polity are indicated in chapter 9.

For an understanding of the data base from which this study has been derived, brief introductions are furnished to the place where the research evolved and to the procedures employed.

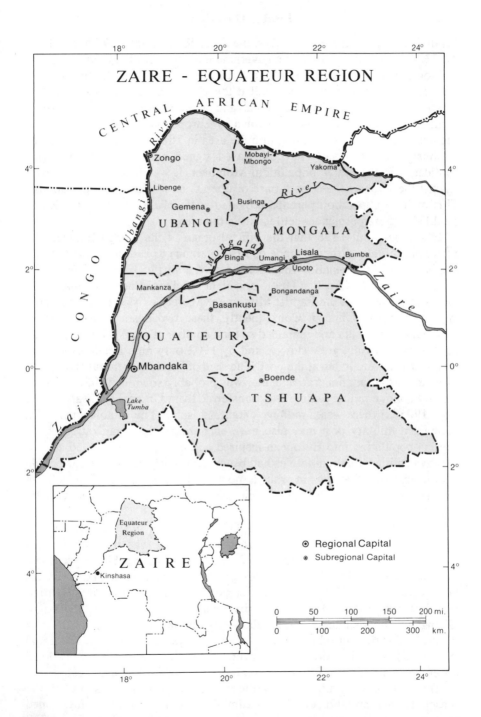

ZAIRE - EQUATEUR REGION

CENTRAL AFRICAN EMPIRE

CONGO

Zongo

Libenge

Mobayi-Mbongo

Yakoma

Ubangi River

Businga

Gemena

UBANGI

MONGALA

River

Mongala

Binga

Umangi

Lisala

Bumba

Upoto

Zaire

Mankanza

Bongandanga

Basankusu

EQUATEUR

Mbandaka

Boende

Zaire

Lake Tumba

TSHUAPA

Equateur Region

ZAIRE

Kinshasa

⊙ Regional Capital
⊛ Subregional Capital

| 0 | 50 | 100 | 150 | 200 mi. |
| 0 | 100 | 200 | 300 | km. |

Lisala: Overview

Lisala is in Equateur Region and on the Zaire River at lat. 2°9" N and long. 21°31" E.[5] First and foremost a government center, Lisala is today the seat of Mongala Subregion and the Zone of Lisala. In addition, it is the site of a local-level urban administration called the *Cité* of Lisala. Lisala's primary functions have always been political and administrative rather than economic. The earliest mention of the town by Europeans probably occurs in an account of a military expedition into the area in 1888, when an outpost was established at "Issala." The post was designed both to pacify and give confidence to the native population. Moreover, it was to serve as a barrier against the Arabs as well as a base of operations for further explorations.[6] This military expedition perhaps provided some of the stimulus needed to establish a more permanent settlement in the area.

It was not until 1898 that the official organ of the Congo Independent State, the *Bulletin Officiel*, made its first reference to Lisala, noting that the post's European population then consisted of a single Belgian. There were two Belgians and a Greek at Upoto and eight Belgians at nearby Umangi. At that time a station of the Baptist Missionary Society existed at Upoto and a military camp at Umangi. Consequently, these two posts were then more important than Lisala and remained so for a number of years.[7] The expatriate population of Lisala grew slowly, and by 1902 only nine Belgians and one Swiss citizen were living at the post. The seed of Lisala's eventual emergence as an important administrative center was probably sown in 1905, when the Force Publique military camp was transferred from Umangi to Lisala. Thus, from 1905 on there was a military detail at Lisala.[8] The establishment of a permanent military post may also have encouraged the organization of the Zairian population into European-inspired and European-controlled administrative entities. Such initiatives had been begun fairly early with the people who lived along the river in what is now the town of Lisala. In 1908 the Belgians organized the Bapoto into four chieftaincies: Upoto, Lisala, Gunda, and Mongo.[9]

Lisala had been part of Bangala District since 1895, and in 1911 it became the district headquarters when the capital was transferred from Nouvelle Anvers (now Mankanza) to Lisala "to facilitate public services and for reasons of hygiene."[10] From this point on, Lisala remained a district headquarters. In 1933 Bangala District gave way to Congo-Ubangi District, but Lisala retained its administrative preeminence. Similarly, in 1956 Congo-Ubangi was divided anew, but Lisala remained the headquarters of the new Mongala District. In addition, Lisala has always been the site of a zonal (territorial) administration.[11] Moreover, in 1935 a new unit of the local government, the Centre Extra-Coutumier (CEC) of Lisala, was created.

The territorial administrator's preliminary report noted some of the reasons for the formation of this new administrative level. First, he mentioned the numerical importance of the population—at that time totaling 1,338 Africans. Second, he argued the benefits of controlling the population by administrative and police regulations that would replace those prevalent in traditional society, which no longer obtained in the town. Third, he believed the creation of a CEC in Lisala would comply with the often expressed wishes of the population to have one. These may or may not have been valid reasons for creating a CEC. Undoubtedly there was at least one other question of no little importance to the Belgians. In October 1935, only seven months after the establishment of the center, it was decided to raise taxes in all the province's CECs. Thus, in Lisala surtaxes of 10 percent, 10 percent, and 20 percent were placed on the capitation tax, the supplementary tax, and the personal tax, respectively. Taxation, a crucially important subject, is treated in more detail in chapter 4.[12]

From 1935 on, Lisala harbored three levels of administration: the district, the territory, and the CEC. This continued throughout the period following independence, although there was some alteration during the *provincette* period (1963–66) when the district was suppressed and Lisala became the provincial capital of Moyen-Congo. With Mobutu's seizure of power and the subsequent reunification of the provinces, Moyen-Congo was reintegrated into Equateur and Lisala once again became the seat of Mongala District.[13] Because the names of various levels in the Zairian administrative hierarchy were changed in 1972, table 1 lists both the old and the new terms.

TABLE 1
ZAIRIAN ADMINISTRATIVE HIERARCHY AND
CHIEF EXECUTIVE OFFICERS, PRE- AND POST-1972

Pre-1972		Post-1972	
Administrative Level	*Chief Executive Officer*	*Administrative Level*	*Chief Executive Officer*
Province	Governor	Region	Regional commissioner
District	Commissioner	Subregion	Subregional commissioner
Territory	Territorial administrator	Zone	Zone commissioner
Sector[a]	Chief	Collectivity[b]	Chief
Chieftaincy[a]	Chief	Collectivity	Chief
Centre extra-coutumier (CEC), or *cité*[a]	Chief	Collectivity	Chief
Groupement (several villages) or quarters[c]	Chief	Locality	Chief
Village	Chief or elder	Sublocality	Chief or elder

[a]Sectors, chieftaincies, and CECs (*cités*) all corresponded to one level in the hierarchy.
[b]Term came into use in 1969.
[c]Subdivisions of collectivities that were once CECs.

TABLE 2

LISALA'S POPULATION GROWTH, 1935–74

Year	Men		Women	Boys		Girls	Total
1935	718		498	289		252	1,757
1937	590		415	235		247	1,487
1938	621		577	292		259	1,749
1944	763		446	236		237	1,682
1946	790		808	434		368	2,400
1947	902		962	539		504	2,907
1948	843		892	469		452	2,656
1949	987		932	539		513	2,971
1950	1,106		1,110		1,251		3,467
1951	1,397		1,345		1,584		4,326
1953	1,582		1,451		1,885		4,918
1954	1,553		1,464		1,878		4,895
1956	1,952		1,768		2,415		6,135
1957	1,926		1,808		2,991		6,725
1958	2,504		2,339		3,967		8,810
—a	—	—	—		—		—
1969		7,369			11,483		18,852
1970		7,941			12,289		20,230
1971		7,815			12,647		20,462
1972		8,049			12,608		20,657
1973	5,238		6,041	7,317		7,270	25,866b
1974	5,471		6,090	8,232		7,896	27,689

SOURCE: Colonial figures are from the *Rapport annuel sur l'administration de la Colonie du Congo belge présenté aux Chambres législatifs,* 1935–58. 1969–73 data are from Zone de Lisala, *Rapport annuel des affaires politiques,* 1969–73, in Archives, Mongala Subregion, Political Affairs Department, Lisala. 1974 figures are from "Tableau synoptique, Zone de Lisala, 1974."

aFigures for decade 1959–68 could not be located, no doubt because of periods of administrative chaos brought on by independence, *provincettes,* and rebellions.

bThere seems to be a discrepancy between totals for 1972 and 1973. In general, post-independence figures must be taken as vague indicators rather than precise data. Although impossible to verify, figures given probably have an error margin of two to three thousand on either side.

Lisala's population growth over the years is shown in table 2. Since 1958 the town's population has more than tripled.

As a government center, Lisala draws its population from all over the surrounding areas of the subregion. Although it is virtually impossible to obtain current data on the ethnic composition of the town, ethnic breakdowns for Lisala's population are available for the colonial epoch.[14] Table 3 presents the data for 1934, the year before Lisala became a CEC.

Table 3 shows, not surprisingly, that in 1934 most people in Lisala came

TABLE 3

LISALA'S POPULATION BY ETHNIC GROUP, 1934

Ethnic Group	Territory of Origin	Men	Women	Boys	Girls	Total	%
Ngombe	Lisala	209	161	66	65	501	37.44
	Gombe	26	16	5	6	53	3.96
Budja	Budja	34	25	11	19	89	6.65
Bwaka [Ngwaka]	Bwaka	10	6	6	7	29	2.16
Ngbandi [Mongwandi]-Banza	Ngbandi	30	17	8	9	64	4.78
Others	Thysville	7	6	6	12	31	2.31
	Ngiri	6	5	—	—	11	0.82
	Uélé	11	9	3	6	29	2.16
	Lulonga	19	12	1	3	35	2.61
	French Equatorial Africa	8	8	2	1	19	1.42
River peoples	Lokele	42	37	27	24	130	9.71
	Yaolema	18	11	11	5	45	3.36
	Basoko	45	39	27	17	128	9.56
	Libinza	17	18	6	7	48	3.58
	Akula	22	20	7	11	60	4.48
Total		537	408	194	199	1,338	99.93

SOURCE: Archives, Equateur Region, Political Affairs Department, Mbandaka. Political Affairs Dossier, Centre de Lisala, "Proposition en vue de la création du Centre Extra-Coutumier de Lisala," 4 October 1934, Territorial Administrator Denis.

from the town's immediate hinterland. The Ngombe alone account for 41 percent of the population; 18 percent are represented by the Budja, Ngwaka, and Mongwandi-Banza groups. Moreover, in that year 31 percent of Lisala's inhabitants were River peoples, who are primarily fishermen. The presence of Sudanic-speaking groups like the Ngwaka and the Mongwandi-Banza may partially be explained by the historical pattern of migrations in northern Equateur. A major study of these migrations has yet to be undertaken, and knowledge of these phenomena is necessarily scanty. In brief it can be said that beginning in the eighteenth century, the Ngombe were pushed south by the Mongwandi. Their migrations and intermittent wars with the Mongwandi lasted from approximately 1750 to 1850, but these population movements were more or less frozen by the subsequent European encroachment and colonization. There is some evidence that had the Europeans not appeared on the scene, these migrations would have continued.[15] By the mid-1930s Lisala was already an administrative center of some importance and had a natural attraction for peoples already living in the area.

The notion of an administrative center drawing its population from out-lying areas is somewhat confirmed by data on the ethnic composition of Lisala in 1958. In the figures presented in table 4, it should be noted that the

TABLE 4

LISALA'S POPULATION BY ETHNIC GROUP, 1958

Ethnic Group	Men	Women	Boys	Girls	Total	%
Ngombe	912	925	781	762	3,380	48.36
Ngwaka	240	226	201	214	881	12.60
Mongwandi	138	121	104	95	458	6.55
Mongo	165	139	105	100	509	7.28
Budja	195	178	87	88	548	7.84
Fishermen						
Lokele	77	54	50	63	244	3.49
Basoko	72	71	67	64	274	3.92
Yaolema	22	16	13	21	72	1.03
Libinza	21	15	16	16	68	0.97
Akula	85	85	73	81	324	4.63
Miscellaneous	81	40	62	47	230	3.29
Total	2,008	1,870	1,559	1,551	6,998[a]	99.99

SOURCE: Archives, Equateur Region, Political Affairs Department, Mbandaka. Political Dossier, Centre de Lisala, "Rapport d'enquête relative au Centre Extra-Coutumier de Lisala," 12 August 1958, Territorial Administrator L. K. Spits.

[a]Discrepancy between this figure and that cited in table 2 may be due to use of different criteria. All statistics must be viewed as tentative.

relative importance of the Ngombe in the population of Lisala remained fairly constant between 1934 and 1958, when they constituted 48 percent of the town's people. On the other hand, the percentage of non-Ngombe ethnic groups from Equateur—such as the Ngwaka, Mongwandi, Mongo, and Budja—increased from 18 to 34. Furthermore, there was a decline in the proportion of fishing populations in Lisala: In 1934 they constituted close to 31 percent of the city's inhabitants, but only 14 percent in 1958. These changes notwithstanding, it may be said that during the colonial period Lisala's ethnic composition was generally characterized by a Ngombe core and an important presence of other major groups from Equateur. There is no reason to believe this situation has changed since independence.[16]

Lisala's hinterland is primarily agricultural. In 1974 the Zone of Lisala produced 76,143 tons of palm products; 9,992 tons of cotton; 6,692 tons of rubber; 3,551 tons of rice; 1,616 tons of cocoa; 1,586 tons of coffee; and 77 tons of peanuts.[17] Most of the palm and rubber production was accounted for by several extremely large plantations, about which more will be said later. The majority of the zone's farmers cultivate rice, cotton, or coffee in addition to staple food crops like manioc and bananas. Cash crops are exported to Kinshasa via the Zaire River. Economically, the Lisala area (and indeed all of Equateur) may be viewed as a logistical appendage of Kinshasa. This has been true since the colonial era; for example, the province's 1957 economic report noted that Mbandaka and the entire region of Equateur were "suburbs" of the capital.[18] The orientation toward the capital was ably summarized by one of Equateur's provincial governors, M. De Ryck:

> Although Equateur has land, men, and capital, I think that Léopoldville's presence is too close and the Province's perfect accessibility by a navigable network naturally oriented toward the capital constitutes a great handicap. The continual amelioration of barge transportation . . . works in this direction.[19]

This was still true in 1974–75, during the period of my stay in Lisala. The town was linked to the capital by twice-weekly river boats. There were also four or five Air Zaire flights per week.

Politically, as well as economically, Lisala has almost always been linked to Kinshasa. In addition to the reasons discussed above, the entire area was subjected to a rather intense missionary effort by the Belgian Scheutist fathers. These Catholic missionaries had a near monopoly on education in the area and often encouraged students to continue studies in Kinshasa. This later resulted in an active and articulate "Bangala" presence in Kinshasa and in Zairian politics.[20]

In 1974 Lisala had a recorded population of 27,689. Because of numerous imprecisions in the existing data and the general problem of conflicting sources, it is difficult to assemble an accurate picture of the town's occupational structure. Table 5 shows that in addition to its role as an administrative nodal point, Lisala functions as an educational center of some importance. There are ten primary schools and as many secondary schools in the city, accounting for the large percentage (36.15) of the population attending school.[21] In this chapter Lisala's importance as an administrative city has been stressed. This is not reflected in table 5 because only 3.15 percent of the townspeople actually work for the state. Administrative dominance is reflected in other ways, however; the administration's grip on the town's economic resources, its dominance of the educational system, and its interpenetration of the commercial sector are discussed at some length in later chapters. This, in brief, is the town of Lisala as I found it in 1974–75.

Procedures

Lisala was chosen with a linkage framework in mind. Initially, however, I had intended to work in either Mbandaka or Kisangani. A visit with Professor Jan

TABLE 5

LISALA'S OCCUPATIONAL STRUCTURE, 1974

Category	Subcategory	No.	%	Total	%
1. Non-school children				6,117	22.09
2. Schoolchildren	Primary	5,361	19.36		
	Secondary	4,650	16.79		
				10,011[a]	36.15
3. Housewives				6,090[b]	21.99
4. Fishermen				1,143[c]	4.12
5. Salaried workers	Agriculture	5	0.01		
	Commerce	87	0.31		
	Transport	72	0.26		
	Office	375	1.35		
	Construction	113	0.40		
	Miscellaneous	918	3.31		
				1,570	5.67
6. State-employed	Bureaucrats	443	1.59		
	Parastatals	145	0.52		
	Teachers	250	0.90		
	Soldiers	36	0.13		
				874[d]	3.15
7. Merchants	Commercial register	31	0.11		
	Small traders	90	0.32		
				121[e]	0.43
8. Unemployed				1,763[f]	6.36
				27,689	99.96

[a]Figures on schoolchildren were provided by JMPR census of school population in Lisala. Total was subtracted from total number of children in Lisala to infer how many children were not in school. These data (and data in this table) must be considered estimates.

[b]Approximately 200 prostitutes are probably subsumed in this figure.

[c]Derived from male population of fishing quarter in Lisala, this figure is probably an overestimate.

[d]There may be some overlap between salaried workers and state-employed. Number of teachers is an estimate.

[e]Number of small traders without stores and not inscribed on the commercial register is also an estimate.

[f]Calculated by adding all other categories and subtracting figure from total population. Because of obvious dangers in this procedure, number should be treated cautiously.

SOURCE: Figures on youth (1, 2) are furnished by untitled JMPR census. (JMPR is the youth wing of the MPR.) Statistics on housewives (3) and fishermen (4) are taken from "Tableau synoptique, Zone de Lisala, 1974." Number of salaried workers (5) may be found in Zone de Lisala, *Rapport annuel des affaires politiques,* 1974, p. 28.

Vansina, then at Louvain, convinced me that perhaps the national-local linkages in a regional capital would be too intense and therefore much more difficult to isolate and study. He suggested that I select a smaller, subregional center instead. When I arrived in Zaire, I asked about facilities and prevalent situations in subregional centers in Equateur. (Equateur has largely been ignored by contemporary scholars, and I had already begun a study of Lingala, the region's main lingua franca.) I ultimately chose Lisala as my primary research site because of the ease with which it could be reached and because it was an area that had given birth to many national leaders.

Because most of the research was done in Lisala and the study is not, strictly speaking, a comparative one, there are several theoretical and methodological issues that merit discussion. First, can we generalize from these data? To what extent are the following findings, suggestions, hints, and musings applicable to other parts of Zaire? In general, I am confident that the data and interpretations presented in the succeeding pages are relevant to most of northern Equateur Region—specifically, Mongala and Ubangi subregions. They are probably applicable to the rest of Equateur as well. Although Zaire is a vast and extraordinarily diverse country, the vestiges of a common colonial heritage and the centralization that has occurred under the Mobutu regime provide the analyst with broad strata of comparable structures and processes. The processes described here are undoubtedly relevant to other parts of the country, although care will have to be exercised because regional and local peculiarities are often important. Second, at some points it will be necessary to take a broader view of the Zairian polity and discuss national policies and their effects on the situation in Lisala. No Zairian locality sits in splendid isolation. Processes of class formation in Lisala cannot be divorced from a broader national perspective. It is hoped that the reader will find the national and local foci felicitously and persuasively interwoven. Moreover, many themes and trends set forth here—though perhaps in a less pointed form—may be equally germane to other parts of Africa.

In purely methodological terms, this study is based upon three methods of data collection that political scientists have traditionally used to study African politics. First, I was fortunate to have some access to the archives and documents of Mongala Subregion in Lisala. I was given a desk in the documents room as well as the unstinting cooperation of Lisala's official community. In addition to reading documents pertaining to the town of Lisala, I consulted those concerning the five zones and twenty-two other collectivities that make up Mongala Subregion. Additional time was spent in

Number of state-employed (6) is derived from numerous administrative documents and from some figures provided by UNTZa, the trade union. Merchants (7) who are inscribed on the commercial register may be found in Archives, Mongala Subregion, Political Affairs Department, Lisala, "Liste des petites et moyennes entreprises zairoises à Lisala," 28 August 1974.

Mbandaka, Kinshasa, and Brussels, where other related materials were studied.

Second, I had numerous opportunities to attend political and administrative meetings in Lisala. There were also frequent occasions to interact informally with bureaucrats, merchants, political officials, and ordinary citizens of the town. These interactions, usually after working hours, contributed greatly to an understanding of Lisala's social dynamics. I was often able to record impressions and conversations in a field log; where possible, this log has been cited as a documentary source.

Third, seventy-three formal interviews were conducted with most of the town's important people: twenty-three subregional service chiefs, fourteen lower-level clerks (zone and *cité*), eleven territorial commissioners (zone and subregion), five party bureaucrats, five educational personnel (inspectors and secondary school principals), thirteen merchants, and two churchmen. The interviews averaged ninety minutes. Numerous respondents agreed to sit for additional sessions, which were usually characterized by frankness and an interchange of ideas. I am confident that the sample—which was not randomly selected—is representative.

Throughout the study, Joel Samoff's impressive book *Tanzania: Local Politics and the Structure of Power* served as something of a methodological guide.[22] Moreover, readers familiar with the extensive body of literature on postindependence Zairian politics will undoubtedly note some mechanical similarities between my study and the school of immediate history that has sprung up around the numerous works of Benoît Verhaegen.[23] This theoretical approach, as well as others, is examined in more detail in chapter 2, which deals with the contextual dimension of social class.

CHAPTER 2
Class and Context

> *By and large the seriously socialistic wing of the NCNC
> sided with Azikiwe. In their view, the national president
> as a man was incorrigibly bourgeois, but as a symbol of
> the national movement and as a leader of the NCNC, he
> was radical, populist, and even worthy of devotion. It
> should be clear by now that Azikiwe's career does not fit
> easily into the traditional Marxian framework of socio-
> political analysis. How does one classify a populist
> banker whose political support lies primarily in the
> peasantry and the working class, and not in the new
> elite of which he is supposed to be the epitome?*
> —Richard L. Sklar[1]

How, indeed? This question, posed fifteen years ago by a perceptive analyst of
Nigerian politics, remains germane today. Similar cases of political actors who
refuse to adhere to the theoretical dictates of their position in the class structure
are quite common and could be cited for virtually every African country.
Unfortunately, failure to deal with what might be called the "Azikiwe paradox"
has generally resulted in two problems. On the one hand, certain analysts of a
doctrinaire Marxist persuasion have chosen to ignore the paradox. This often
results in an excessive reliance on ownership of the means of production an as
explanatory crutch. The famous Marxian variable is thought to explain
everything, and deviations from the master's predictions are simply attributed to
false consciousness. All this is done at the cost of violence to the facts.

The second problem is the mirror image of the first. Political analysts of the
pluralist persuasion have noted the paradox (or other shortcomings of Marxist
theory) and have decided to ban class from their conceptual lexicon. This, too, is
done at the risk of distorting the facts. Why these two strands of thought have
sprung up and why they have existed in isolation from each other will be
discussed later. For the moment, my purpose is to set forth a possible
explanation of the Azikiwe paradox. To achieve this I shall first comment on
some of the particular problems that students of Zairian politics have
encountered in their quest for theory and the frameworks that have resulted from
their efforts. The extraordinarily fluid and shifting nature of postindependence
Zairian politics confronts would-be theorists with only the slickest surface on
which to erect their analytic structures. In addition, because class analysis is no
newcomer to the study of Zairian politics, an attempt will be made to place some
earlier work in perspective. Some of the broader philosophical and empirical
problems involved in the adoption of class as an analytic framework must also be

raised. Finally, relying heavily upon the work of European anthropologists and sociologists, I shall present a situational, or contextual, notion of class and class consciousness. Under this rubric, definitions of social class and class action will be put forward and discussed.

Zaire: Frameworks and Issues

In the methodological appendix to *Politics in the Congo*, Crawford Young notes that the fruitful application of any conceptual framework depends on the existence of an agreed-on body of data. Although his work went a long way toward filling this gap, Young's position at that time was essentially atheoretical. He did not embrace any particular model of political change for organizing his data because, in his view, none then evolved provided a "felicitous scheme for scaling the significance of the multifold facts pressing for the attention of the student of Congo politics."[2] Whether this position was justified at that time is beyond the scope of my concern here, and in fairness it must be mentioned that Young has subsequently moved away from this point of view.[3] Even if it were true then, it may not be true now. Although at present no single political theory can completely explain the complexity of politics in Zaire, it is nonetheless incumbent on researchers to provide readers with the information on which conclusions are based as well as a theoretical framework that permits meaningful interpretation of their finding.

There is a twofold responsibility for the analyst of Zairian politics. First, as a social scientist, the analyst should illuminate and further elucidate—however imperfectly—an aspect of the fundamental ambiguity of the human condition. The Azikiwe paradox presents just such an opportunity. Second, as a political scientist, the analyst should begin to develop a conceptual framework that can shed light on the exceptional fluidity of politics in Zaire. Let me add here that Young is correct on this point. Change and flux are indeed the crucial aspects of politics in Zaire. Moreover, in this situation, "the task of seeking comprehension of the dynamic would seem to merit priority over rigorous analysis of the static."[4]

Zaire's chaotic political history has provided analysts with a remarkable challenge. A hastily arranged and ill-conceived decolonization, the massive departure of Belgian personnel, the revolt of the Force Publique, the Katanga secession and the intervention of the United Nations, the division of the country into four autonomous and competing poles of authority, the ethnic polarization common during the *provincettes*, the Mulelist and Eastern rebellions, the November 1965 military coup, and the subsequent course of events under the Second Republic are diverse political phenomena that are difficult to subsume under any one theoretical rubric.[5]

Serious, sustained attempts to do so have been made, however. One of the most important and ambitious of these has been the continuing efforts of Verhaegen and his students, who have called their approach "immediate history." Verhaegen's aim is to present a qualitative methodology, and he defines immediate history as a discipline at the confluence of history, anthropology, and sociology, [which] has as its object the scientific knowledge of contemporary societies, insofar as these are in crisis and engaged in a more and more conscious manner in the practical transformation of their conditions of existence.[6]

This school of thought deals with contemporary society because it is a living history, which presupposes that those who have shaped and experienced the past can still be interviewed. In addition, only societies in flux and crisis are thought to be suitable for this methodology. Immediate history also depends heavily on the dialectical method, which Verhaegen believes to be "absolute and permanent." Commitment to the dialectic ensures that scholars are not cut off from the people they study and that they are actively engaged not only in trying to explain social phenomena, but also in trying to transform the world.[7] Verhaegen's approach is noteworthy for its emphasis on movement, its attention to crisis, and its concern with what political actors say and think.[8] Certainly Zaire has been characterized by flux, and a certain dynamism will have to be built into any conceptual framework that hopes to explain this aspect of Zairian society.

Jean-Claude Willame has selected a different way of dealing with the fluidity of the Zairian polity. His *Patrimonialism and Political Change in the Congo* represents an intriguing effort to comprehend Zairian politics by imposing a Weberian framework on it. Denying that the Zairian experience is unique,[9] Willame seeks to impose order by applying the patrimonial formulas of Max Weber. Briefly, the key elements in this idea are that patrimonialism is a system of rule in which the appropriation of political office is the elite's major source of prestige and reward; territorial fragmentation develops through the salience of primordial and personal loyalties; and private armies, militias, and mercenaries are the chief instruments of rule.[10] The rebellions that swept through Zaire in the mid-1960s resulted in the breakdown of decentralized patrimonial authority and sired the Mobutu regime, or what Willame chooses to call a "Caesarist bureaucracy." This is "a type of rule characterized by a single authority figure at the head of a bureaucratic governmental structure."[11]

In general, although Willame's work is a laudable attempt to solve the puzzle of the polity's perpetual motion, it ultimately misses the mark. The study is overconceptualized. There are important aspects of Zairian politics that simply will not be poured into the Weberian mold. As stated earlier, no theory can account for everything. This is understandable. What is not understandable, however, is Willame's attempt to relate diverse, irrelevant, and un-Weberian politial phenomena to his central tenets. His chapter on conditions for political change, for example, correctly stresses the international dimension of domestic politics as well as the difficulties inherent in Zaire's largely dependent position vis-à-vis Western capital. This is an important point and certainly needs to be mentioned, but it stretches the imagination to suppose that it has anything whatever to do with the author's patrimonial framework. It is only one more proof that political science can make strange bedfellows as easily as politics. These two strands of thought, patrimonialism and dependency, rest in uneasy juxtaposition throughout the study.[12] I would argue, too, that by failing to relate Weber's notion of closure to events in Zaire, Willame has missed a key Weberian concept that could be of great utility. More will be said of this later.

The efforts of Verhaegen and Willame contain much that is useful, stimulating, and valuable. Any conceptual framework, however, must ultimately pass the acid test: Does it successfully illuminate the information at hand? In answering this question one must admit that a host of factors comes into play. The researcher's personal preferences, ideological orientations, and general view of the world and the people in it certainly play a role. The importance of these predispositions should not be minimized, the canons of American social science notwithstanding. Although the approaches of Willame and Verhaegen explain certain aspects of politics in Lisala, if either framework were adopted in its entirety, many important political processes would be missed. But these gaps will not be so great if social class is used as an organizing principle.

Class Analysis and Zairian Politics

A study of class analysis and the uses to which it has been put in Zaire should begin with the colonial period. In general, the preindependence writing on class in Zaire was preoccupied with indigenous merchants and artisans—with emphasis on their wealth and political loyalty and on whether they constituted a middle class. This question was asked with a practical rather than an academic frame of reference. As Mukenge Tshilemalema has pointed out, the colonial concern was to elaborate the role this middle class might play in the continuation of Belgian rule in Zaire. Or, in Mukenge's words, "In what way could the African Middle Class constitute an element of social stability and peaceful cohabitation between blacks and whites in a Belgo-Congolaise community?"[13]

The studies of the middle class cited above indicate that the Belgians did not tend to include Zairian priests, clerks, primary school teachers, and others who worked for the state under this rubric. In short, the crucially important *évolués* were not perceived as being part of any middle class. Indeed, one post-independence analyst, Paule Bouvier, makes the same distinction, explicitly excluding those white-collar workers who were directly dependent on the colonial state from consideration in the middle class. She reserves this category for those merchants and artisans who were able to maintain some independence from the colonial administration. She thus observes that the Zairian middle class of the 1950s had its origins in the commercialization and development of indigenous agriculture on the one hand, and in the extension of commerce and artisanal activities in the urban centers on the other. At independence this so-called middle class was poorly organized, numerically weak, and without any significant economic power.[14] Her reasons for arbitrarily distinguishing between the independent artisans and traders, on the one hand, and the *évolués* and state employees, on the other, escape me because both groups had similar economic levels. In political terms, moreover, the *évolués* were far more important, and the members of this group were to form the core of the dominant elements in Zairian politics under the First Republic.

Other scholars, however, have been extremely concerned with the important role played by the *évolués* in the struggle for independence and in the immediate aftermath of decolonization. Young, for example, notes that "elite satisfaction was the central issue in colonial policy."[15] The term *évolués* was vague, and the criteria for being accepted as a member of this group probably varied from place to place in Zaire; inclusion may have depended on some kind of outward acceptance or labeling of the status either by the European missionaries or by the administrators.[16] What is clear, though, is that by the end of World War II the number of *évolués* was large enough to constitute a distinct social grouping. Roger Anstey even suggests that in some respects their behavior displayed certain characteristics of class consciousness. Indeed, the *évolués* were acutely aware of belonging to a group completely distinct from the mass, and they profoundly desired to be accepted as equals by the Europeans or, failing this, to be treated differently from the majority of their compatriots. Their goals were a closer association with Europeans as well as a separate status. By the late 1940s the *évolués* increasingly had the means to emulate the life-style of their most salient reference group, the European colonialists. This, of course, had important social and political consequences when independence was obtained and members of this group moved to fill the administrative and political vacuum left by the departing Belgians.[17]

In all the works cited thus far, even though the words *class* and *middle class* are bandied about, there is almost no attempt to define these terms analytically. Nor is there the slightest effort to relate the position either of the merchants and artisans or of the *évolués* and clerks to the totality of Zairian society. For this latter task we are indebted to Christian Comeliau and Jean-Louis Lacroix. Comeliau's work, *Fonctions économiques et pouvoir politique,* is a case study of the *provincette* of Uélé in 1963–64. Unwilling to resort to the term *class*, he describes the social "groups" present in Uélé during that period. Eight groups are mentioned; the criterion for delineating the position of each group is its relation to the monetary economy.

Comeliau's first group is the Europeans, who still controlled much of the area's economic activity. The second is the bourgeoisie, which includes both independent merchants and cadres in the pulic and private sectors. Unlike some previously cited authors, Comeliau emphasizes the importance of the politico-administrative section of the bourgeoisie, which he considers the most highly differentiated of all the Zairian social groups. In his opinion it is only this group in which one can discern the existence of a social class in formation. The core of this group is all those, especially the *évolués*, who moved into places that had previously been occupied by the Europeans.[18] Comeliau's third group, the "underbourgeoisie," is composed of the lower levels of the state administrative machinery and salaried workers in the private sector. Merchants and other independents form the fourth group; the fifth contains the stabilized urban mass, particularly the salaried manual workers. Salaried agricultural workers on European plantations are placed in the sixth group. Comeliau's last two groups have little or no contact with the modern cash economy. Specifically, they include the members of rural traditional society and the urban unemployed—especially the young.[19]

Comeliau correctly notes that this kind of classification presents some dangers. First, the criterion of participation in the monetary economy results in the crystallization of a complex and shifting reality into a static table. The danger here is that it becomes all too easy to ignore the *evolution* of these groups. Second, the author observes that multiple allegiances, participation, and attitudes characterize a social situation in transition. It thus becomes difficult to place each individual in an exact location in any outline of social groups. I find this point particularly suggestive and shall return to it.[20]

Jean-Louis Lacroix has also tried to present a more global view of Zairian society since independence. Like Comeliau, Lacroix refuses to use the word *class*. An agnostic in this regard, he states it is beyond his competence to determine whether postcolonial Zairian society has classes, or whether these putative social classes have succeeded in integrating social groups to their complementary interests. He does maintain, however, that the notion of class is far richer than that of group and that class consciousness is more or less a prerequisite of class formation.[21]

Nonetheless, Lacroix obligingly provides us with a list of social groups. First, there are the foreign enterprises that control the principal means of production, with the exception of land. Capitalist companies and foreign colonials are included in this category. Members of the second social group are foreigners earning salaries whose interests tend to be associated with the owners of capital. In the third social group there are salaried Zairians who work for the private sector. Fourth, there are those Zairians who own their own means of production and who produce goods and services for the domestic market. These are primarily peasants, transporters, artisans, and some entrepreneurs. All intermediaries, foreign and national, who are responsible for lengthening the nation's distributive circuits compose the fifth group. Zairian peasants who produce for export and are unusually involved with crops, such as cotton, palm, and coffee, form the sixth group. The seventh and last group contains all those who drink from the public trough: politicians and their clients, administrators, teachers, soldiers, and police.[22]

A number of points should emerge from the preceding few pages. Unlike Comeliau, Lacroix's criterion for designating his social groups seems to be their relation to the means of production. Like Comeliau, Lacroix seems impressed with the degree of overlap between certain of the social groups he has delineated. He mentions that there is a certain osmosis between politicians and their clients on the one hand, and between merchants and entrepreneurs on the other. Moreover, he underlines the vagueness of the boundaries separating the intermediaries from other social groups and particularly those holding political power.[23] The imprecision of group boundaries—or of class boundaries, for that matter—receives more detailed attention later. For the moment, it may be noted that although both Comeliau and Lacroix have tried to encompass the totality of

Zairian society with their seven or eight social groups, neither has made use of social class as an organizing principle. But some analysts have tried to apply this notion to Zairian politics and society and, of these, Nzongola-Ntalaja is among the keenest.

In 1970 Nzongola published an article entitled "The Bourgeoisie and Revolution in the Congo."[24] Beginning with a review of the relevant Marxist literature, he basically accepts the definition of class set forth by Marx in the third, and uncompleted, volume of *Das Kapital*. The identity and source of revenues thus become one of the keys in the theoretical structure he wishes to elaborate. Nzongola then tries to apply this notion to a specific historical and social situation, the political events that led to Zairian independence in 1960. To do this he first refers to the social groups delineated by Comeliau and then to the widespread political perceptions and vocabulary used in Zaire. There is thus an attempt to include both subjective and objective elements in his picture of the Zairian class structure.

He emphasizes five terms in the Zairian political vocabulary: intellectuals, workers, traders, villagers, and unemployed. The intellectuals correspond roughly to Comeliau's bourgeoisie; traders refer to merchants and other independents; workers subsume both the urban and agricultural salaried employees that Comeliau discusses; villagers are the peasantry, or cash crop farmers and others in the countryside; and the unemployed refer to adults and youth who have no permanent position in the monetary economy.[25]

Nzongola then distills these social groups and social categories into five social classes. The national bourgeoisie includes politicians, bureaucrats, cadres, independent entrepreneurs, and wealthy traders. The second class, the petty bourgeoisie, corresponds roughly to Comeliau's underbourgeoisie and is composed of clerks, teachers, nurses, soldiers, and policemen. The working class encompasses rural and urban salaried workers, and village farmers are in the peasantry. Finally, the fifth class includes the lumpenproletariat, or the unemployed. He recognizes that the five social classes do not emerge evenly in their pure form and that this accounts for the discrepancies in their relative importance as sociopolitical forces. In basing his social classes on the social groups put forth by Comeliau, Nzongola notes that these groups can be considered classes-in-themselves, which have recognizable structures. They may, if conditions merit, become classes-for-themselves through political organization and the development of class consciousness. Nzongola elects to use the word *class* because of its value in the analysis of social change and political conflict.[26]

In his later and more elaborate study of urban administration in Kananga, Nzongola advances essentially the same class structure of Zairian society. In this work, however, he seems to place greater weight upon objective elements in determining his social classes, and the criteria used are externally observable. Using residential neighborhood and means of transportation as empirical indicators, social classes are easily discernible in the city of Kananga.[27] Once again, five classes are present. First, there is the national bourgeoisie, which includes political, military, and judicial authorities; wealthy merchants and entrepreneurs; managers or top bureaucrats of parastatal enterprises or private firms; senior civil servants; secondary school principals; and expatriate teachers. This class was exclusively European before independence and is filled today by those who were *évolués* under colonial rule or by postindependence university graduates. In general they live in modern houses, have at least one domestic servant, and have at least one car.

The second class is composed of traders and independent artisans who have employees; middle-level bureaucrats and lower-level political authorities; secondary school teachers; nurses; and primary school principals. Nzongola assigns these people to the petty bourgeoisie and notes that although many of them have modern houses, they are usually smaller than those occupied by the national bourgeoisie. The motorbike is their most common form of locomotion.

Somewhat strangely, Nzongola does not elaborate on the three remaining classes, which, after all, contain most of the Zairian population. The proletariat is made up of skilled workers, low-level administrative clerks, salespeople, and unskilled workers who have some job tenure and security. The lumpenproletariat contains domestic servants, petty traders, petty artisans, unemployed school leavers, as well as hard-core unemployed. Finally, there are the peasants and agricultural producers who live in the rural quarters of Kananga. Nzongola does not mention what kind of housing or transportation these three lower classes enjoy, but it is safe to assume that they live in the poorer sections of the city, do not live in concrete houses, and own no means of transportation other than perhaps a bicycle. The influence of these three poorer social classes is not felt on the workings of the urban administration.[28]

Nzongola's treatment of urban administration in Kananga is both exciting and depressing—exciting because it represents a major effort to apply class analysis to Zairian society, depressing because the attempt is only partially successful. Despite the author's reluctance to discuss his ideas on class and class structure at length, there is an attempt to relate the study to the literature on Marxism and the role of the state. Althought the first part of his work is well elaborated, he fails to link this macrotheory with the microdata presented on the workings of administration in Kananga. While he lists lower administrative clerks as members of one of the three exploited classes, much of the second part of his work is an examination of the ways in which these officials exploit those who are lower than themselves in the sociopolitical pecking order. There are thus paradoxes that are not resolved in terms of the Marxist theory Nzongola sets forth. To explain these, he resurrects Fred Riggs' view of administration in developing countries.[29] Moreover, the links between the various classes are never really detailed or explained. Thoughtful theory and intriguing data are uncomfortably coupled, and the whole is thus less than the sum of its parts. Last, the fluid nature of class composition in Zairian society is not dealt with in terms of the situation in Kanaga. But as will be shown, some of these problems are not insurmountable and could be overcome with a contextual approach to class analysis.

While Nzongola has devoted his attention to the urban areas, other class analysts have focused on the rural sectors of Zairian society. Notable in this respect is the work of Paul Demunter, *Luttes politiques au Zaire*. Demunter's study is a conventional Marxian attempt to treat the historical dimensions of class formation in Ngeba Sector in Bas-Zaire. The author sees the history of colonialism in Zaire as essentially the decline of precolonial modes of production before the onslaught of the "universal expansion of the capitalist mode of production."[30] He argues that many of the seeming inconsistencies in colonial policy can be explained by realizing the Belgians had neither the means nor the personnel to effect an immediate and massive shift from one mode of production to another. They were, for example, forced to rely on indigenous chiefs; although their legal texts demanded respect for traditional society and its institutions, their agents often subverted and weakened these same social arrangements when it became necessary to expand capitalist relations. Village elders were to be respected, but were never consulted when Ngeba Sector was formed, even though the colonial statutes required it.[31]

At the end of his book Demunter describes the class structure he finds characteristic of First Republic Zaire. Unfortunately these pages are added almost as a postscript and are not really an integral part of the preceding analysis. In short, he perceives a Zairian oligarchy—a petty bourgeoisie composed of merchants, transporters, and salaried workers in rural areas; and a peasantry. Demunter's work is occasionally stimulating, but often disappointing for his analysis fails to capture the dynamic processes of rural class formation and the fluidity of the Zairian situation. Moreover, with the exception of the rise of the *évolués*, he does not come to grips with the important question of social mobility and closure. Demunter does call our attention to the fact that the Zairian oligarchy does not own the means of production. Rather, its economic advantages come from control of key positions in the state apparatus.[32]

Class: Some Analytic Problems

Were it asserted that, broadly speaking, class analysis of African politics has had an undistinguished track record, there probably would be little disagreement. There are reasons for this and not all of them have to do with the analytic properties of the concept. Immanual Wallerstein believes that class analysis in Africa has had a somewhat "shaky" history. In his view, before World War II most students of politics and society did not wish to apply an essentially European term to a new and very different situation in Africa. The lone exceptions, it seems, were French Marxists. They applied the term *class*, but in a far too mechanical way; in general their efforts along these lines were unconvincing. The early years of African independence brought with them two phenomena. On the academic side there emerged among younger European and American scholars a liberal-modernist-pluralist school of thought. These students of African politics were interested primarily in modernization, nation building, integration, elites, and political development. Class was not perceived as an important part of the nascent pattern of politics. On the political side the rush to independence brought with it the political dominance of a number of African leaders who claimed that class was a divisive concept and a foreign ideology, not at all suited to Africa, where, of course, there were not any classes at all. Lost in the confusion, excitement, and expectations of the early 1960s was the realization that this position on the existence and applicability of social class invariably served to bolster the political fortunes of the ruling groups in the new nations.[33] What occurred, then, was a situation in which the political needs and rhetoric of African politicians coincided with the ideological predispositions of many students of African affairs. This observation is neither new nor startling. Georges Balandier, for one, has noted that the idea of social classes in the African context has often been confused by ideological considerations.[34] In a similar vein, Colin Leys writes that

> people who can swallow words like "charisma" and "integration" (or indeed "modernization") without flinching sometimes have a surprisingly strong aversion to some others, such as . . . "class" or "oppression."[35]

Another important reason for the generalized failure of class analysis on the African scene is the overall complexity of African society. In addition to the citation from Sklar's work that began this chapter, Leys' writings might also be mentioned. He notes:

> Any attempt to present Kenyan politics purely in terms of antagonism between classes tends to appear artificial. This is partly because of the difficulty of finding Kenyan equivalents for the most familiar Marxian class categories. While it may be possible to talk of an embryonic haute bourgeoisie, it is extremely difficult to speak intelligibly about a proletariat, and the classic problem of analysing the all-important and diverse socio-political characteristics of the peasantry must always be solved afresh in this context; while all of these concepts tend to obscure the equally obvious patterns of relationships based on lineage and locality which cut across the objective bases of class identification.[36]

Leys' observations are relevant; his points are well taken. This does not mean, however, that it is impossible to utilize class analysis in the study of African politics. Unfortunately, some analysts have noted these diverse and most non-Marxian phenomena and have decided that class is not important in the political dynamics of African society. R. H. Jackson, for example, believes that most African societies have only one class, the one that governs. He arrives at this conclusion because he insists on a strict application of class consciousness and the emergence of political organizations to represent the interests of the diverse classes. In his view, then, to make class analysis meaningful, social groupings must have already been transformed into classes-for-themselves. These conditions are rarely met. Furthermore, concerning the general applicability of class analysis in societies that are largely rural and unindustrialized, he argues that both the social ranking of groups and the articulation of political interests tend to follow cultural channels that reflect principles of social structure significantly different from those that most industrialized class societies rest upon.[37]

By asserting that "political interests tend to follow cultural channels," Jackson is maintaining that in Africa ethnicity is a key sociopolitical phenomenon that cannot always be subsumed under the rubric of class, and properly so. Ethnicity is a widespread phenomenon in Africa (as in other more industrialized areas of the world), and it is an important variable in its own right.[38] Recognition that "cultural channels" are of great importance should not rule out the possibility that other factors, class among them, may be significant in the analysis of postindependence politics.

It should be apparent that I do not agree with writers like Georges Gurvitch who maintain that classes appear only in industrialized societies.[39] My position resembles that of Anthony Giddens, who believes that

> a class society is not one in which there simply exist classes, but one in which class relationships are of primary significance to the explanatory interpretation of large areas of social conduct.[40]

Throughout this study I argue that Lisala represents a partial microcosmic view of such a class society and that attention to the vagaries of class formation can contribute much to our understanding of political dynamics.

There have thus been heated debates about the applicability, or inapplicability, of the concept of social class in an African context. Unfortunately many writers who have espoused this term have not contributed to its wider acceptance because their analyses are too rigid and lack contextual flexibility.[41] This lack of suppleness can be illustrated by a number of concrete examples. First, intellectuals and their role in the class structure are a case in point. As noted earlier, Nzongola lumps those Zairians who are popularly called intellectuals into the national bourgeoisie. More specifically, they are a

> generalized grouping of all the educated groups, from primary school teachers to highly trained cadres such as medical assistants, doctors, lawyers, scientists, and university professors. It also includes secondary and university students, clerks in public and private employment, and politicians.[42]

Another Zairian, V. Y. Mudimbe, has tried to study intellectuals and their world view. His preliminary results are reported in a short article that appeared in 1974. Although he conducted a sample survey among university graduates and cadres in Kinshasa, there is no indication of what selection criteria he used. Moreover, the total sample size remains a mystery because results are conveyed only in percentages. Mudimbe defines the term *intellectual* more vaguely than Nzongola does and merely notes that both cadres and university graduates qualify.[43]

At first blush there is nothing objectionable about these two definitions. The problem comes only when there is an attempt to relate them to the class structure of the whole society. For example, is an intellectual in Kinshasa the same thing as an intellectual in Lisala? Neither author deals with this question. Ali Mazrui, however, observes that the answer to the question "What is an intellectual?" in large measure depends upon the society at which one looks.[44] In addition, although level of education may have little to do with one's intellect, rightly or wrongly, the more highly literate and industrialized the society, the more formal will be the criteria for inclusion in this category. To carry this line of thought one step further, this same principle might also be applied to different locations within the same society. It thus seems very unlikely that Mudimbe included in his survey those who, in Lisala, would consider themselves intellectuals and, more important, be regarded as such by everyone else. To give only one example, primary school teachers in places like Lisala are widely perceived to be intellectuals. But in Nzongola's definition, it would be practically impossible to include these teachers in the national bourgeoisie even though they are intellectuals; their financial resources are too meager. The basic problem here, then, is a failure to adapt class categories to the diversity of contextual situations, as well as an inability to draw precise class boundaries that accurately reflect situational complexities.

Many writers who have used class in their analyses have found themselves forced to resort to the standard Marxian dichotomy: oppressor versus oppressed. This second rigidity has characterized much of the work done on class. Ralf Dahrendorf writes that theories of conflict have to include only two competing parties, for a two-class model is implied in the very idea of conflict.[45] Indeed, this seems to be the position of many sociologists who have devoted serious thought to the question. Frank Parkin, for example, is concerned with the relationships between the dominant and subordinate classes and with the exploitative nature of these interactions.[46] Aidan Southall states that although a "mere dichotomy is much too crude a term to cope with the empirical realities of complex stratification, . . .we must retain it as a fundamental starting point."[47] Nonetheless, criticisms of the dichotomy are legion. The major one is that dichotomous conceptions of the class structure tend to hinder our vision of the so-called middle classes.[48] In other words, the analytic bifurcation of society into those on the top and those on the bottom can scarcely reflect the complexities of the empirical evidence.

In Lisala there is the policeman who works for the collectivity and makes approximately $16 per month. Chances are good that this policeman will not be paid on time, if at all. To make ends meet, he is likely to extract money or other resources from the farmers who live in his jurisdiction. In this context he is clearly an exploiter. On the other hand, when asked, he might well reply that he is being exploited by the officials who run the collectivity and are unable to pay him regularly because they are pocketing the funds destined for his salary. Here, the same policeman sees himself as exploited by the collectivity chief. Exploiter or exploited? The dichotomy breaks down when confronted with a situation of this kind. Some students might assert that although the objective life conditions and economic status of the policeman are closer to those of the farmers than to those of his masters, he exploits them because he is suffering from false consciousness and has not yet realized his affinity with the other members of his class. Such reasoning neither provides a way out of the dilemma nor contributes significantly to our understanding of human behavior. This argument, moreover, is scarcely subject to empirical refutation.[49]

A third rigidity in much of the work on class in Africa is reflected in an excessive preoccupation with the ownership of the means of production. Property relationships throughout much of Africa are often difficult to reduce to statements of who owns what. This has traditionally been so for land. More recently, however, many African states, including Zaire, have been engaged in ambitious programs of nationalization. As a result of this continent-wide trend, it is becoming increasingly apparent that the "control of the means of production is more important in the current social restratification than effective ownership of the means of production."[50] To put the point more precisely, it might be stated that nationalization has made the traditional question of ownership irrelevant. In addition, control over the means of distribution and exchange merits more attention than it has previously been given, a point Robin Cohen has cogently argued. These factors must be understood to discern the structure of exploitation, and exploitative relationships in Africa may often rest predominantly "on the *control* of the means of production, distribution and exchange, rather than on ownership."[51] Control, not ownership, is the key in contemporary Zaire. Political conflict often centers around control over money-generating enterprises and distributive networks. The case studies of the political economy of beer in chapter 5 and the nationalization of commerce and agriculture in chapter 7 speak directly to these issues.

These concerns lead naturally to a fourth, and final, area of rigidity—the bureaucracy. In classic Marxian terms the bureaucracy, or state, is perceived as "the form in which the individuals of a ruling class assert their common interests."[52] In this view the state does not have an existence independent of the ruling class. This, however, is not borne out in the African context. In Zaire, as in most other African countries, there has been a reversal of the traditional Marxian pattern. Whereas Marx saw political dominance as a manifestation of economic power based on ownership of the means of production, in Zaire such a situation does not obtain. Politico-administrative position and control are often used by those who hold them to increase their personal access to, and control over, the society's economic resources.[53] In this respect Balandier perceives the emergence of a new class, the managers of the modern state. In a similar vein, it has become increasingly obvious that elites are becoming bourgeois far more rapidly than workers are becoming proletarians.[54] One implication of this dynamic is that class consciousness is likely to emerge in the upper levels of the bureaucracy before it does among either farmers or workers. Much of the evidence presented below indicates that this is true in Lisala. The bureaucracy is of crucial importance also because it maintains a monopoly over the society's means of violent control.

The state's coercive capabilities and their effect on the germination of class consciousness are discussed at greater length in chapters 4 and 8.[55]

For a number of reasons much of this study is concerned with the bureaucracy and its role in the political dynamics of class formation. First, the bureaucracy is of crucial import in these dynamics since it now controls most means of production, distribution, and exchange and thus shapes the societal framework in which social relations occur. Second, the coercive capabilities of the bureaucracy are often used to close off upward mobility by village farmers, thereby preserving and hardening certain segments of the class structure. Third, the politico-administrative segment of the population, although small, is politically significant because it is the focal point of much of the fluidity that has characterized the Zairian polity. Furthermore, interviews with village farmers or industrial laborers were not arranged because my early focus on linkage theory did not lead down those paths. The analysis that follows therefore deals—directly or indirectly—with various segments of the bureaucracy and especially with the interconnections between the bureaucrats, on the one hand, and the merchant princes, on the other.

Rigidity and lack of contextual flexibility characterize much of the writing on social class in Africa. Because of the rapid rate of political change since independence, analytic flexibility and contextual awareness would seem to be requisite ingredients of any conceptual orientation that hopes to explain features of Zairian society. In advocating a contextual approach to class analysis, I have been strongly influenced by those social scientists who have successfully noted the complex, shifting, and extremely situational nature of the ethnic phenomenon. Their studies of situational ethnicity provide a starting point for further analysis of social class.

As early as 1961 Paul Mercier observed that all regions of the continent could furnish examples demonstrating that one is not simply a member of a single, immutable ethnic group. Individuals, lineages, and clans are constantly becoming part of new ethnic groupings just as the old groupings are simultaneously disappearing. Relying heavily on a subjective definition of ethnicity, Mercier wrote that an ethnic group could be defined in whatever way its members chose.[56] In Zaire the fluid and nonpermanent aspect of the ethnic structure of society has been persuasively set forth by Jan Vansina, who argued that the "notion of the perennial tribe is meaningless" because tribes appear and disappear—often without population movements or even changes in the "objective cultures" of the relevant communities. A classic example is the division of the Luba-Kasai into Luba and Lulua groups. Before the colonial era the Lulua had had no independent existence.[57] Perhaps the most detailed and empirically convincing case for this argument has been submitted by Crawford Young in *The Politics of Cultural Pluralism*. The central idea behind Young's work is that "the processes of integration and disintegration, and crystallization of identity are dynamic; that the definition and boundaries of cultural groups are fluid rather than static."[58] He presents three relevant propositions.

> (1) The set of groupings which constitute the plurality are not necessarily permanent, frozen collectivities, but in a state of flux in response to long-run forces of social change, shorter-run alterations in the political context, and continuous processes of interaction with other groups; (2) The individual actor is not necessarily assigned by birth to a single cultural aggregate; the possibility exists of two or more simultaneous cultural affiliations or more than one layer of meaningful identity or cultural migration from one identity to another when social circumstance alters; (3) Each cultural aggregate may vary widely in the degree to which its identity pattern is given ideological formulation, ranging from highly developed theories of a group's collective history, cultural heritage, and common destiny to amorphous, ill-formed and only barely manifest self-awareness.[59]

If situational complexities and changing contexts can be incorporated into studies of ethnicity, social class might also benefit from such an approach. First, though, the terminological disputes that surround the concept of class deserve attention.

Class and Context

Dahrendorf has shrewdly observed that the problem of the applicability of the notion of social class is purely terminological.[60] Definitions of social class abound in the literature; they are probably as numerous as those who have investigated the subject. This conceptual minefield must be entered with utmost care. Much of the debate that has raged over the definition of social class has occurred in the shadow cast by Marx. Because Marx's definition was incomplete, those who have followed in his wake have tried to interpret his voluminous writings in such a way as to tease out a consistent meaning. For our purposes here, Marx's classic description of the French peasantry provides us with at least a partial definition of what he meant by social class.[61]

Numerous writers have reflected Marx's concern with economic factors in their own definitions. Typical of these are the works of Poulantzas, Dos Santos, Giddens, and Weber.[62] There are, in addition, scholars who have chosen to stress the internal aspects of the Marxian view in their definitions. Richard Centers is a case in point as is, to a certain extent, Georges Gurvitch.[63] Others, like T. H. Marshall and Frank Parkin, have tended to work a bit farther from the Marxian paradigm and have dealt with class as a component of social stratification.[64] Finally, some authors have used the concept without bothering to define it.[65]

There is a strong temptation to say that throughout this work an undefined concept will be adopted, because there are convincing arguments to be put forward for intellectual flexibility on this subject. Nonetheless, in the following pages social class will be defined as the manifestations of a process by which allied actors obtain or lose, open up or close off, become increasingly or decreasingly conscious of access to life and mobility chances. Because this definition is moderately complex, each component will be explained in detail.

The term *allied actors* refers to political cooperation. These alliances may be either tacit or explicit and probably vary at different points in time and space. Often they may simply take the form of mutual cooperation, according favors to others who might someday be in a position to return them. In general most such alliances are between people who share similar economic lifestyles and enjoy comparable levels of economic wealth, but this is not essential. As we shall see, the exchange of favors that occurs both between bureaucrats and between bureaucrats and merchants is an example of this phenomenon. In addition, it should be noted that there is nothing permanent about such alliances. They may be either long- or short-lived and they are not necessarily mutually exclusive. It is entirely possible to participate simultaneously in any number of alliances. Implicit here is the hypothesis that such alliances will change as the social context does and that class membership—or at least the perceptual, subjective components of it—may shift as the alliances do.

In resorting to life and mobility chances I am, in effect, hoping to include a degree of ambiguity in the definition. In some cases they may constitute access to educational facilities for one's children; in others they may be access to political office, budgetary revenues, taxes, quasi-legal forms of bureaucratic graft, or common indices of wealth such as income or transportation. All these topics are discussed in later chapters. The common thread that unites these diverse themes is a general concern with the economic and social standards of one's self and family. The ways in which such standards may be raised and the obstacles that may tend to prevent this are also important.

The obstacles to better social and economic conditions, or closure mechanisms, will receive detailed attention since they have much to do with social mobility in Zaire. In elaborating this aspect of the definition of social class I have been heavily influenced by Frank Parkin's interpretation of Weber's notion of social closure:

> By social closure Weber means the process by which social collectivities seek to maximize rewards by restricting access to rewards and opportunities to a limited circle of eligibles. This entails the singling out of certain identifiable social or physical attributes as the justificatory basis of exclusion. ... Social closure can be effected by groups located at any level in the stratification order.[66]

Access to opportunities and benefits is far from being wide open in Zaire. Those on top of the social hierarchy are generally intent on maintaining restricted access to the educational, financial, and political rewards the system can offer. In many instances privileged elements will consciously act or decide either to increase their own access to life and mobility chances or to restrict them for others. Later, when discussing access to party office, distribution of beer revenues, and acquisition of nationalized enterprises, we shall comment on this feature of the Zairian system. But at this time such acts or decisions will be defined as class actions. A class action is an act or decision that deliberately aims to increase access to life and mobility chances by either opening them up for self or closing them off for others.

In general these class actions should be perceivable by an outside observer. Although this emphasis on class action deliberately stresses the process-oriented nature of the class phenomenon, there is also a question of structures involved. Through the evolution of manifold factors over time, structures may arise in social situations that tend to reproduce access to life and mobility chances for some while denying them to others. These structures may be manipulated by means of a conscious class action, but they do not always have to be, for latent consequences may have much the same effect as a class action. In chapter 3, for example, we note how access to educational facilities has been translated into high occupational status across three generations. Similarly, in our treatment of local administration we observe the interactions between structures and conscious decisions that create situations in which resources are extracted from the village farmers, thus preventing them from rising in the social system.

To cite Parkin again, the idea of closure

> refers to the *processual* features of class, thereby directing attention to the principles underlying class formation. This processual emphasis gives due acknowledgement to the essential fluidity of class arrangements, something not readily captured by standard dichotomies.[67]

I am particularly impressed with this process-oriented approach to class. Emphasizing class formation as a process makes it possible to deal with the fluidity that is part of any set of social dynamics. This approach, furthermore, is particularly well suited to the Zairian scene, where coping with constant change and flux is a major analytic task.

To this point, only the objective aspects of the definition of social class have been discussed. It will be remembered, however, that a subjective element is also included, and this part of the definition is of equal importance. In varying situations people will become either increasingly or decreasingly aware of the degrees of access they have to life and mobility chances as well as the access enjoyed by others in the society. Such consciousness can be manifested in any number of ways. It may be verbal; it might well be present in associational preferences. Popular language and folk categories are yet other means of tapping this part of the class phenomenon. Political organization is not necessarily a key empirical referent in determining class consciousness. It is entirely likely that people can be conscious of their access to life and mobility chances—of their class—without necessarily banding together to form an organization to represent their interests. Although certain analysts insist on this point, in doing so they fail to consider adequately the repressive role of the state apparatus. In short, people may be fully conscious of their class interests, but still do nothing to further them for fear of the consequences.

Since both objective and subjective dimensions have been included in the definition of social class, it seems appropriate to consider the relations between them. In general the two are initimately connected. Usually, when access to life and mobility chances are either gained or lost, the people most immediately concerned will be conscious of the fact. During my stay in Zaire I was repeatedly impressed by the ability of ordinary folk to see beneath the smoke screen of government publicity and official pronouncements. It seems reasonable to maintain, therefore, that both the objective and subjective elements must be present before there is a social class. In other words, there will have to be both differential access to, and unequal distribution of, life and mobility chances as well as social consciousness of these patterns. The problem we shall have on this score is primarily one of measurement and weighting. How much inequality of access to life and mobility chances should there be to compensate for a low degree of class consciousness? This question cannot be answered with any real precision, as Stanislaw Ossowski reminds us.

> There is no objective measure which would enable one to establish the degree of originality in a work of art which would make up for a degree of technical deficiency. Nor is there an objective measure which could establish the degree of rigidity of class boundaries which could off-set, say, a lack of consciousness. As the criteria are not commensurable, the final decision as to what is and what is not a social class must ultimately be reached by intuitive judgments made in a given milieu about the importance of various criteria.[68]

My own intuitive judgments and sense of the situation will therefore be applied whenever necessary.

The two dimensions of social class interact in another important way. The objective social and economic aspects of the class phenomenon usually provide an overarching framework within which the immediate perceptual dynamics of the class experience occur. In Zaire the basic economic fact of life is scarcity. There are not enough resources to go around, and the existing few are unevenly distributed throughout the society. Jean-Paul Sartre provides insight on this question.

> Exploiter and exploited are men struggling in a system in which *scarcity* is the principal characteristic. Of course, the capitalist possesses work instruments and the worker does not: that is a pure contradiction. But, precisely, this contradiction does not take into account each event: it is the framework, it creates a permanent tension in the social milieu.[69]

Thus, specific political events and phenomena may not be explicable in terms of a pure opposition of interests between those who have and those who do not, but the phenomenon of scarcity does provide a framework in which social dynamics may be understood. Awareness of scarcity often leads to feelings of insecurity. Robin Cohen observes that the "major activity of the ruling groups is an attempt to use the benefits of political power in an attempt to redress the insecure position they find themselves in."[70] One result of this, of course, is the *embourgeoisement* of the ruling elements. This theme is discussed at various points in the study; for the moment, suffice it to say that scarcity and insecurity are the twin engines that motor the social dynamics of the Zairian polity.

The rest of this work will be informed by three propositions: (1) Social classes are constantly changing in response to differing sociopolitical contexts. (2) The individual actor can, and does, belong to differing class alliances at the same time. (3) The degree of class identity will vary depending upon the geographic, social, political, and economic junctures of the moment in question.

We have already seen that other authors have noted complexities in the Zairian class structure that tend to support these propositions. It will be recalled that Anselin observed the rotating composition of the middle class in Lubumbashi; that Comeliau was concerned with the question of multiple allegiances and the problems inherent in placing specific individuals in precise positions in the overall outline of social groups; and that Lacroix had some difficulty in determining group boundaries with any degree of precision. It also seems apparent that these propositions run counter to many of the assumptions that have previously guided students of social class.[71] More specifically, then, the rest of this work will focus on the processes of class formation and dissolution. Indeed, Giddens maintains that the main difficulties in the theory of class can be sought in the "*structuration* of class relationships" and that the most serious gaps in class theory "concern the processes whereby 'economic classes' become 'social classes,' and whereby in turn the latter are related to other social forms."[72] Voicing a similar concern, Lucien Goldmann reminds us that at any given moment social and historical reality "always presents itself as an extremely tangled mixture, not of structures, but of processes of formation and dissolution."[73] Quite simply, classes are constantly appearing and disappearing, a circumstance that exists in both the objective and the subjective dimensions.[74] Once this basic fluidity is accepted as given, it becomes possible to address the question of class boundaries. Giddens has noted that class boundaries have often posed an analytic problem. They are all too often drawn with remarkable precision by those who study various forms of social stratification.[75] If, however, it is possible (and often likely) for one's class to change according to context, the uselessness of such precise schemata and boundary lines quickly becomes apparent. One could no more draw an accurate class map of Zaire than one could draw an accurate ethnic map. Similarly, if these propositions are accepted, it becomes exceedingly difficult to answer the question "How many social classes are there in Zaire?" Comeliau's eight groups, Lacroix's seven groups, Nzongola's five classes, and Demunter's three classes all become meaningless scholastic exercises if we adopt a contextual and process-oriented approach to the study of class.

Such an approach to the study of social class can provide a possible answer to the Azikiwe paradox, which introduced this chapter. It is likely, moreover, that the paradox disappears if one realizes that Azikiwe, like all of us, can best be understood as a creation of his particular context. When the situation shifts, so, too, does an individual's class identity. Azikiwe may well have felt little or no tension in his role as a populist spokesman even if he was a banker, a newspaper editor, and the epitome of the rising new class in Nigeria. The case of the collectivity policeman is similar. Exploiter or exploited? To which class does he belong? The answer would appear to depend upon the political, social, and economic contexts of the moment. It especially depends on whom he interacts with at any particular time. The same might be said of the Kananga clerks. Although Nzongola sees them as members of the oppressed classes, they nonetheless prey on those lower than themselves. But in this case, as in the others, their class identity must be viewed contextually. Viewed from the top down, they are oppressed. Viewed from the bottom up, this is less clear.

This stand on the contextual dynamics of class has some important implications. If a situational approach to questions of class and class formation lead us away from the traditional dichotomies and the usual oppositions posited between different classes, how then should we perceive class conflict? Though difficult to resolve, a partial solution may be found in some of Sartre's writings. Sartre affirms that we should be looking for a "supple and patient dialectic which espouses movements in their truth and which refuses to consider a priori that all conflicts experienced oppose contradictions or even oposites."[76] In other words, there may not be a synthetic resolution that lies beyond the dialectic. This slant on social class successfully illuminates data gathered from Lisala and Zaire. In addition, this way of treating the subject may be of use to others looking at different social situations. Of more immediate importance is the need to relate this notion of class to the Zairian polity in a manner that will permit greater appreciation of the contextual flexibility of class dynamics.

To understand more fully the historical basis of these dynamics it will be necessary to cast a look backward. Balandier believes that the colonial period affected old social structures and implanted the generators of new social classes while at the same time inhibiting their formation.[77] Moreover, since access to mobility chances is one of the theoretical foci selected here, the occupational mobility of families across time ought to be of interest and importance.[78] An examination of the family histories of certain key segments of Lisala's population could, therefore, provide an occasion to gauge this kind of social mobility. In addition, it will provide us with an opportunity to assess the weight of history on the political dynamics of class formation in Lisala.

CHAPTER 3
The Weight of History:
Family Background and Social Mobility

> *Behind the features of the landscape, behind tools or machinery, behind what appear to be the most formalized written documents, and behind institutions, which seem almost entirely detached from their founders, there are men, and it is men that history seeks to grasp. Failing that, it will be at best an exercise in erudition. The good historian is like the giant of the fairy tale. He knows that wherever he catches the scent of human flesh, there his quarry lies.*
>
> —Marc Bloch[1]

The preceding chapter stressed a contextual approach to the politics of class formation in Zaire. It is also important to bear in mind that the current context of politics in Zaire is the result of a concatenation of past events, the perceptions of past events, and the evolution of social structures over time. In this chapter social history is viewed neither in terms of the broad sweep of political currents nor in terms of the lives and actions of a handful of prominent men. Social history ought to be the sum of its individual parts: the stories of the people alive during the era under examination. For Lisala the best way to approach the subject of the weight and influence of the past on the dynamics of class formation is through the career histories of the seventy people I was able to interview formally.[2] Detailed attention will be paid to their lives, careers, and family backgrounds. Throughout, the emphasis will be upon both intra- and intergenerational mobility. How much personal mobility has there been in each career? How much family mobility—up or down—has occurred across generations? These are obviously key questions if one is to deal with access to life and mobility chances in the theoretical context chosen.

To answer these questions seven composite, or modal, career patterns are constructed. These are not the real lives of seven people, but fictional life stories extrapolated from the patterns that emerged from a careful reading of the careers and family histories of my respondents. This protects the anonymity of the people who were kind enough to share their experiences with me. To preserve the flavor and nuance of the interviews, as well as the human dimension, the first-person pronoun has been retained. To be sure, data and generalizations are presented, but it is hoped that readers will find this modal-biographical procedure equally informative.

The seventy respondents fall into six broad groups, based largely upon occupation. Subregional service chiefs, lower-level clerks, territorial commissioners, party bureaucrats, educational personnel, and merchants are dealt with separately. This division conforms to my own sense of the situation, based upon familiarity with the people and the patterns involved. It also corresponds roughly to the way the actors tend to perceive themselves. This self-perception was most apparent every morning at the flag-raising ceremony. The flag is raised and the national anthem sung every workday in front of the subregional and zonal headquarters in Lisala's administrative quarter. Before beginning, all the people present sort themselves and line up according to their occupational status. The territorial commissioners are together, as are the subregional service chiefs. Union officials and magistrates are present in this second group as well, and I have accordingly treated them as service chiefs. The clerks and typists of all departments merge in a third group. A fourth group consists of all the manual workers employed by the Department of Public Works. This group, I was informed, is thought to be representative of "the people." In all these groups there is a physical merging of those who work for the subregion and those who work for the zone. This merger probably occurs on the symbolic level as well because many residents have difficulty in distinguishing the two levels of government.[3]

For the interview respondents not present at this daily ceremony I have been guided by their occupations. I have included those who work for the local collectivity in the group of lower-level clerks. They are similar in terms of career patterns, and there is also much exchange of personnel involved at that level. Educational personnel are not present, either, but it makes sense to group them by occupation. The same can be said for the party bureaucrats and merchants.

Each of the modal career patterns sets forth data on family background, age, ethnic heritage, religious affiliation, educational attainments, professional career, motivations, and salary level. Each pattern is discussed individually, and observations are made concerning the mobility patterns, the interpenetration of the commercial and political sectors, the pervasive sense of insecurity, and the role of education in determining future patterns of access to mobility and life chances.

Subregional Service Chiefs

Twenty-three subregional service chiefs, or at least two-thirds of the people occupying these positions during the time of my stay in Lisala, were interviewed. Because the N for this group is relatively large, two modal career patterns will be examined. The first, career pattern A (N = 11), represents those who joined the administration before 1960. The second, career pattern B (N = 12), is typical of those who joined after independence.[4]

Pattern A

I was born in 1930, toward the end of that year, in a small village about forty-five kilometers from Mbandaka. My native language is Lomongo; I am a Mongo of Equateur. I never saw my grandfather, but I was told he was a man who just lived in the village. He had his fields and he fished a bit, too. My father was a carpenter for the state. He was in the Public Works Department. I was born in the maternity hospital run by the Sisters in our village, and I went to the primary school the Fathers had there. I went to secondary school in Mbandaka itself. I started at the minor seminary since I originally wanted to be a priest. I changed my mind after two years, though. I finished the rest of secondary school in a different school. It was still taught by the Fathers, though. So I did four years of secondary school and I finished in 1951. I stayed for a few years at the mission and then I joined the administration. While I was still at the mission, I did odd jobs for the Fathers.

To join the administration you had to take an examination. I saw at the post office that the exam was going to be given. I took it and passed first of all those who took it when I did. When I found out the results, I was very happy. I was officially hired on 3 June 1953 and I still have the original paper. I wanted to be in the administration to have a better life. The state agents had more money than anyone else. The state really took care of you. We would see the state agents with their uniforms and they were really envied. There was more security working for the state, too. You were taken care of; there was a good pension when you retired. I also wanted to serve my country. This was a reason too.

I was first sent to Bumba where I was a clerk-typist. I was also in charge of the classification of mail when it arrived. I did this to the satisfaction of the Belgians and I was sent to Basankusu, where I did pretty much the same thing. There was a Belgian who showed me how to do everything and took an interest in what I did. I was in Basankusu for three years when independence came and the Belgians left. I was called back to Mbandaka, where I was promoted and given a more responsible post in the administration of the department. I had a lot of agents working under my orders. A few years later I was sent to Gemena, but that did not last long because of the *provincettes*. The people there wanted their own province and I was a stranger, so I went back to Equateur. It was very difficult when the rebels came to our province. I was in Boende and I had to hide in the forest for two months; but eventually I made it back to Mbandaka, where I stayed until 4 April 1972, when I was sent to Lisala. I have been in Lisala ever since.

Yes, I think this position I have now is an advancement in my career on the administrative plane. Not true in terms of salary, though. I get only Z86.60 a month.[5] For a man like me that is not even a taste. In the time of the Belgians we worked less and had more money. Now it's the reverse. We work more and have less money. I have four boys and four girls. I want my sons to be doctors, agronomists, or engineers. The country needs people in those jobs. They are noble professions and the children will be well situated. People with those skills have no trouble finding a job. To help my children get there, I help orient their studies, I pay their school fees, and I have put one son in a boarding school. That especially is very expensive.

Pattern B

I was born in a village in the Zone of Gemena, Ubangi Subregion, Equateur Region, in 1941. To be exact, 9 May 1941. I am Ngwaka and that is my native tongue. I went to primary school for six years in the school that was a few kilometers from the village. The school was run by the missionaries. I also did six years of secondary school at the Groupe Scolaire in Mbandaka. It was maintained by the Brothers of the Christian Schools, a Catholic order. I don't remember him very well, but my grandfather was a *chef médaillé* under the Belgians.[6] My father was a small farmer, but he also worked as a catechist for the missionaries around the village.

I finished secondary school in 1964. Since I was a good student, the Fathers did not want to let me go, so I began teaching for them. I did this in the orientation cycle for a year, and the next term I was the head teacher in the sixth year of primary school. There is not much chance for advancement in teaching. It is a career without any future. You reach a certain level of pay and there is little chance of moving up. It's a flat career from that point of view. I wanted to teach for a year or two and then go on to the university, but I couldn't do this because there was a crisis in the family. My father died and I had to help out with the family responsibilities. I needed more money, so I left teaching to join the administration, where the pay was quite a bit better. There was also a question of security involved. If you work for the state, you really have to commit a major blunder before they fire you. This is not the case in the private sector, where you can be fired for any little thing.

I joined the administration in 1966 and I was sent to Boende, Tshuapa Subregion, on February 4 of that year. I was there for almost three years and I was then sent to Mbandaka, the regional capital, for an accelerated training program. I managed to stay there for some years, and I was next sent to Lisala, where I arrived in November 1972. At each post I was given progressively more responsibility until today. Now I am in charge of all this service for the entire subregion. This, of course, is due to the confidence my chiefs have in me and the good work I have done wherever I have been sent. Yes, this post is an advancement in my career. If my superiors like my work here, I hope to be given another advancement.

My salary is Z112.25 per month. That figure includes all my allowances and bonuses for the family. I have four children and it is really not enough money. If you go by the amount of time I have been working and major responsibilities I have, it is not enough. In my case, the work I do is worth more than the salary I receive. I have to educate my children and schooling is very expensive. I want my children to be doctors or engineers. I try to take care of their fees and buy them notebooks, but it is not enough money. In terms of money, this job is not an advancement.

A number of points emerge from an analysis of these two modal career patterns. In terms of family history, eight of the twenty-three respondents had grandfathers who were various kinds of chiefs, while many others had grandfathers who were involved with the colonialists in different capacities. There were some cooks, masons, and artisans who were employed with the administration or the other agencies of Westernization in Zaire, the church and the businesses. Ten of the twenty-three claimed grandfathers who were simple villagers or fishermen, so it would be wrong to assume that all these families had established occupational contacts with the colonial structures so early. Nonetheless, the number of chiefs is striking. In the fathers' generation, the picture was slightly different. Here there was only one chief, but many either were state agents or had jobs that centered on the local mission or a local company. Twelve could be identified in this way. In this second generation there were eight villagers and fishermen. Under colonial rule positions with the state, church, and private firms held the highest status and (church excepted) were the most rewarding financially. Many of the grand-fathers were able to translate their initial contacts with the colonial estab-lishment into benefits that were transmitted to their sons. This process might have consisted only in ensuring that the child was exposed to the missionaries and was able to attend their school. In turn, the generation of the fathers was often able to do the same thing for their children, who are the bureaucrats I interviewed.

One theme that emerges from these career patterns is the influence of the church. Four of twenty-three respondents had been to a minor seminary. Virtually all had been educated in schools run by the Catholic church, and many were quick to relate incidents where they were helped, guided, or influenced by missionaries. Though perhaps a banal observation, it is none-theless true that those families who were exposed early to the missionaries and the church seemed to have better chances of getting their children started upward on the ladder.

In terms of their own careers, bureaucrats in both groups began their service for similar reasons. Money, service to the nation, and security were the factors most often mentioned. When the pervasiveness of corruption in Zairian government is discussed in later chapters, it should be remembered that many bureaucrats enter the service because of a sincere desire to serve their countrymen and not all are responsible for the excesses that occur.

Many older service chiefs (pattern A) were bitter about their situations. They would remember the "good old days" under the Belgians when, they believed, their services were better appreciated. Specifically, they would often criticize their better-educated younger colleagues who were advancing more quickly. One complained that "people are sent to Europe to perfect their work. When they return, they speak impeccable French but apart from that, it is zero."[7] Even a younger service chief recognized that his advance-ment had been slowed because of his failure to get a university education. "I don't advance like the university graduates," he noted, "but like a tortoise."[8] For their part the younger university-trained service chiefs were quick to criticize those they worked with because they were not adequately educated.[9] Real tension exists between the young and the old, between the better-educated and those who were brought up under colonial rule and never had a chance to receive university training. This tension affects the ways in which the bureaucracy operates and may contribute to conflicts over substantive matters.

Their own educational attainments aside, there was virtual unanimity on the importance of schooling where their children are concerned. When the respondents were asked what they would like to see their children become, the answers were fifteen doctors, seven agronomists, and four engineers, with a host of miscellaneous occupations thrown in as well. When they were asked how they could ensure that this comes to pass, almost all replies had something to do with education or with saving enough money so that educational costs could be met. In fact, the role of education in a child's life and mobility chances is recognized by every group.

Lower-Level Clerks

Seven of fourteen lower-level clerks interviewed during my stay in Lisala worked in the zone office; the remainder formed part of the collectivity administration. They are together because of the similarities in their functions, life-styles, and career patterns. They represent only a small percentage of the clerk-typists in Lisala, but I am fairly confident that they are representative. There is much interchange of personnel among the three levels of government in Lisala, and particularly competent clerks found at the collectivity or zone may be appropriated by the subregion. These changes do not constitute promotions and do little to alter their outlook on life.

I was born here in Mongala, here where my home is, in a small village just on the other side of the Zaire River in Bongandanga. I was born around 1937, but a lot of the records have been lost or destroyed so I am not really sure. I speak Lingombe because I am a Ngombe. My grandfather was a notable in our village. Whenever there was a problem, people came to hear what he had to say about it. My father was a farmer in the village, but he was also a small merchant and sold things to the women. He would sometimes go to Lisala to buy, and then return home to sell.

There was a primary school in the village, but I had to walk a few kilometers to go to the secondary school that the Fathers had. I was able to do only four years of secondary school because my father died. We did not have much money, and when he died, I had to support the family. When I left school in 1955, the Fathers said I could stay there and work for them as a primary school teacher. I did this for about a year. Then I crossed the river to go to Lisala, where I found a job working for one of the trading companies. At first I worked in the warehouse, but later I was promoted to clerk and I was even taught some accounting. Two years later I was transferred to Bumba, where I did pretty much the same thing. In Bumba I switched companies because I had a chance to be a full-time accountant. I was still not making very much money, however. At Bumba I had a friend who was working for the administration as a clerk. He was making more money than I was and he said I could get a job with the Belgians. I took the exam and I passed because of my training as an accountant. I started as a clerk in the Bumba office of the territorial administration.

I had been there for about a year when independence came and all the Belgians left. I was promoted and became a *chef de poste* in one of Bumba's collectivities. I had a lot of responsibility in that position. I had to see to the roads, taxes, justice, and I really did everything. In 1963 there were the *provincette* troubles. Since I was Ngombe, the Budja did not want me there in Bumba. They were part of Moyen-Congo but they wanted their own *provincette*. I had to come back to Lisala, where I was safe and there wasn't any trouble for me. When I got back to Lisala, I managed to see the provincial officials whom I knew, and I was named an assistant territorial administrator at Binga. I did that for a year and was then called back to Lisala because of my good work. I was promoted to bureau chief of the Interior Department of the province and I supervised all the customary authorities.

When the provinces were reunified, I went back to Mbandaka to see about my new job. I was sent back to Lisala and put under the district commissioner. He sent me to be a *chef de poste* in Businga. This did not last long and I then worked as a typist and clerk in Bumba, Mobayi-Mbongo, and Businga again. I finally came back to Lisala in 1971, and I have been a clerk-typist here ever since.

Advancement? This job? Let no one deceive you. There is no advancement if you are a clerk-typist. Well, I might get a promotion, but it is not likely. I earn Z36.92 a month and that is not enough. I have a lot of children and it costs me Z2 a day only to eat. How can such a salary be enough for the family? I'd like one of my sons to be a doctor, but it is hard because there isn't much money for his pens and notebooks.

A few observations need to be drawn from this modal career pattern. The family histories of the clerks are in some ways similar to those of the subregional service chiefs. In the generation of the grandfathers there were four chiefs and notables, six farmers and fishermen, one blacksmith, and one boat captain. In the following generation there was one notable, one healer, five farmers and fishermen, two catechists, two workers, one merchant, one teacher, and one soldier. Although not so sharply pronounced in this case, there is still a tendency for traditional status in the grandfathers' generation to translate itself into an involvement with the agencies of Westernization then present in Zaire. The generation of the fathers benefited in terms of access to education and often became low-level salaried workers for the state or the companies. Their sons, my respondents, also reaped the rewards of this involvement when their time came.

One of the salient features of the career patterns of lower-level clerks is their early involvement with the private sector. Many of them were initially employed with large expatriate companies. For some there was a tendency to seek this employment and to leave school because of a specific family crisis and a consequent need for money. In any event, they generally abandoned the private sector because the pay was better working for the state.[10]

The career patterns of these clerks provide an extraordinary example of intragenerational mobility. The occupational position of these men has very closely followed the political ups and downs of the country as a whole. Most joined the administration before independence and were then promoted when the Belgians left and a personnel vacuum was created. In addition, there was a second wave of promotions resulting from the administrative and political expansion that occurred during the *provincettes*. During this period many of the clerks moved into real positions of command and authority. When the provinces were reunified, however, their status in the hierarchy returned to what it had been during the early years of independence. Having once tasted the prerogatives of power, the clerk-typists are not content with their present lot. One of them expressed it this way: "Typing especially does not please me at all. I would like to have other duties. I especially want to have a position of command like the zone commissioner."[11]

Much of the discontent felt by lower-level clerks centers on the question of money. Although better off financially than most of their compatriots, they unanimously maintained that their salaries were totally inadequate. Many realize that financial problems could limit the occupational alternatives open to their children since, at this level, few have the funds necessary to put their children in boarding schools and, for many, even paying the standard school fees is a problem. Nonetheless, they have the same dreams for their offspring that the service chiefs do; nine of the fourteen would like to see at least one of their children become a doctor.

Territorial Commissioners

This composite career pattern is based on interviews with all eight of Lisala's territorial commissioners, and includes those working at the zone and those assigned to higher positions at the subregion. In addition, the modal career is based on the biographies of two former territorial commissioners who are now bureaucrats in the Department of Political Affairs at the subregion. Therefore, N = 10.

I was born on 28 August 1935 in Bas-Zaire—more precisely, in Cataractes Subregion and the Zone of Madimba. My maternal language is Kikongo, but I also speak Lingala and French, and I think I remember a bit of Latin and Greek, too. My grandfather was a farmer around Madimba, and I'm told he was a very good Catholic who was well liked by the missionaries. My father was a soldier for many years and retired as a sergeant. I went to primary school in Equateur because my father was stationed there at that time, but I had six years of secondary school in Bas-Zaire. I was in the ancient humanities section and we studied Latin and Greek with the Fathers. I finished my studies in 1957. I was a good student and the Fathers made me teach in their school for a few years. They wouldn't give me my diploma before I had done this. Similarly, I had to marry in the church before I could receive my diploma. I had once wanted to be a priest, but I changed my ideas on that subject shortly before I finished school. After teaching for two years I went to Kinshasa, where, with a bit of luck, I was admitted to Lovanium University in 1959. I spent two years there studying political and social science.

Independence had come in 1960 and there was a need for qualified people to replace the Belgians who had left after the events. So I prepared my applications and presented myself at the Department of the Interior in Kinshasa. I could have finished my college education, but there was a real need for people then and I wished to serve my country during that difficult time. I also felt that since I had studied political science, I had been more or less prepared for the territorial service. I passed some time in Kinshasa in the ministry attending a rapid training program, and then I was assigned, on 3 July 1962, to be an assistant territorial administrator in Mbanza-Ngungu, ex-Thysville. I was there for some three years and then I was promoted to territorial administrator at Tshela. There weren't many ethnic-political problems for me because I was Kongo, in Bas-Zaire, and everyone there was in ABAKO [Alliance des Bakongo] at that time.

In 1969 there was a reshuffling of personnel and I was sent to Equateur, where I had the same functions in the Zone of Kungu. I spent five years in Kungu and then, in November 1974, I was transferred to Lisala.

Now we are called politico-administrative officers and, to a great extent, it is true. We have both political and administrative functions. I feel, though, more political than administrative. Now the party takes precedence and we are given five-year mandates that can be revoked at any time. This is why it is hard to think of this position as an advancement. If the president likes me and my work, he could make me a regional commissioner. On the other hand, he could choose someone who has no real experience in the territorial service. I make Z200 a month less 10 percent, which goes to the party, so that comes out to Z180 a month. Yes, that's what our chiefs have decided, so it is enough for us. Of course, if I were to be offered a raise, I would not refuse. I have seven children right now: two boys and five girls. With all those women the house is really a convent. Most of them are still pretty young, but I hope that there will be at least one doctor and perhaps an agronomist among them. In those professions they will have an easier life and will never be faced with unemployment. The nation needs doctors and agronomists. The key to their future is in their schooling, and I try to orient their studies and see that they have whatever they need.

The ancestry of the territorial commissioners is quite illuminating. Eight of the ten were able to identify their grandfather's occupation. Of these eight, two were chiefs, five were village farmers and fishermen, and one was a catechist. In the succeeding generation, that of the fathers, there were one chief, three state agents, three employees in the private sector, one teacher at a mission school, one catechist, and one village farmer. The noteworthy aspect here is the almost complete absence of farmers and fishermen in the generation of the fathers. Nine of the ten commissioners had fathers involved with either the state, the church, or the private expatriate business sector. In this case, even more clearly than the two previous ones, early occupational association with the agencies of Westernization has tended to translate itself into higher occupational status over time.

It should also be pointed out that, in general, the commissioners are even better educated than the service chiefs. At least five of the ten have had some years of university training. Here, too, the influence of the church and particularly of the mission-based educational system has been decisive.

The motives expressed by the commissioners for joining the territorial service differ in emphasis from either of the two previous patterns. Money is mentioned less frequently, and a desire to serve the nation becomes all-important. (Only two commissioners cited money as a reason propelling them to join the service.)

The commissioners are the first explicitly political group thus far examined, and this becomes evident in their life stories. Most of them perceive their roles as primarily political; as the modal biography makes clear, there is a certain amount of career insecurity because of their dependence on the political favor of their superiors, a point worth returning to later. Like the clerks and service chiefs, most of the commissioners want their sons to be doctors or agronomists. Moreover, education is almost universally seen as the key to fulfilling this ambition.

Party Bureaucrats

This modal career pattern is based upon interviews with all five MPR bureaucrats in Lisala. It includes those working at both the subregion and the zone. More specifically, it is based on interviews with directors of the Jeunesse du Mouvement Populaire de la Révolution (JMPR) and MPR secretaries. During the course of my stay in Lisala the MPR secretaries were absorbed into the state apparatus and given purely administrative posts. There may thus be some question as to the validity of including these secretaries with party bureaucrats rather than with lower-level clerks. Until 1975, however, they did constitute a distinct category of worker, and it is for this reason that they are treated separately here. Because the total number is small ($N = 5$), some care should be taken in interpreting the following modal career pattern.

I was born in Djolu on 3 September 1939. Djolu is in Tshuapa Subregion of the Region of Equateur. My native language is Lomongo and most of the people where I was born belong to that tribe. I, too, am a Mongo. The father of my father was a farmer in the village. He did not really have an occupation or a profession as such. He just tended his fields. My father is still alive and retired from his service a few years ago. He was an agronomist for the state. I went to primary school for six years in Djolu. There was not much of a choice there so we all attended the school run by the Catholic Fathers. For secondary school, though, I spent four years in a teacher-training college in Bamania, nine kilometers from Mbandaka. The school was managed by the Brothers of the Christian Schools. I was in school for four years; that was all we could do at that time. I was graduated in 1959.

Since the school was really designed to furnish teachers for the state, we all had to work for some time and I became a teacher for the Force Publique. I did not go to work in a mission school because the Fathers did not want any Zairian working there who was not married. They were afraid that I would sleep with all the girls. So I was sent to the instructional center of the Force Publique at Irebu. I taught French and math there for two years, and after that I was called to Mbandaka by the provincial governor, Engulu. He assigned me to work in the penitentiary service in Ikela. I was there for a couple of years, but then the rebels came and I had to flee for my life. The people in Kinshasa and Mbandaka did not understand what it was like out there and I was fired because I abandoned my post. There was really no other choice, though. It was flee, or be killed.

After the rebellions were put down, I was without a position in the administration; so I went back to Djolu, where I started a small plantation and tended my crops. I did this until the president announced the creation of the Corps des Volontaires de la République (CVR). I volunteered immediately and was named head of the CVR for the Territory of Djolu. A year later this became the youth wing of the party, the JMPR. As a former teacher I was still interested in the youth of the nation; this might also lead to a paying job, so I joined the JMPR at once. This was in 1967 and I stayed in Djolu until 1970, when I was transferred to Basankusu. It was only at that point that I began to receive a salary. In Djolu I worked for free and was supported by my plantation. In late 1973 I was finally transferred to Lisala, where I have been ever since.

No, I would not say that my salary is enough to live on. I make Z69.50 a month. We are waiting for the state to make an adjustment upward. My children have to be educated, and I would like at least one of them to be a doctor. That way he will be able to live better as well as care for the family. I have to save money for that, and it is difficult when you consider the current cost of living here. At the moment we are paid flat rates. We do not receive any family allotments, benefits, or provisions for our retirement. I am not like a state bureaucrat. I have a political mandate that can be withdrawn at any time. If it is, I'll go back to Djolu and tend to my plantation. I am a politician and I really do not have any career, therefore. Today they may think I am doing a good job; tomorrow I could be sent home.

As mentioned, it is difficult to draw compelling generalizations on the basis of five individuals. It can be said, however, that none of the findings previously set forth for the other occupational categories is contradicted by the model career pattern. In terms of family history, in the generation of the grandfathers there were three village farmers, one chief, and one blacksmith. In the succeeding generation there were two farmers, one blacksmith, one plantation worker, and one agronomist. Here, too, there is a slight tendency for those in high positions today to have had fathers and even grandfathers involved with the agencies of Westernization in Zaire. The tendency is less discernible in this occupational category than in others, but this may be because of the somewhat restricted N.

Four of the five respondents were dissatisfied with their salaries and fringe benefits; it seems clear that this colors their outlook on life and their jobs. As with the other groups already examined, the fate of their children is a prime concern. All recognize the importance of education in the future advancement of their descendants. Furthermore, the ambitions they hold for their children are all but identical with those held by most of the other groups. All five replied that they would like to see at least one son become a doctor. Other occupations mentioned were agronomist, soldier, mechanic, and carpenter.

Motivations for choice of a career in the party apparatus varied. In general the main themes were money and an expressed desire to serve the nation. Although impossible to document precisely, while other groups such as subregional service chiefs and commissioners were usually sincere in citing service as a motive, the party bureaucrats were not. It is hard to escape the impression that these men are opportunists. Experts at *débrouillez-vous* and Article 15, they will always manage to land on their feet.[12] If the MPR were to fall tomorrow, most of them would undoubtedly end as militants in the forefront of whatever new political movement might happen to arise.

Finally, party bureaucrats, like territorial commissioners, are an almost exclusively political group. As such, they are wont to emphasize the instability inherent in their current positions. Like commissioners, they are given a five-year mandate and can be fired at any time. This insecurity is rarely far from their minds and has an effect upon the way things happen in Zaire.

Educational Personnel

This category is another small one. The modal career pattern presented below is based upon interviews with five secondary school principals and educational inspectors. Although twelve principals and inspectors were resident in Lisala, I was unable to conduct formal interviews with all. Fairly frequent interaction with most of them occurred on an informal and a social basis. Despite the small N, this modal career pattern is reasonably representative.

I was born on 31 August 1942 in Bumba. My maternal language is Budja, but I speak Lingala better. Sometimes when I go home I talk Budja with my mother, but she is the only one with whom I speak that tongue. I am really far more comfortable in Lingala. With my father, brothers, and sisters I speak Lingala. Lingala is also the language of my own household. Even though my wife is also Budja, we speak Lingala. It is the language we are teaching our children as well. I really do not have a clear memory of my paternal grandfather, but he was a villager and lived from the crops he grew on his own farm. My father died several years ago; he was an important government functionary. His last official post before retiring was assistant district commissioner of Equateur Subregion. I attended primary school here in the Mongala—more precisely, here at the Catholic mission in Lisala. My father was a bureaucrat even then, and he was stationed in Lisala at that time. My primary schooling lasted for six years and I continued my education in Kinshasa at the Collège ex-St. Joseph. I completed the prescribed course of study in six years. At that time, in Kinshasa there was a Scheutist Father who influenced me greatly. He took me under his wing and encouraged me to continue my studies. His example taught me what a good teacher should be to his students. In any event, after graduating from secondary school, I enrolled in the Faculty of Letters at Lovanium in Kinshasa. Four years later I had successfully completed the degree requirements for a *licence* in French literature with a minor in African culture. That was in 1967.
There was really never much doubt in my mind about what I wanted to do after graduation. I felt that I had a vocation for education. It was the profession for which I had been trained; the nation had a great need for good teachers; and I felt I could do a very good job. Thus, almost immediately after the final results were published, I went to the Catholic Education Bureau and tried to find a teaching job. I had lived much of my life in Kinshasa and I wanted to see some other parts of the country. Initially I had wanted to go to Kivu because of the climate and interesting culture there; but there were political difficulties at that time, so I went to Mbandaka instead. I began working at one of the Catholic secondary schools there that very year. I taught in Mbandaka for four years. In

1971 I was transferred to Lisala and two years later I was named principal of the school.

This job is an advancement for me in terms of my own education. As a principal I have learned many things about people that cannot be found in books—things about how they act, think, and feel. This has been an especially valuable formation for me. In terms of money, however, it is not much of an advancement. My base pay is Z93.25 plus a Z50 bonus for my university degree. The total, therefore, is Z143.25 per month, which is not enough, given the high cost of living in this part of the country. I have three children, all boys. The are still very young and it is too early to say what they will want to become. I would like to have one become a doctor and perhaps another decide to become an agronomist. These will be the indispensable professions of the future. The nation will have great need of people trained in these areas. Again, my children are still very young, but when the time comes, I will try to make sure that their studies are in order. I shall also see that they benefit from my advice. In short, I hope to orient them and guide them toward these paths.

It is worth observing that four of the five respondents were able to furnish the occupations of their grandfathers. In that generation there were two village farmers, one blacksmith, and one Catholic catechist. In the generation of the fathers there were one miner, one soldier, one houseboy, one artisan, and one assistant district commissioner. It is particularly noteworthy that there were no village farmers or fisherman in the second generation. This would also tend to support the basic proposition that early occupational involvement with the agencies of Westernization has tended to be associated with high occupational status throughout the history of the family in question.

Another distinctive trait of this group is their relative youth. At the time of these interviews their average age was only thirty-three. In part because they were born later than their counterparts in other branches of state service, they had the opportunity to receive a university education. As might be expected, this was the group with the highest level of education. There has been almost no shifting between services or between the public and private sectors. Concomitantly, this group seems to be the one with the strongest feeling of vocation for their profession. Most cited vocation, preparation, and service to the nation as reasons for entering the teaching profession.

There are similarities between educators and other groups surveyed. Although highly paid in the context of Lisala, all believed their salaries were insufficient. When asked what they would like their children to become, they cited doctors three times, agronomists twice, engineers once, and teachers once. Their vision of their children's future is thus the same as that of the other groups. The educational personnel, too, recognize the importance of schooling in assuring their offspring's access to future life and mobility chances.

Merchants

The thirteen merchants interviewed in Lisala were all inscribed on the commercial register. In 1974–75 thirty-one traders were registered with the state in this way, so the total N represents more than one-third of the more important and wealthier businessmen in town. Included in the interview group are nine independent traders. Most of these own bars, stores dealing in basic trade goods, or small plantations outside the city. Two of the thirteen are managing directors of wholesale houses and receive salaries from their respective companies. The two remaining merchants are independent traders of Portuguese nationality. When their businesses were nationalized in 1973, they remained to run the stores for their wives, who had succeeded them. They are included in this sample because of their importance in the local commercial picture and because—nationality excepted—aspects of their career patterns do not differ markedly from those of their Zairian counterparts. This modal career pattern and biography should be representative of Lisala's commercial elite.

I first saw the light of day on 17 January 1934. I was born in my father's village, which is about thirty-five kilometers from Lisala on the Lisala-Akula road. My native language is Buela, which is a lot like Lingombe. When someone speaks Lingombe, I can understand it. I feel I am both Buela and Ngombe at the same time. I cannot really say what my grandfather did because I do not remember him at all. My father told me that he was a farmer who lived in the village and lived off his fields. He grew corn and manioc for his own family. My own father was a merchant in the general area of Lisala. He would buy small things in Lisala, like candles, sardines, and soap, and then sell them from village to village. He was always moving around the area and he had friends wherever he went. I went to primary school at the Catholic mission at Umangi, which is down the road from Lisala. I did six years there. After that I came to Lisala to go to secondary school here. I spent three years here at the secondary school next to the mission. I had to repeat one year, so I only finished the two years of the orientation cycle. I stopped going to school in 1952.

The Fathers taught us some basic skills in school, which enabled me to get a job, but I did not finish the full course so it was a bit more difficult for me than for some of the others. I was unemployed for two years and just tended my fields in the village. After that I was lucky and got a job working in the warehouse of a wholesale firm in Bumba. This firm must have liked my work because the next year I was transferred to their office in Kivu. Once there I switched companies. Now I worked for a small Portuguese company. The Portuguese did not have many employees and he taught me a lot about business. From him I learned some accounting and bookkeeping. I was with him until about 1957, when I went to Kisangani for family reasons. The family needed more money and the Portuguese did not want to give it to me, so I left. I could have had a job like that one in Kisangani, but I thought the pay would be better working for a big company. I was hired as a clerk-storekeeper for a Dutch firm there. That job lasted for two years.

In 1959 I decided that I needed more money and I took the exam for the state. I passed with good marks and became a clerk for the territorial administration. The state paid better than the private sector and that was why I wanted that job. I worked in Kisangani itself until independence, when the troubles came, and I was transferred to Buta at that time. It was hard for me there at that time because I was a foreigner to that area. In Buta, though, I was able to begin a small commerce with some of the money I had earned as a clerk for the government. I went back to Kisangani in 1962, still as a clerk for the state. There I opened a small *buvette* [backyard bar] in my house. Unfortunately, it was destroyed when the rebels came in 1964. That was a difficult time for me. I was a foreigner there and the rebels liked neither merchants nor state employees. I had to hide for several months in order to escape from them. Everything I had was lost and one of my children died.

After the recapture of Kisangani I quit the government and came home to Lisala because I knew I could be tranquil here. I started in Lisala in 1966 with just the little money I had been able to salvage from what I had in Kisangani. I bought four cases of beer and began another *buvette*. Beer sold well in Lisala, and I was soon able to open another store with the profits from the bar.

In 1966 the president also announced the CVR. I enrolled right away and became a charter member. The next year came the MPR and I was very active in that. I was named party leader in one of the quarters of Lisala. This was because everyone knew me very well. My bar was also popular with the other party officials in the city and meetings would often be held there. I was a good militant and often provided free beer for the MPR officials. At about that time I opened a small plantation in my village. That was for my retirement. In 1970 I was a candidate for the National Legislature, but I was not successful. I thought I would be, and everyone in town was surprised that I was not accepted, but I am still a very good militant in the party.

I have a lot of children. There are seven boys and four girls—all with the same wife. I would like each one to choose a different profession. I want one to be a doctor, another a judge, and another an agronomist. That way their lives will be assured. I have two boys in boarding school and I have opened a bank account for each child. That way they will have something when I am gone.

One trader was unable to identify his grandfather; among the other twelve there were six village farmers and fishermen, two chiefs, one merchant, two salaried workers, and one carpenter. In the following generation four of the respondents' fathers were merchants, three were farmers and fishermen, two were state agents, one worked for Gécamines (a mining company), one was employed by ONATRA [Office National des Transports du Zaire], one was an accountant, and one was a church deacon. Again, the prominent trend here is the decline in the number of village farmers from the first generation to the second. The generation of the fathers shows only three of thirteen men living off the land; the rest were either merchants or employees of the state or private sectors. In general the same patterns hold for the traders as for the other groups examined. The immediate ancestry of the merchants shows a tendency for fathers and grandfathers to have been occupationally involved with, and dependent on, the three main agencies of Westernization in colonial Zaire. This high occupational status seems to have been transmitted across generations. In several cases the occupation of merchant passed directly from father to son. Interestingly, none of the merchants was descended from a blacksmith.[13]

The modal career patterns presented for the traders highlight a few additional points. In the lives of many merchants interviewed, there has been an extraordinary degree of intragenerational mobility. Like lower-level clerks, merchants have shown themselves to be extremely sensitive to the political turmoil through which Zaire has passed since independence. In 1960 many were forced out of work when their expatriate employers left the country. If they managed to establish themselves later, they often lost all they had worked for in the upheavals that accompanied the *provincettes* and the rebellions. Many of those with whom I spoke were financially destroyed during this period and had to recommence their commercial enterprises after calm was restored. In the space of one career, dramatic variations in wealth and status have occurred. This pattern closely resembles that of lower-level clerks.

There is another point of similarity between the careers of merchants and lower-level clerks. Clerks often came to state service via a stint in the private sector working in some large expatriate company. Merchants often gained commercial experience in exactly the same kind of positions. Six of thirteen merchants interviewed also worked for the state at one time or another. Often, though, they would use this employment to accumulate a bit of capital so that they might begin commerces of their own. Another source of initial capital was provided by their fathers, particularly when they were merchants themselves. In both groups there has been a tendency to move back and forth between the private and public sectors, depending upon the requirements and context of the moment. Those who have been able to make a go of it in the private sector are, in general, better off today than their counterparts who have remained lower-level employees in the state bureaucracy.

Another factor of note is the early involvement of merchants in the political life of the Second Republic. Many of Lisala's traders got in on the ground floor, so to speak. They were early activists in both the CVR and the MPR, partly, it seems, because many responsible positions in the early party structure were not salaried and to fill them one would have had to have an independent source of income. A merchant with a bar or a small store could often afford to donate his time and effort to party matters; a subsistence farmer or salaried worker would not have been able to do so. While their independent financial situations permitted them an involvement in politics, many traders, at least initially, were doubtless genuinely attracted to the Mobutu regime and its political arm because they had suffered under the unstable conditions of the First Republic. Whatever the reasons, it is beyond question that the career patterns of merchants in Lisala reflect a substantial mixture of politics and commerce. This interpenetration of sectors was certainly present under the old regime, but has been carried to new heights under Mobutu.

Merchants share the same desires and hopes for their children that the other five groups do. When they were asked what they would like to see their children become, their responses were as follows: five doctors, two agronomists, two technicians, one engineer, one magistrate, two merchants, one soldier, one teacher, and one tailor. Furthermore, like their counterparts in government or party service, they felt that education was the key to their children's future advancement. Most responses mentioned the importance of advanced education; others dealt with amassing the financial resources necessary to ensure that the child will receive the educational training required to increase future mobility chances.

Modal Careers and Indices of Wealth

The composite careers emphasize the importance of family history, the tendency for social structures to reproduce themselves over time, the importance of educational access as an avenue upward, and the interpene-tration of sectors that—at least in one sense—may be seen to date from the colonial epoch. Thus far the modal biographies have not been ranked in terms of either occupational status or salary levels. It might be wise to attempt a rank order of these six occupational groups on the basis of certain indices of wealth. The first index to be considered is monthly salary; these data are set forth in table 6.

TABLE 6
AVERAGE SALARIES OF INTERVIEW RESPONDENTS, LISALA, 1974–75

Group	N	Salary/Month[a]
1. Territorial commissioners	10	Z183.60
2. Educational personnel	5	Z143.25
3. Subregional service chiefs		
Pattern B	12	Z112.25
Pattern A	11	Z85.80
4. Party bureaucrats	5	Z69.50
5. Lower-level clerks	14	Z36.92
6. Merchants	13	no data[b]
Total N	70	

SOURCE: Interview data, Lisala.

[a]To a certain extent these figures are misleading because some salary averages were obtained from base pay and others from net pay. Shortly before my departure slight upward revisions were made in salaries of lower-level clerks, which are not included here.

[b]Although it is impossible to estimate monthly intake of merchants, data obtained from business receipts indicate they generally earn more per month than do commissioners.

Table 6 requires no elaboration. The financial hierarchy stretching from the lower-level clerks at the bottom to the territorial commissioners at the top is readily apparent. It should be borne in mind, however, that the figures cited represent the actual monthly salaries and not the real income or purchasing power. As of January 1969 the real income of state bureaucrats equaled less than one-third of the administrative salaries paid in 1960.[14] The erosion of purchasing power notwithstanding, it is still apparent that all six groups form part of a relatively advantaged minority. Although there are sharp gradations of salary among the groups, even lower-level clerks are well off compared with the majority of Zairian citizens. A subsistence farmer living in a village and earning a *yearly* income of Z12–25 might well regard an administrative clerk-typist as a member of the privileged elite.[15]

Land is a second index of wealth, and for purposes of land attribution, Lisala is divided into two sections. The center of town, which contains the administrative residential areas and the commercial center, is governed by the Subregional Cadastral Office. Unfortunately, land ownership records are hopelessly out of date, and it is therefore impossible to estimate accurately which occupational categories possess which part of the town's land. A general reading of these records convincingly shows that much of the land in the wealthier part of the city is held either by merchants or by those who work for the state. Though it is offered as a personal observation, some support for this notion can be deduced from the procedures for obtaining land. First, there must be a written request for each plot. Then, there are two assessments. The first is called *taxe achat terrain* and is Z34 per parcel. The second is a Z12 surveyor's fee. The total required, even without considering the necessary *matabiche*,[16] is beyond the reach of all but the most affluent elements. The second section of the town, the so-called popular quarters, is managed by the land office of the collectivity. At this level the allocation fee per parcel of land is Z15, and there is an additional assessment of Z1 per year levied on each inhabitant of the lot. Although the amount is considerably less than the rate for residential and commercial sections, most Zairians would find even this outlay an enormous burden.[17]

A third index of wealth is the distribution of automobiles and motorbikes among Lisala's residents. Obvious symbols of wealth, cars can be counted without difficulty in such a small town. The results of this census are reproduced in table 7. It is obvious that most of these resources are owned by traders and state employees. This further confirms the picture that has already emerged from an examination of salary structures and the cursory investigation of land ownership: Wealth in Lisala, and in Zaire, is concentrated in the hands of merchants and bureaucrats.

It might be added that there were three Mercedes in Lisala at the time of my stay. One belonged to the subregional commissioner, a second was driven by the Catholic Bishop, and a third was owned by a wealthy merchant. On a symbolic level, these three luxury automobiles demonstrate where Lisala's wealth lies.[18] On an empirical level, one might also say that the concept of the colonial trinity advanced by Crawford Young still has some utility in ordering information.[19] Throughout the modal career patterns it is evident how each of the three sectors has touched the lives of the respondents. The influence of the church may be seen through its control of the educational appartus. No fewer than eight (slightly over 10 percent) of the seventy respondents had attended seminaries. Moreover, most of the people interviewed had attended schools

TABLE 7

CAR AND MOTORBIKE CENSUS OF LISALA'S POPULATION, 1974–75

Group	Cars & Trucks	Motorbikes	Total
1. Merchants	27	10	37
2. Subregional service chiefs	10	6	16
3. Territorial commissioners	6	2	8
4. Educational personnel	4	4	8
5. Lower-level clerks	1[a]	8[b]	9
6. Party bureaucrats	0	2	2
Total	48[c]	32[d]	80[e]

SOURCE: Personal observation.

[a]The clerk is the subregional accountant.

[b]Four of these eight clerks either are accountants or work in offices dealing with finance. Two others were once interim collectivity chiefs.

[c]This may be a slight underestimate.

[d]Counting the number of motorbikes in town proved difficult. This may be a serious underestimate.

[e]Vehicles belonging to the state and the church are not included. Multiple ownership, especially among merchants, is not considered. It should be mentioned that the census includes people in some categories who were not interviewed.

in the Catholic educational network and had been taught by priests at the secondary level. Of some importance, too, is the fact that seven of the respondents had either fathers or grandfathers who were catechists at the local mission station.

The interchange of personnel that has occurred, and is occurring, between the commercial and politico-administrative sectors should also be noted. These, of course, were the other two prongs of the colonial trident. Lower-level clerks have often passed by way of the private sector before beginning their careers in administration. Some merchants began careers in colonial administration and then struck out on their own as independent merchants. In the latter case, traders have often converted their economic advantages into political influence by financing early MPR activities. One result is that today it is sometimes difficult to draw a discrete line between the realm of politics and the kingdom of commerce. The interpenetration of the two sectors makes such distinctions and divisions purely analytic and, thus, to a certain extent academic.

If the interpenetration of sectors is one major theme to emerge from the modal biographies, the quest for security is a second. A number of respondents, particularly some of the subregional service chiefs, cited the desire for security as a motive for entering the administration. It was also clear that territorial commissioners and party bureaucrats often felt insecure in their jobs because they knew that their positions were primarily political and that they could be fired at any time. More generally, many interviews suggested that respondents were anxious about job tenure and income level in one form or another. All these adults had grown up with their nation. Zaire's infancy and early childhood have been characterized by a series of frequent and recurring political and economic upheavals, a turbulence that has affected virtually every citizen. The careers of lower-level clerks and merchants would often rise and fall with the then current political and economic context. In these two groups there has been a remarkable degree of intragenerational mobility. This movement—both up and then down again—may be responsible for the genuine desire for a secure and stable niche that emerged from many interviews. On a more theoretical plane, it also makes it extremely difficult to place these individuals within any particular social class. The up-and-down movement characteristic of the careers of many respondents means that there is a fairly continuous and rapid change in the composition of certain social classes. It is fair to say that their social class has depended largely on the sociopolitical context of the moment.

The search for security and stability was particularly apparent where their children were concerned. It will be remembered that almost all those interviewed shared the same vision of their children's future. When asked what they would like to see their offspring become, forty-one of seventy replied that they hoped at least one of their children would become a doctor.[20] Yet, when asked, in another context, to name the people in Lisala who were most respected and listened to, only two of seventy named the town's one doctor. This seeming occupational paradox can be explained in terms of a greater desire for a secure situation than for prestige. Although the medical profession may not be well respected or listeded to in Lisala, it is a steady job, which permits a relatively high standard of living. Many interviewees said that doctors would always be in demand and would always have work. Furthermore, some responded that if their child were a physician, he or she would be able to take care of the family when the parents became old and infirm. In short, medicine is perceived as a long-term and stable profession. Ironically, the position many cited as the most well respected and listened to in Lisala is generally perceived as short-lived and unstable. Twenty-eight of the seventy people I spoke with mentioned the subregional commissioner as the man most people listened to in Lisala. Fourteen others mentioned the zone commissioner. Although these positions are powerful and prestigious, few parents wish to see their children follow this route. If nothing else, the practice of politics in Zaire has proved to be volatile.

There is good reason for territorial commissioners and party bureaucrats to feel insecure in their positions. In addition to the general political instability that has characterized Zaire during much of its postindependence history, President Mobutu's method of handling personnel problems is somewhat reminiscent of Lewis Carroll's Queen of Hearts.[21] Territorial commissioners especially have a great deal to lose if their mandates are revoked. Many hold low-level positions in the administration, to which they would presumably return if they fell from grace. Others are purely political appointments without any permanent position. In either situation the loss of personal revenue, as shown in table 8, would be staggering. These figures do

TABLE 8

SALARIES OF TERRITORIAL COMMISSIONERS, LISALA

Current Position	Current Salary	Permanent Position	Salary if Political Mandate Revoked
1. Subregional commissioner	Z270	Division chief	Z143
2. Assistant	Z225	First-class office attaché	Z86
3. Assistant	Z225	None	0
4. Assistant	Z225	None	0
5. Zone commissioner	Z180	Bureau chief	Z115
6. Assistant	Z135	Bureau chief	Z115
7. Assistant	Z135	None	0
8. Assistant	Z135	First-class auxiliary agent	Z26
9. Division chief[a]	Z180	Division chief	Z180
10. Bureau chief[a]	Z126	Bureau chief	Z126
Average	Z183.60		Z79.10

SOURCE: Interview data, Lisala.

[a]Administrators, former commissioners.

not even hint at the loss of fringe benefits and quasi-legal perquisites of which the commissioners have been known to avail themselves. One result of this insecurity is an urge to accumulate as quickly as possible whatever resources one can, a factor that helps explain certain aspects of Zairian administrative behavior.

Insecurity of job tenure is by no means restricted to territorial commissioners and party bureaucrats. Lower-level clerks also are usually in fear of their jobs. When Mobutu radicalized the revolution on 30 December 1974, he announced that unemployment would cease to exist in Zaire. In response to this policy line, Lisala's trade union secretary gave a speech to the workers asserting that henceforth no one could be fired because the president had banned unemployment. Unfortunately, several weeks later there were massive firings of lower-level clerks in all branches of government in Lisala.[22] Job tenure is certain nowhere, and this naturally affects the way people perceive their world and the way in which they envisage the world of their children.

A third major theme to emerge from the modal careers is the tendency of the Zairian social system's mobility patterns to reproduce themselves over time. The fathers and grandfathers of almost every group of respondents tended to enjoy high occupational status under the Belgians. Most were able to transmit their initial advantages to their children and grandchildren, usually through early exposure to the missionary-based educational system. It became clear during my stay in Lisala that while the colonial system inhibited the development of certain social classes by arbitrarily closing off avenues of upward mobility, it nonetheless laid the foundations of the current class system. The modal biographies demonstrate the impressive number of respondents with fathers and grandfathers who were occupationally involved with the agencies of Westernization in colonial Zaire. This has surely contributed to the present elite status of all my respondents in Lisala. The family histories of these men are summarized in table 9.

TABLE 9
SUMMARY OF FAMILY HISTORIES

Group	Grandfathers	Fathers
1. Subregional service chiefs (N = 23)	8 chiefs..............	1 chief
	1 houseboy	
	1 mason	
	1 artisan.............	
	1 woodcutter	
	....	5 state agents
	....	2 workers
	....	2 catechists
	10 farmers and fishermen	8 farmers and fishermen
2. Lower-level clerks (N = 14)	2 chiefs..............	
	2 notables	1 notable
	1 blacksmith	
	1 boat captain	
	....	1 healer
	....	2 workers
	....	1 teacher
	....	1 merchant
	....	1 soldier
	....	2 catechists
	6 farmers and fishermen	5 farmers and fishermen
3. Territorial commissioners (N = 10)	2 chiefs..............	1 chief
	1 catechist	1 catechist
	....	3 state agents
	....	3 workers
	....	1 mission teacher
	5 farmers and fishermen	1 farmer
4. Party bureaucrats (N = 5)	1 chief...............	
	1 blacksmith	1 blacksmith
	....	1 state agronomist
	....	1 worker
	3 farmers	2 farmers

TABLE 9 (continued)

Group	Grandfathers	Fathers
5. Educational personnel (N = 5)	1 blacksmith	
	1 catechist	
	....	1 miner
	....	1 houseboy
	....	1 soldier
	....	1 artisan
	....	1 assistant district commissioner
	2 farmers	
6. Merchants (N = 13)	2 chiefs..............	
	1 merchant...........	4 merchants
	2 workers.............	3 workers
	1 carpenter...........	
	....	2 state agents
	....	1 deacon
	6 farmers and fishermen	3 farmers and fishermen

SOURCE: Interview data, Lisala.

The conclusion that high occupational status tends to reproduce itself across generations is scarcely earthshaking. Nonetheless, this exercise has proved useful because it demonstrates just how important family background has been. One caveat is in order. The argument as stated here assumes that the mass of Zairian village farmers did *not* have fathers and grandfathers who were occupationally involved with the three prongs of the colonial system. Because my interviews did not touch on this sector of society, this remains a plausible, but untested, assumption.

It has long been known that the extended African family acts as a social security system, providing certain forms of solidarity in times of crisis.[23] It is less widely recognized that this can act as a drag upon the upward mobility of certain individuals. Eight of seventy respondents mentioned that they were forced to seek salaried employment and abandon their education because of family difficulty. The death of a father or older brother would often provoke the search for employment and the end of formal education. Of these eight, four are lower-level clerks, two are service chiefs, one is a merchant, and one is a territorial commissioner. Taking note of their family histories, we find that in the generation of the grandfathers there were six farmers and fishermen, one notable, and one chief. Similarly, in the generation of the fathers there were six village farmers and fishermen and two workers. It seems that those coming from the poorer segments of society are less able to cope financially with these crises. For some, these family responsibilities may act as a barrier to further advancement in the social hierarchy.[24]

A fourth major theme underlines the importance of education. The key role of access to educational facilities has appeared in virtually every one of the modal biographies. Perhaps even more important is the almost universal perception of the significance of education in assuring the children's life and mobility chances. One subregional service chief informed me that "even the children of villagers become big men since the state is in charge of the children's education, especially at the university level."[25] The view is exaggerated. While there has been an extraordinary expansion in the educational infrastructure since independence,[26] access to educational facilities—for reasons to be discussed—is becoming more and more problematical for those at the lower levels of the social hierarchy; opportunities are closing off fast. Tables 10 and 11 present information on the occupations of the parents of primary and secondary school children in Lisala.

TABLE 10

PARENTS' OCCUPATIONS, PRIMARY SCHOOL STUDENTS, LISALA, 1975

School	State-Employed	Peasant	Private Sector	Total
1. Ebabo-Zozo	232	150	128	510
2. Boboto	412	274	91	777
3. EPN/Lisala	345	291	152	788
4. Mama Zairoise	212	162	152	526
5. Upoto	193	426	142	761
6. Monyele	536	384	94	1,014
7. Kaba	272	123	9	404
8. Mobateli	32	31	30	93
9. Ngombe-Doko	105	121	15	241
10. EPN/Mika	103	100	44	247
Total	2,442	2,062	857	5,361
Percentage	45.55	38.46	15.98	99.99

SOURCE: JMPR census of schools, 2 February 1975.

In interpreting tables 10 and 11, it should first be noted that only 11 percent of the school-age youth in Mongala Subregion are currently attending school.[27] Available positions seem to be disproportionately filled by those whose parents are employed by the state; 45.55 percent of the primary school students and 43.87 percent of the secondary school students have parents who work in the state sector. This is in a region of the country where easily 90 percent of the population is engaged in agricultural pursuits. The reasons are not difficult to find. Economics are of unquestioned importance; parents who have a steady source of income will be better able to cope with school fees and other mandatory expenses.

Political factors also help explain this disproportion. When President

TABLE 11
PARENTS' OCCUPATIONS, SECONDARY SCHOOL STUDENTS,
LISALA, 1975

1. Anuarita	95	87	52	234
2. Ado	71	479	53	603
3. Athenée de Mika	452	258	22	732
4. Monyele	162	222	37	421
5. Ngomba ya Elikya	129	247	1	377
6. Monzoto mwa Ntongo	100	28	34	162
7. Upoto	133	134	10	277
8. Likomu	842	503	120	1,465
9. 24 novembre	12	193	74	279
10. Centre Agricole Officiel des Jeunes	44	39	17	100
Total	2,040	2,190	420	4,650
Percentage	43.87	47.09	9.03	99.99

SOURCE: JMPR census of schools, 2 February 1975.

Mobutu took office in November 1965, an important task facing him was the creation of a sense of national unity. One way in which he strove to achieve this was the systematic rotation of political and administrative officials. The goal was to have bureaucrats work outside their respective areas of origin. It was believed that the forces of ethnicity would thus be contained and people would develop a sense of confidence in the local representatives of the national government. Although the policy merits a sustained treatment and evaluation, only one unintended consequence should be noted. When a bureaucrat is transferred, his children, if they have been attending school, must automatically be admitted to a new school. This is normal and desirable. It would be most unjust were the schooling of the children of bureaucrats disrupted because their parents are rotated. If the child's papers are in order, the bureaucrat has the option of installing them at the school of his choice upon arrival at a new post.[28] The effect has been that in administrative and educational centers like Lisala, the best schools tend to have a disproportionate number of students whose parents work for the state. Furthermore, largely because such places are administrative centers, the schools there tend to absorb the lion's share of the available resources from the education ministry. Few funds, if any, are left over for the schools in the interior, which generally have a higher proportion of students whose parents are village farmers.[29] The obvious result is that both the schools and the students in rural areas suffer from a lack of finances, while schools in educational centers like Lisala are better off financially and have a much higher percentage of students whose parents work for the state. They also tend to have a higher percentage of their graduates pass the state examinations and go on to the university.[30]

Moreover, deliberate actions are taken by individual state employees to ensure their children educational benefits. Some school principals complain that they are interfered with by political authorities wishing to enter their children in certain schools. Such class actions are not uncommon; I witnessed one incident in which a territorial commissioner sought to pressure a secondary school principal into admitting his daughter even though her marks on the entrance examination were insufficient.[31] These class actions also tend to increase the proportion of students whose parents work for the state.

On the basis of this evidence it may be argued that educational opportunities, wide open after independence, are now beginning to close. In the future it will become increasingly difficult for children of village farmers and fishermen to attend school because of the problems involved in raising the necessary money to pay tuition fees. This is but one result of the manipulation of the rural economic and political systems, which seems designed to prevent farmers from accumulating economic resources.

CHAPTER 4
Collectivity Administration and the System of Rural Exploitation

As far as taxes are concerned, people are economically weak. The Cité *[collectivity] compels people to pay.*
—A lower-level clerk[1]

Volunteers pay [the CPM] easily, but supervision is necessary. But to get volunteers is difficult.
—A collectivity chief[2]

We have advantages in the cash box.
—A collectivity chief[3]

I am very surprised to learn that certain Zone Commissioners, while on tour in their respective administrative entities, take pleasure in effecting deductions from collectivity accounts.
—The state commissioner for political affairs[4]

It is desirable that authorities reinforce the popularizing actions of the agronomists and agricultural agents by the efficacious system of imposition and not persuasion.
—Regional Agricultural Division[5]

Most Zairians live in rural or semiurban areas, which, like Lisala, are governed by collectivity administrations. Life in these administrative entities is, for the most part, not very pleasant. Economic, social, political, and physical abuse are the normal components of everyday existence. This chapter contends that collectivity administration is a driving force behind a vast system of rural exploitation, oppression, and violence. To avoid misunderstandings, following Giddens, exploitation is defined as "any socially conditioned form of asymmetrical production of life chances."[6] Certainly, the local administrative system is structured and manipulated to inhibit the accumulation of resources by the village farmers.[7] As a result, opportunities for upward social and political mobility are effectively closed. Support for these ideas is furnished by a close examination of collectivity budgets. The study of taxes and expenditures has proved a productive way of highlighting the class dimensions of the political process in rural areas. In addition, the effects of what I call budgetary capitalism are studied, particularly as they pertain to agriculture.

The national budget is devised in Kinshasa. Within the categories of this document, funds are delegated to regions and subregions. Regional and subregional service chiefs are thus involved in the elaboration of budgetary estimates for their respective services each year. At each of these levels the principal territorial commissioner has overall control of the financial resources that happen to arrive from Kinshasa. He can, and often does, make significant changes in the allocation of funds among the services he controls. The zones depend on the subregions and have no budgets of their own. Therefore, if it is said that perhaps 70 to 80 percent of the national budget is spent on administrative salaries, the reference is to the Kinshasa budget and the delegations made to all the nation's regions and subregions. The collectivity budgets discussed in this chapter are separate and distinct. They have nothing to do with the allocation of funds at the national level. The only money the collectivity receives from Kinshasa is the Z50 per month for the chief's salary and the very occasional delegation of funds for the locality chiefs. Collectivity resources are generated by taxes levied on the people who live within its boundaries. Thus, with the exception of the two cases noted above, the collectivities are financially autonomous. In theory, financial autonomy was ended with the important territorial reform enacted on 5 January 1973.[8] In practice, however, the Kinshasa government does not have enough funds to take over the financial administration of Zaire's more than eight hundred collectivities. The situation described below, then, will probably continue for at least some time. Before we begin a discussion of these budgets, one further clarification is in order. Although it is difficult to have complete confidence in the data on specific budget items, the figures provided here appear to be basically correct and furnish a reasonably typical picture of the politics of resource distribution at the collectivity level.

Collectivity Budgets

Taxes

The main pillar of collectivity finance is the *Contribution Personnelle Minimum* (CPM). Direct successor to the old colonial head tax, the CPM was instituted in 1960.[9] It is designed to tax those whose income is currently less than Z240 per year and who are not subject to an income tax collected by withholding part of a salary. Although it is difficult to reconstruct the fate of this tax during the troubled years immediately following independence, there are some indications that while the tax was collected by the collectivities, at least 60 percent of the proceeds were handed over to the central government. Of course, during the *provincette* period tax collection was, at best, intermittent. In 1969 it was decided that the central government would no longer require the collectivities to remit a portion of these revenues. Total CPM receipts thus belonged to the units of local administration. Nonetheless, it was still incumbent upon territorial authorities to supervise its collection and ensure that no abuses occurred.[10]

Since salaried employees in both state and private sectors have their taxes withheld at the source, the major burden of the CPM falls squarely on the shoulders of village farmers. This has been true since the colonial epoch, and one historian of that period has noted that this tax was a principal means of coercion. Although it was impossible to calculate accurately, he estimated that the head tax would relieve the village farmers of one-quarter to one-half of their revenue in any given year.[11] Current figures are not available, but the percentage taken today is certainly no less and might well be more, particularly if other taxes and exactions are considered. The state commissioner for political affairs is responsible for establishing the CPM rates; in terms of the tax table, villagers are currently required to pay a fixed rate of Z2.80 per able-bodied man each year. This tax presupposes an annual income of Z60–69, although most village farmers earn considerably less in an average year. Furthermore, since it is invariable and bears no relation either to the villager's ability to pay or to his subsistence needs, the tax may cause great hardship. As James Scott has superbly demonstrated for Southeast Asia, the fixed tax can be an enormous burden on the village farmer in bad years because it can force him below the subsistence level. It is "an *expanding* proportional claim on his diminishing resources" and a cause of rebellion in rural areas.[12] The authorities are well aware of this dangerous situation. One zone commissioner in Mongala reported that the rate of taxation was too high for the villagers to bear without considerable suffering. In his zone few, if any, local farmers háve incomes of even Z40–50. In 1974, a particularly difficult economic year, there was a revolt in this zone when the villagers refused to pay their taxes because they did not have the money. The revolt was put down quickly and decisively.[13]

The overall dependence of the collectivities on the CPM is shown in table 12. Although the *Cité* of Lisala is used as an example, similar percentages obtain for virtually all collectivities in Mongala Subregion.

TABLE 12
CPM RECEIPTS AND TOTAL RECEIPTS, CITÉ OF LISALA, 1968–74

Year	CPM Receipts	Total Receipts	CPM as % of Total
1968	Z2,656.45	Z7,302.34	36.37
1969	1,995.39	5,586.97	35.71
1970	1,353.59	6,745.83	20.36
1971	10,543.20	14,799.59	71.23
1972	9,415.80	18,302.94	51.44
1973	10,438.80	22,067.80	47.30
1974	7,583.80	15,417.34	49.19
Total	Z43,987.03	Z90,222.81	48.75

SOURCE: Cité de Lisala, *Comptes des recettes et des dépenses*, 1968–74.

Given that almost 50 percent of the *Cité*'s income is generated by the CPM, it would be reasonable to assume that the planning and collection of this vital source of revenue would be accomplished with some degree of foresight. This is almost never the case, however. The data presented in table 13, and depicted graphically in figure 1, indicate that there is usually a considerable shortfall between the budgetary estimates made at the beginning of each fiscal year and the amount of money actually collected by the end.

TABLE 13
CPM, BUDGETARY ESTIMATES AND ACTUAL RECEIPTS,
CITÉ *OF LISALA, 1968–75*

Year	Budgetary Estimates	Actual Receipts
1968	Z2,602.35	Z2,656.45
1969	4,101.95	1,995.39
1970	11,535.10	1,373.59
1971	11,400.00	10,543.20
1972	10,200.00	9,415.80
1973	17,680.00	10,438.80
1974	20,080.00	7,583.80
1975	41,784.00	no data

SOURCE: Cité de Lisala, *Comptes des recettes et des dépenses* and *Prévisions budgétaires*, 1968–75.

FIGURE 1
CPM, BUDGETARY ESTIMATES AND ACTUAL RECEIPTS,
CITÉ *OF LISALA, 1968–75*

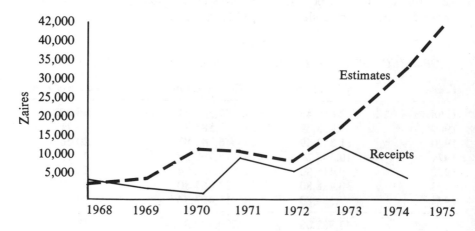

Once again it should be understood that although the figures pertain to the *Cité* of Lisala, this pattern of overestimation is widespread throughout Mongala Subregion.

While the CPM is the major source of collectivity revenue, it is not the only source. Each collectivity, with the consent of the subregional commissioner, can levy a diverse panoply of taxes on its inhabitants. As seen in table 14, the collectivity authorities often systematically overestimate these other revenues as well.

TABLE 14

SELECTED TAX RECEIPTS AND ESTIMATES, CITÉ *OF LISALA, 1974–75*

Tax	1974 Estimates	1974 Receipts	1975 Estimates
1. Birth, marriage, divorce certicates	Z410.00	Z130.40	Z500.00
2. Notarization fees	1,100.00	236.80	1,200.00
3. Public works	2,700.00	882.55	3,510.00
4. Palm wine tax	680.00	58.00	500.00
5. Transit permits	850.00	307.30	800.00
6. Land tax	3,000.00	859.80	5,000.00
7. Water consumption	200.00	0.00	500.00
8. Social tax	390.00	43.95	390.00
9. Boutique tax	300.00	76.90	500.00
Total[a]	Z9,630.00	Z2,595.70	Z12,900.00

SOURCE: Cité de Lisala, *Comptes des recettes et des dépenses, 1974; Prévisions budgétaires, 1975.*

[a]These taxes have been chosen from a long list. The totals do not represent the complete intake or estimates of the *Cité*. They are illustrative only of the general pattern.

Table 14 makes certain things clear. There appears to be little relationship between receipts and estimates on any given budget line. Thus, even though the actual revenues for 1974 were well below the estimates for that year, the 1975 estimates were, if anything, even higher than those of the preceding year. Surely, then, these budgetary predictions have almost no links with reality. Moreover, one can assert that this system has little to do with the theoretical school of incremental budgeting, which has grown up around the works of Charles Lindblom and Aaron Wildavsky.[14] The budgetary data for the *Cité* of Lisala are provided here merely for purposes of illustration. While they are more exaggerated than those of other collectivities in Mongala, the inflation of budgetary estimates is prevalent throughout the subregion.

The question must now be asked why the actual tax revenue rarely attains the budgetary estimates the collectivity officials elaborate and the zone and subregional commissioners approve. There are several possible explanations for the persistent pattern of resource overestimation. First, primary responsibility for drawing up the yearly budgetary estimates lies with the key officials of the collectivity. This means that the chief, the accountant, and the secretary will have the most influence on the budget. Most of these officials are not well educated, and ignorance may partly explain the repeated overestimates. Although lack of education is certainly part of the problem, it is only a small part.

More important is an understanding of both the mechanics of the budgetary process and the motives of the most important collectivity personnel. The information presented above in tables 13 and 14, as well as my own observations of the process, suggest that the overestimation of tax revenue is a deliberate ploy by those who manage the collectivity. If, as F. G. Bailey would have us believe, politics is a competitive game of stratagems and spoils, this overestimation is merely a stratagem.[15] What are the spoils?

The spoils are an ever-ready and ever-open cash box for those who run the collectivity. The mechanisms involved are fairly simple. At the end of the year, when the budgetary documents are established, there is a rather systematic overestimation of the next year's resource intake. When the new fiscal year arrives, those in charge of the collectivity consult their documents and see that on the basis of their own estimations they can expect to gather in an enormous amount of money. Their next impulse is to pay themselves most of the fringe benefits that have been previewed into the budget by the estimates. For example, one collectivity chief wrote various indemnities totaling Z6,429.00 into his 1974 budget. Included were entertainment costs, a cost-of-living allowance, a car indemnity, a travel allowance, additional funds for his family, medical expenses, and other, miscellaneous items.[16] Another collectivity chief extracted important sums each month for the upkeep of his two automobiles, which, he claimed, were being used on official business. In reality the chief did not own even one vehicle, let alone two.[17] This is what is meant by "*avantages dans la caisse*," to use one chief's felicitous phrase. So widespread is this sytem that upwardly mobile bureaucrats figure these *avantages* into their own career calculations. One party bureaucrat confided to me that he had been recommended for two positions: one as bureau chief in the Political Affairs Department at a salary of Z125 per month and one as a collectivity chief with a salary of Z50 per month. He unquestionably preferred the latter alternative because of the *avantages*.[18]

Such overestimations are common coin in Mongala. Although the zonal and subregional commissioners are well aware of this, they do nothing to bring the situation into line. Each year they can almost always be counted on to approve the resource predictions drawn up by the key collectivity personnel. Harsh commentaries are occasionally written, but these have little or no effect upon the chiefs. The commissioners, too, have a vested interest in the continuation of this system, for they, as well as other bureaucrats from the zone and subregion, use the collectivity cash box as a general drawing fund for their own personal needs. Arriving on periodic inspection tours, they often "borrow" money from the collectivity strong box. In the unlikely event that the chief or the accountant should refuse their "loan," it will be pointed out that on the basis of this year's budgetary estimates, the coffers are overflowing. Consequently, there should certainly be no harm in "advancing" just a few zaires because something special has come up and the money is needed for a good cause. Some effects of this kind of budgetary capitalism are obvious; others are less readily apparent. To gain a fuller appreciation of these results it is necessary to pay attention to the expenditure side of the budgetary process.

Expenditures

When asked what services the collectivity administration provides to the population, a former chief was unable to answer directly. After thinking about the question for several minutes, he replied that law and order was the main service and that there was also some popular education through *Salongo*.[19] He might also have added that the collectivity provides employment for a large number of relatively unskilled people. Most expenditures made by the rural and the semiurban collectivities concern personnel and salary costs, and only a very small percentage pertain to infrastructural development of any kind. This is demonstrated in table 15.

TABLE 15
ACTUAL EXPENDITURES, CITÉ OF LISALA, 1974

Rubric and Line Expenditure	Sum	%
1. Administration		
Administrative salaries	Z3,669.16	
Police salaries	3,521.72	
Salaries of collectivity and locality chiefs	913.35a	
Travel for administrative personnel	475.77	
Office supplies	162.10	
Office supplies census office	92.51	
Total	8,834.61	57.30
2. Justice		
Judges' salaries	Z940.51	
Court clerks' salaries	747.46	
Prison maintenance	4.53	
Office supplies	17.18	
Total	1,709.68	11.08
3. Public works		
Maintenance administrative buildings	Z613.99	
Maintenance judicial buildings	6.40	
Maintenance medical buildings	20.90	
Salaries of roadworkers	2,074.80	
Transportation of materials	1.20	
Total	2,717.29	17.62

TABLE 15 (continued)

Rubric and Line Expenditure	Sum	%
4. Hygiene		
Salary for technical personnel	Z89.38	0.57
5. Accidental and diverse		
Good works	Z459.75	
Public festivities	406.14	
Miscellaneous	1,200.46	
Total	Z2,066.35	13.40
Total	Z15,417.31	99.97

SOURCE: Cité de Lisala, *Compte des recettes et des dépenses, 1974.*

ªThis line actually refers to "premiums" and other *avantages*, not to salaries.

Table 15 indicates that most of the *Cité*'s expenditures are accounted for by the salaries of the collectivity personnel. If we were to recalculate the figures provided and lump all the salaries under one heading, we would find that 77.55 percent of the total expenses are to pay personnel. This general tendency is by no means restricted to the *Cité* of Lisala. Almost all the other collectivities in Mongala Subregion manifest the same kinds of expenditures. Table 16 provides an example. Here, too, it will be noted that most of the collectivities' expenses pay the monthly wages of the personnel. Those categories dealing specifically with developmental expenses such as education, hygiene, and economy are all but ignored. It should also be noted that the majority of the funds allocated under the rubric of public works are earmarked for salaries as well. There can thus be little question that although a few occasional services are furnished, collectivity administration is basically parasitic. It lives off the tax revenues collected from village farmers, but fails to return much to them in the way of developmental activities. The major "service" apparently rendered the local people is a plethoric bureaucracy whose main concern is the extraction of resources so that its own life might be extended. A somewhat closer look at the personnel employed by the collectivities is in order. Data on the employees of twelve of the twenty-three Mongala collectivities are in table 17. Almost all the figures in table 17 exclude locality chiefs and judges and should, therefore, be considered underestimates of the total number of people employed by the units of local administration. Moreover, with the possible exception of the collectivity chief, virtually all the personnel are from Equateur Region. More specifically, most of those who work for the collectivity come from either the collectivity itself or its immediate environs. Perhaps the most important fact to be gleaned from table 17 is that 44 percent of the employees are policemen. These "agents of order," as they are termed, are under the direct control of the chief.

TABLE 16
BUDGETARY EXPENDITURES BY RUBRIC, FOUR COLLECTIVITIES, ZONE OF LISALA, 1969–74

Rubric	1969	1970	1971	1972	1973	1974	Total	%
Administration	Z23,725.93	20,903.37	40,012.76	47,010.76	55,806.74	47,002.64	234,462.20	56.37
Justice	5,093.09	6,303.72	7,841.61	8,962.33	9,020.98	11,644.48	48,866.21	11.74
Public works	6,405.39	5,709.66	10,152.92	13,211.64	16,272.62	8,985.78	60,738.01	14.60
Economy	1,225.05	1,165.17	1,196.86	9,075.51	2,017.38	796.91	15,476.88	3.72
Education	1,939.18	153.32	0.00	0.00	313.19	497.74	2,903.43	0.69
Hygiene	555.91	153.48	1,147.38	1,054.50	791.54	0.00	3,702.81	0.89
Diverse	1,620.58	1,586.31	4,279.58	14,712.34	11,273.42	16,278.44	49,750.67	11.96
Total	Z40,565.13	35,975.03	64,631.11	94,027.08	95,495.87	85,205.99	415,900.21	99.97

TABLE 17

COLLECTIVITY ADMINISTRATIVE AND POLICE PERSONNEL,
TWELVE COLLECTIVITIES, MONGALA SUBREGION, 1974

Collectivity	No. Administrative Personnel[a]	%	No. Police Personnel	%	Total No. Employees
1. Lisala	41	59	29	41	70
2. Gombe-Doko	28	48	30	52	58
3. Ngombe-Mombangi	18	37	30	63	48
4. Mongala-Motima	57	68	27	32	84
5. Yandongi	54	62	33	38	87
6. Boso-Melo	26	57	20	43	46
7. Boso-Djanoa	62	67	30	33	92
8. Hotto-Banza	32	54	27	46	59
9. Yakoma	47	55	39	45	86
10. Mobayi-Mbongo	22	37	37	63	59
11. *Cité* Businga	21	58	15	42	36
12. Businga	34	52	31	48	65
Total	442	56	348	44	790
Average for 12 collectivities	37	56	29	44	66

SOURCE: Collectivity personnel documents, 1974.

[a]Including manual workers.

By any standards, collectivity personnel are not well qualified for their
tasks. The average educational level of the administrative personnel is about
two years of postprimary education. Few policemen have had more than five
or six years of primary school, and the overall average is closer to two or
three years of primary education. For all intents and purposes, they are
functionally illiterate.[20] While it cannot be said that education is the sole
criterion for determining the quality of an employee, it is an important one.
Other indicators, discussed below, support my initial conclusion on this
point. The personnel ratings of the various collectivities emphasize that those
employed are inadequate for the tasks they are supposed to perform.
Alcoholism is widespread at this level of the administrative structure, and
drunkenness does nothing to facilitate administrative performance, as the
evaluations of five different bureaucrats demonstrate:

> . . . must avoid popularizing himself with the beverage salesmen. He leaves his
> office and abandons the work that his chief has given him to saunter about the
> *Cité*, entering one house after the other, looking for a drink.

> . . . must avoid consuming arack [the local home brew] which is for him the
> most important food.

... must also avoid excesses of drinking. ... This will save him from com-
mitting adultery with a free woman during the hours of work as was the case not
long ago.

Inebriate of the first order.

All his ideas are focused on drinking and he has not one minute to lose for the
interests of his work.[21]

While these evaluations deal with the purely administrative workers, the
same shortcomings can be imputed to the police. The alcoholic exploits of
collectivity policemen are so well known throughout the area that a single
example can suffice as an illustration. One evening a collectivity policeman
was assigned to guard the administrative offices. During the day some arack
had been seized. That night the policeman on guard was cold, so he broke into
the office to have some arack, hoping that it would warm him. Apparently this
did the trick, and he consumed all the liquor. He was found sleeping it off in
the office the next morning.[22]

Qualified or not, efficient or not, sober or not, all the administrators and
police who work for the collectivity draw a monthly salary. In many
instances, however, this salary is not paid. Or, if it is paid, the workers receive
it only after delays of six to twelve months because the chiefs, accountants,
secretaries, and territorial commissioners do not hesitate to appropriate the
major portion of the collectivity's resources for themselves.

One result of this behavior is that there is not enough money left over to pay
the less-privileged collectivity workers. Police, tax collectors, and roadworkers are sometimes forced to go without their salaries for extended
periods. This is a common feature of life in Mongala Subregion. During
1973, forty-four roadworkers in one Mobayi-Mbongo collectivity were not
paid. In May 1974 the police of the *Cité* of Lisala had not been paid for ten
months. The personnel of one collectivity in Businga received no money at all
between January and June 1975.[23] These are but a few examples of a
widespread phenomenon. What this means in financial terms is shown in
tables 18 and 19.

What are the implications of this shortfall? As seen in table 18, the yearly
average difference between salaries promised and salaries paid to the police
of the *Cité* is Z1,188.12. In individual terms, this means that each of Lisala's
twenty-nine policemen will not be paid Z3.40 per month to which he is
entitled.[24] Since the average salary for policemen in Lisala is on the order of
Z8–10 per month, he will have to provide for his family on approximately
Z5–7. Most of these men have wives and at least three children. It is
inconceivable that they could make ends meet on only Z5–7. The implications of this pattern are staggering. Because the police are not well paid to
begin with and, even then, do not receive all their salary, they have to find
ways to support their families. Given their positions of authority and ability to
make life miserable for those under them if they so choose, when the end of

TABLE 18

POLICE SALARIES, PROMISED AND ACTUAL, CITÉ OF LISALA, 1968–75

Year	Promised Salary	Actual Salary
1968	Z1,177.61	Z690.59
1969	2,135.17	735.53
1970	4,025.20	1,532.71
1971	5,507.89	3,730.20
1972	3,870.41	2,414.60
1973	4,336.90	4,038.68
1974	3,927.68	3,521.72
1975	7,925.29	—
Total 1968–74	Z24,980.86	Z16,664.03
Yearly average 1968–74	3,568.69	2,380.57
Average yearly difference between promised salary and paid salary	1,188.12	

Source: Cité de Lisala, *Comptes des recettes et des dépenses* and *Prévisions budgétaires,* 1968–75.

TABLE 19

ADMINISTRATIVE PERSONNEL SALARIES, PROMISED AND ACTUAL, CITÉ OF LISALA, 1968–75

Year	Promised Salary	Actual Salary
1968	Z2,109.96	Z1,709.94
1969	1,998.43	1,588.34
1970	2,472.58	1,567.09
1971	4,276.36	3,054.25
1972	3,176.93	3,062.02
1973	3,568.16	3,937.91
1974	5,392.67	3,669.16
1975	6,111.01	—
Total 1968–74	Z22,985.09	Z14,919.55
Yearly average 1968–74	3,283.58	2,131.36
Average yearly difference between promised salary and paid salary	1,152.22	

Source: Cité de Lisala, *Comptes des recettes et des dépenses* and *Prévisions budgétaires,* 1968–75.

the month rolls around, they extract what they can from the local populace to tide themselves over until the next payday. Ultimately, it is the population—the ordinary villagers—who suffer because of the *avantages* the chief and his cronies enjoy.

Table 19 demonstrates that other administrative personnel have the same problem. Particularly ironic is the situation of the tax collectors. For the individual there is likely to be a difference of approximately Z2.30 per month between what he should be paid and what he actually receives.[25] These officials, like their colleagues in law enforcement, are not well paid and receive from Z10 to Z12 per month. The money they do not get because of the financial mismangement of the chief probably means a great deal to them. They therefore resort to violence to extract money from the population so that they can feed their families. Tax collection in Zaire is a brutal affair in which the police and party youth wing often collaborate with great gusto. In no society is the tax collector a well-liked figure. In Zaire, however, people literally run when they see him approach. Once again, the *avantages* of the chief result in brutality by the bureaucrats and suffering for the people.

The failure to pay lower-level collectivity personnel regularly has other serious consequences. If, for example, a tax collector is not paid on time, he may well try to remedy the situation himself. This means that if he collects, say, Z300, he will turn over only a small percentage to the collectivity accountant, claiming as justification that the amount he has refused to turn in constitutes the arrears of his unpaid salary.[26] Consequently, the amount of money coming into the coffers will seriously be reduced and the collectivity will perpetually find itself in a financial hole. Once in this position, the collectivity finds it difficult to get off the treadmill, and the arrears owed to other employees will only grow. In addition to what they can extract from the local population, the agents are also then dependent upon the chief and the accountant for "advances" on their salaries. This is a frequent occurrence throughout Mongala and creates a situation where personnel are constantly required to borrow money from the collectivity in return for IOUs. The problem here is that the agents usually wind up borrowing more than they can ever hope to repay, for the amounts loaned are often more than the monthly salary itself.[27] Again, this creates a predicament from which it is difficult to escape, even though a small portion of the loan might be withheld from the worker's salary. There are few collectivities in Equateur Region that are free from this situation; IOUs are invariably found in the cash box. This money is more often than not unrecoverable, and most collectivities have perpetual deficits.

To this point, the discussion has been limited to aspects of collectivity finance that, although they have a seamy side, are perfectly legal. The advantages and fringe benefits the chiefs claim may be ill-advised, but are usually approved by the superior echelons of the administration and are not illegal. The resulting deficits, however, are compounded by embezzlements by the chief and other key personnel. A few examples, largely drawn from budgetary documents, illustrate the point. In 1975 one collectivity in Mongala previewed an expense of Z1,500 for magazine subscriptions for the local youth center. Unfortunately, there is no local youth center in that particular collectivity.[28] The inference that such funds ultimately make their way into the pockets of the chief and his immediate collaborators is virtually irresistible. Other items written into the budgets are equally suspect. The categories of good works, public festivities, and diverse expenditures are particularly important in this context. The chiefs and their accountants rarely bother to provide detailed justifications for these expenses but, when furnished, they make interesting reading. In 1974 one collectivity in Bongandanga submitted the following justifications for diverse expenses of Z6,053.59:

JMPR encouragement premiums	Z563.15
Arrival regional commissioner	266.00
Bills at plantation stores	1,001.37
Unrecoverable advances to personnel including the zone commissioner and his assistants	2,109.54
Cheerleading festival	625.54
Payment CND official	333.60
Arrival of president	366.80
Diverse	787.49
Total	Z,6,053.59[29]

It will be noted that over 50 percent of the total (bills and advances) benefited the local cadres. In addition to this sort of irregularity, special collections that the national authorities institute from time to time are rarely put to the uses for which they were intended. A case in point is the yearly social security payments of collectivity workers. Each month a small sum is withheld from the salaries of the collectivity personnel. In principle, this money is to be held at the collectivity and then sent to the social security office in the regional capital. This yearly fund can reach Z1,000 to Z2,000 per collectivity. In practice however, this money rarely makes its way to the appropriate office.[30]

Collectivity authorities have other illegal means of raising funds. People throughout Mongala, and indeed in all Equateur, have to contend with a series of frequent and completely illegal taxes levied by the chiefs and their associates. In 1975 the chief of a collectivity bordering the *Cité* of Lisala imposed a Z2 tax on all manioc sellers. During the same year the chief of the *Cité* set up barricades along the main roads leading into Lisala and required a supplementary road tax of all those coming into town either to sell their produce or to visit the hospital. Examples abound. One collectivity even went so far as to impose a tax on concubinage. The population, of course, has little recourse and virtually no means of ending such exactions.[31]

The difficulties described in this section are only compounded by territorial comissioners who are supposed to prevent them. In brief, commissioners are usually implicated in these corrupt practices, and administrative correspondence on this point is voluminous. In the words of one regional commissioner:

As far as the collectivity cash boxes go, irregularities in the management of funds are legion; bookeeping is not done daily, or even monthly; nor is it controlled by

Zone authorities who, for the most part, are immersed in these management irregularities.[32]

Such irregularities are common occurrences throughout Equateur Region. An inspection team dispatched in 1974 discovered that no fewer than twenty-three collectivity chiefs had embezzled funds ranging from Z26 to Z7,606.76.[33] Furthermore, there is much evidence indicating that these phenomena are not limited to Equateur. A region-wide inspection of collectivity finance in Kasai Occidental found that all but one of the collectivities had serious deficits. In addition, it found that the pattern of resource overestimation was prevalent everywhere. The overall situation was deemed "catastrophic."[34]

These aspects of collectivity financial administration are an important part of the overall rural exploitation system. But while detailing the dimensions and mechanisms of financial mismanagement and corruption, I have not intended to give the impression that all who hold positions of authority at these levels are corrupt. There are some politico-administrative cadres who are acutely aware of the problems involved and are trying to redress the situation. Unfortunately, their hands are tied. As one cadre put it:

> But we are on the political plane. There is bad management. If I try a judicial process there will be more bad than good. Between two evils we must choose the lesser. We cannot arrest everybody.[35]

This same official uncovered an embezzlement of Z13,371.40 in one of the collectivities under his jurisdiction, but since another politico-administrative official was involved (the chief), he asked the regional commissioner for instructions on how to proceed. The latter in effect instructed him to take administrative rather than judicial action. Official policy on this question is now based on *Ordonnance-Loi* no. 74–255 of 6 November 1974, which maintains that collectivity chiefs cannot be brought to justice without the express written consent of the state commissioner for political affairs. The regional commissioner made it known that

> in practice it must be retained that this [judicial] option can only be executed when it is a question of important affairs, for considering the volume of work that the State Commissioner for Political Affairs is called on to do, it is important to spare him the examination of minor problems.[36]

In effect, the application of this policy gives the chiefs carte blanche. They can continue their activities without fear that they will be called before the bar of justice.

Villagers are the immediate victims of such activity. It is their money that is misappropriated, and it is they who bear the brunt of the excesses committed by the police and the bureaucrats when they are not paid. Moreover, they receive few services in return for their taxes. Collectivity administration even has difficulty in performing the much vaunted law-and-order function. In addition to the normal exuberance of the police, the population must bear the weight of the prison system. Each collectivity has its own jail. More often than not, this consists of a wooden shack from which it is not at all difficult to escape. In Lisala prisoners amuse themselves by tunneling through the prison's corroding walls. The police are unable to control prisoner escapes, and the result is a reign of terror for those who live in the vicinity of the prison.[37] Even if the physical premises are secure, there are other serious problems. Because of the financial and budgetary mismanagement prevalent in the collectivities, there is rarely enough money to feed prisoners. The meager funds consecrated to that purpose are often skimmed off the top by prison directors. Since it would be inhumane to let prisoners starve, they are released for the day and sent out among the population to fend for themselves. Such foraging expeditions usually result in the inmates stealing what they can from local villagers. The situation has become so serious that a territorial commissioner informed me one of his main priorities for Lisala was to eliminate banditry.[38]

All these processes result in widespread insecurity. The local citizenry is forced to live in a state of quasi-permanent insecurity because they never know when the next exaction will occur, or what precise form it will take. Will it be an illegal manioc tax by the chief? The visit of a tax collector in search of funds? The brutalities of a policeman who has not been paid? Or the theft by a prisoner who has been released because the authorities do not have enough money to feed him?

Feelings of insecurity are by no means restricted to local villagers. The chiefs, their entourage, the lower-level clerks, and the policemen are in a similar vise. The chiefs, like other politico-administrative cadres, have an insecure hold on their positions. They serve under a political mandate that can be revoked at any time. Because they know their *avantages* can go up in smoke from one day to the next, there is a tendency to extract what they can, while they can, for they may no longer be in power on the morrow. The same can be said of other collectivity employees, no matter what their particular job. Chiefs are changed fairly often, and the new man will usually wish to have his own cronies and collaborators in the positions he can fill. Since most collectivity personnel are not permanent civil servants, they can be fired at virtually any moment. This is no idle worry, and administrative records show numerous instances of such happenings.[39] Collectivity bureaucrats thus have real concerns about their future. So they, too, believe that they had best accumulate as much capital as possible, since their stay in authority may be brief. The changeover of collectivity personnel in this manner thus heightens their feelings of insecurity and, unfortunately, the population must pay the price in the form of frequent and varied abuses. Naturally, this occurs in addition to "normal" insecurities that result from being paid irregularly and never having enough money to make ends meet. Although the turnover in the composition of a social class is by no means restricted to the collectivity level and has been a feature of Zairian social dynamics since independence, the perpetual rise and fall does create problems for the people who have to put up with the extractions accompanying this fluidity. Such problems are not unique to the administrative sphere, as an examination of the system's effects on agriculture will demonstrate.

Agriculture

The continuing shortfall in collectivity finance results in a renewed effort to get village farmers to pay their CPM because it is the main source of collectivity funds. The villagers' only real supply of income, however, is from the sale of agricultural products to state agricultural offices and other approved intermediaries. These agencies are primarily interested in buying cotton, rice, coffee, and cocoa, which can be exported. Most of these products cannot be eaten, and for this reason (among others to be discussed) the population is not particularly interested in cultivating them. The state's answer—now, as in the past—is obligatory cultivation. At various times during the colonial period villagers could be forced to grow these crops from 45 to 120 days per year. This requirement had the dual effect of forcing villagers into the cash economy (they also needed the money for their taxes) and of providing the crops necessary for export to the metropole. Mulambu Mvuluya persuasively argues that this system has never really been modified. The 1969 ordinance organizing collectivity administration notes that a total of forty-five days per year can be required of villagers for such "educational work." This limit, however, may be exceeded if there is urgent work to be done. Forced labor is still a reality in Zaire. In Equateur, for example, each able-bodied villager is required to cultivate one-half hectare of cotton per year. One result of this system, especially in the cotton-growing areas, is that farmers do not have enough time to grow their own food crops, and the incidence of malnutrition increases dramatically.[40]

Villagers need money to pay school fees for their children; to buy clothing, beer, agricultural tools, food, and other first-necessity items; and to pay their local taxes. Such needs could be met if farmers were given a fair price for their crops and a just return on their labor. Regrettably, they are not. The system does not place money in the hands of villagers, mostly because a large percentage of the harvested products never find their way into the hands of buyers.

Coffee is illustrative. The 1974 agricultural report for Equateur Region noted that coffee stored in the villages had been rotting since 1971. The Office National du Café (ONC) bears much of the responsibility for this. In 1974, for example, the ONC branch office in Lisala was to have bought 5,138,055 kilograms of coffee from villagers in the zones of Lisala, Businga, and Mobayi-Mbongo. At the end of that year it had actually purchased only 284,508 kilograms, or roughly 5 percent of the total harvest. Like most of the state's agricultural offices, ONC suffers from serious organizational and financial defects. The Lisala branch has only one truck for its three zones, and in addition there are not enough sacks to distribute to village farmers.

There are human problems here as well. In the rare instance when an ONC truck manages to arrive in a village where sacks had previously been distributed, the agents—seeking personal profit—require a *matabiche* from each farmer. Should a villager refuse this small consideration, the agent will not buy his produce. As the ONC holds a complete monopoly on coffee-buying, villagers have little choice but to pay. The bureaucrat in charge of Lisala's ONC office claims he is not given enough money to buy all the coffee in the area, and this may well be true. But local skeptics dismiss this excuse by pointing to the thriving commerce of the bureaucrat's wife and wondering aloud where she got the money to begin her commercial ventures.[41]

The difficulties in getting rice to market are similar. Until recently the subregional commissioner was responsible for assigning buying zones to local rice merchants. Each merchant was granted a monopoly on the products of his zone. Unfortunately, these rice merchants are often incapable of getting the rice out to market. Here, too, there are not enough sacks to go around. In addition, there is fierce competition among rice merchants to be granted a buying zone close to one of the more passable roads. If a merchant should have the ill fortune to be given a zone that is not serviced by a passable road network, the tendency is to write off the exercise for another year and make no attempt at all to reach the villagers. The reasoning behind this attitude is that the trucks will break down, the costs will multiply, and the potential profit will decrease and no longer be worth the effort. Consequently rice, like coffee, will remain in the villages, and farmers will not be able to get a return on their labors.[42]

One result is that the field is opened up for speculators who own their own trucks. If the ONC and the rice merchants are either unwilling or unable to get into the villages, farmers, in desperate need of money, are forced to sell to whoever comes along first. Speculators arrive in the villages and purchase the products at rates well below even the meager government price. Upon completing the transaction, they then return to towns like Lisala and sell the products to accredited state buyers at the official price, thus realizing a tidy profit.[43]

Unsold products are a great problem in all parts of Mongala. In 1975 officials in the Zone of Businga recorded that 1,300 tons of coffee, 181 tons of corn, 35 tons of peanuts, and 18 tons of rice remained unsold in the villages. Similar conditions obtain throughout Equateur Region, and there is evidence that the same problem exists in both Haut-Zaire and Shaba.[44]

As suggested above, a complication is the lamentable condition of the local road infrastructure. One of the main reasons there are such difficulties in evacuating harvested crops is that many local arteries are impassable at best, nonexistent at worst. The terrible state of the road network is a constant subject of administrative concern. Both collectivity chiefs and territorial commissioners are perpetually exhorted to get to work on the roads. Many villages in Mongala are accessible only by land rover—and then only during the dry season. It is all but impossible for large trucks to come into villages and pick up the coffee, rice, and cotton that have been harvested.[45]

Some collectivities devote a portion of their budget to hire roadworkers. These lower-level employees are paid poorly and irregularly because of the chiefs' budgetary capitalism. Not surprisingly, this lessens their devotion to duty. After all, why work on the roads if you are not going to be paid for it? Often the task is simply ignored. Moreover, should road conditions deteriorate to the point where a chief's superiors are likely to lean on him, the local citizenry is pressed into involuntary service to remedy the situation. Villagers are thus forced to do the job for which roadworkers are ostensibly being paid. Naturally, they are constrained to volunteer their services without pay. There is, of course, resistance to these "revolutionary imperatives," but the alternative is a jail sentence. A report on one collectivity in Mongala noted somewhat dryly that "the decision taken by the Regional Committee to incarcerate whoever would refuse road repair work was well-applauded by all the leaders of this [collectivity]."[46] Villagers are therefore forced to take time off from their fields to work without hope of recompense.

The overall failure to get the crops to market has very serious implications. If villagers cannot sell their crops, there will be no money to buy basic trade goods. Money for the CPM will not be available, and this alone is enough to bring the wrath of local officialdom down on their heads. The chiefs and their cohorts will redouble their efforts to get taxes from the population because their own salaries and other benefits depend on them; their extractive methods will become still more brutal. The combined impact results in a disincentive to produce. Economically rational, villagers will correctly deduce that there is no sense in farming if the fruits of their labor are going to be left unsold in the villages. At that point, all the work necessary to produce cash crops becomes absurd. Unfortunately, this failure to produce will engender the anger of the national authorities, who need the crops both for export and to feed the population in metropolitan areas. The government in Kinshasa thus pressures territorial authorities and agronomists to coerce the villagers into even greater productive efforts. Those at the bottom of the ladder, the village farmers, are badgered from all sides to produce crops that will not be sold. If they cannot be sold, the villagers will take crops like corn and rice and make alcoholic beverages from them. Alcoholism thus increases in areas where crops are not evacuated.[47]

Under such circumstances there are several options open to villagers and none of them is pleasing. On the one hand, they can submit to the system and produce. But because of the low prices, bad roads, inability of the government to buy the crops, excessive taxation, and "normal" financial pressures of collectivity officialdom, farmers will not be able to accumulate capital. What few funds they do receive and manage to retain will barely enable them to meet current needs and expenses. This option provides no incentive to produce and no way off the treadmill.

On the other hand, they can refuse to produce, but this decision may entail any number of serious consequences. First, since failure to comply with what the authorities term "educational work" (or forced labor) is illegal, they may very well wind up in jail. This is not a remote possibility and the collectivity court systems are quite active in such matters, as table 20 bears witness.

TABLE 20

PRISON SENTENCES, CUSTOMARY COURTS,
ZONE OF LISALA, BY INFRACTION, 1969–74

Infraction	Number of Sentences[a]							
	1969	1970	1971	1972	1973	1974	Total	%
1. Matrimonial affairs	196	189	297	269	226	151	1,328	10.56
2. Assault	191	177	210	271	243	294	1,386	11.02
3. Theft	158	164	121	135	188	214	980	9.49
4. Failure to register with local authority	72	73	38	64	40	30	317	2.52
5. Disobedience to authority	84	86	79	154	113	59	575	4.57
6. Public drunkenness	61	64	118	105	123	76	547	4.35
7. Sorcery, superstitious practice	73	62	37	76	80	36	364	2.89
8. Forced cultivation	74	68	96	181	179	104	702	5.58
9. Village hygiene	109	98	183	250	119	1	760	6.04
10. Failure to register births or deaths	200	198	87	211	90	35	821	6.53
11. Defamation	194	198	172	194	95	133	986	7.84
12. Insults	112	114	114	202	236	197	975	7.75
13. Gambling	16	12	0	17	1	2	48	0.38
14. Debts	46	47	61	86	36	22	298	2.37
15. Felling palm trees	36	28	5	8	12	29	118	0.93
16. Setting bush fires	0	0	0	1	5	1	7	0.05
17. Diverse	390	396	417	636	320	200	2,359	18.76
Total	2,012	1,974	2,035	2,860	2,106	1,584	12,571	99.91

SOURCE: Zone de Lisala, *Rapport annuel des affaires politiques,* 1969–74.

[a]Customary courts can levy prison sentences of 1 to 60 days. Most sentences here were from 1 to 30 days.

Table 20 shows the number of convictions handed down by customary courts in the Zone of Lisala from 1969–1974. Briefly, each collectivity has one or more of these courts, presided over by judges who are usually older men well versed in the customs of their own ethnic groups. In general, however, chiefs usually have a great deal of influence over the way the customary courts function in any given locality. Moreover, recent territorial reforms have attributed to them the powers of Officers of the Judicial Police, and they can now arrest wrongdoers themselves. It should be noted that offenses such as failure to register with the local authority, disobedience to authority, sorcery, forced cultivation, village hygiene, failure to register births or deaths, felling palm trees, and setting bush fires are infractions that generally call into question the authority of the chief. Regardless of how they are labeled, most crimes concern the failure of citizens to comply with agricultural regulations like forced cultivation. If all these categories are totaled, we see that perhaps 25 percent of the prison sentences meted out are the result of agricultural infractions. To this total could also probably be added many of the crimes listed under "diverse." It is thus clear that the local court system serves to uphold the authority of the chief in agricultural matters. Any villager who refuses to participate in the required cultivation effort is more than likely to be placed behind bars.

There are numerous chances for abuse to creep into this system. As mentioned, the chief is the dominant figure in the collectivity even though he does not sit on the court. A brief word to the judges can usually be counted on to produce the desired results. In theory, the Subregional Tribunal and the Public Prosecutor's Office are supposed to inspect the work of the courts. But customary courts are numerous, and judges at the subregional level are almost never able to perform this task. There are many instances of judgments that ought to be quashed but never are. This lack of inspection is almost legendary, and the courts in one zone in Mongala were visited for the first time since independence only in 1974.[48]

In some isolated collectivities, chiefs can pretty much do as they please. In Bumba, for example, there is one chief who defines "educational work" to mean forced labor on his own plantation. Obviously, failure to comply with his directives on this subject can result in a lengthy jail sentence without hope of appeal. Such arbitrary arrests are quite common, and higher authorities are constantly warning their subordinates about such excesses. To make matters worse, while in jail a villager might be subject to various kinds of physical abuse. Cases of flogging and other forms of corporal punishment are by no means unknown in Mongala. Once a villager is placed in confinement, many chiefs require the payment of exorbitant fines before seeing that the culprit is released.[49] Declining to participate in forced cultivation is a dangerous option to pursue.

A second consequence of refusing to participate in forced cultivation is flight. Many villagers flee to the deep forest or the river islands to avoid the burdens—agricultural and financial—of the collectivity. These withdrawals, which might be called tax flight, are usually temporary and end when the immediate danger has passed.[50] There are, however, permanent communities that spring up in the deep equatorial forest and zealously guard their independence from the political authorities of the regime.[51] Equally often, the consequence of rural oppression brings a more permanent exodus to urban areas. The situation in rural collectivities has become so desperate that, rightly or wrongly, many believe the only solution is to leave for the large cities. Another factor that often pushes people to migrate to urban areas is *Salongo*. In theory, *Salongo* is a voluntary method of civic education that takes the form of communal labor on projects of public interest. In practice, it is simply another form of forced labor. Very little about the operation of *Salongo* is voluntary, and territorial authorities often have to call out the police and army to ensure active participation. Moreover, governmental authorities have restricted travel on the river between Kinshasa and Lisala to make certain that citizens "respond in great number to the call of the Father of the Zairian Revolution concerning *Salongo*."[52]

A third option villagers can choose is revolt. As mentioned earlier, there are occasional instances of revolt against the exactions of collectivity administration. But rural communities are widely scattered, and the forces available to the authorities greatly outnumber those upon which the population can call. In addition, most adults remember the anarchistic years of the *provincettes* and the rebellions in the mid-1960s. The violence of the army and police against the populace was then widespread; as Scott says, "the tangible and painful memories of repression must have a chilling effect on peasants who contemplate even minor acts of resistance."[53] The fear of armed intervention is very real in these rural areas, and no community wishes to see the army descend on it. While the Zairian army has rarely distinguished itself against opponents who can fight back, it still has the capability of making short shrift of an essentially unarmed opposition.[54]

Indeed, throughout the system of rural exploitation described here, the Zairian army and gendarmes function as a free-floating source of oppression. Their behavior is usually less than exemplary and abuse abounds. In Lisala drunken soldiers have been known to release all the prisoners held in detention; levy illegal taxes on merchants and other citizens; and arbitrarily arrest innocent people until such time as their friends or relatives can pay exorbitant and highly illegal fines. Civil-military relations are not good anywhere, and civilian justice is incapable of bringing a halt to these activities.[55] State Commissioner Engulu noted that in general most territorial authorities (and we can certainly add the military to his assessment) behave in their districts as though they were in a conquered territory.[56]

Conclusion

The picture painted here of collectivity administration is bleak. It has not been my intention to be morbid, but merely to present things as they are. In the course of research I had access to documents on almost all of the twenty-three collectivities in Mongala. Consequently, data from all these administrative entities are interspersed throughout this chapter. While particular features of the oppressive system pertain more to some collectivities than to others, the general image is accurate. In a sense, my aim has been to elaborate certain aspects of collectivity administration in the rural and semiurban areas of Zaire. I should like to present a preliminary model of local administration in the form of a propositional summary.

1. Village farmers need money for first-necessity items and to pay their CPM.
2. The only way they can obtain this money is by cultivating and selling cash crops.
3. Village farmers are forced to sell their produce to the state agricultural offices. Conditions of monopsony obtain.
4. If produce is sold, the prices received are extremely low and do not permit any accumulation of capital.
5. Crops are often left unsold because of inefficiencies and corruption in the state agricultural offices and because of the poor state of the road infrastructure. The farmers then have no money to pay their taxes, and an accumulation of capital is not possible.
6. Because of low prices and unmarketed harvests, villagers have no incentive to produce, and agricultural output declines.
7. Unmarketed crops mean there will be no money to pay the CPM.
8. Collectivities depend on the CPM for about one-half their monetary intake.
9. Chiefs and their associates appropriate funds for their own use.
10. This bureaucratic capitalism results in a shortage of money for other collectivity employees. Police and tax collectors are not paid on time.
11. These employees will then extract what they can from the people in their jurisdictions, often resorting to violence.
12. Unsold crops mean that there will not be enough food to feed the cities or to export for foreign exchange.
13. National authorities pressure the territorial and collectivity officials to increase production and to repair the roads.
14. Agronomists and local officials force villagers to cultivate cash crops and to work without pay on the roads.
15. Villagers comply grudgingly, serve time in prison for refusing, escape to the islands and the forest, migrate to the cities, or revolt.

It is clear that the system of rural exploitation does not permit villagers to accumulate significant economic resources, since the collectivity administrative apparatus siphons off what it can. The entire extractive system acts in such a way as to close off opportunities for those villagers who would like to move up either socially or politically because such mobility is virtually impossible without money and access to education. Village farmers are, in effect, placed on a treadmill from which they cannot escape. Since villagers cannot accumulate much money, they are often unable to pay school fees. The real tragedy, then, is reserved for village children. We have already seen that there is a disproportionately small percentage of village children in Lisala's primary and secondary schools. One reason is that they are expelled from school when they cannot pay the fees. The long-range result is that the sons and daughters will probably be unable to escape the fate of their fathers and mothers.[57] The rewards and opportunities provided by the economic, political, and social systems will thus continue to be systematically denied to the majority of the population.

As Nzongola correctly observed, the postcolonial state in Zaire "has failed to improve the material conditions of life of its citizens."[58] The administration is not part of the solution, but part of the problem. To use Wittfogel's term, many of those who work for the state—regardless of level— are "bureaucratic capitalists."[59] This is certainly true of budget-padding collectivity chiefs and their tax collectors. It is also true of those who hold higher positions in the administrative apparatus. At higher levels occasions often arise to translate politico-administrative authority into commercial opportunity. These commercial-political interactions are particularly evident in the example of the politial economy of beer in Lisala.

CHAPTER 5

The Political Economy of Beer: Reflections on Policy in Zaire[1]

Si vous avez de la bière, vous avez de l'argent.
                                                    —A Lisala trader[2]

In Lisala—and in Zaire generally—if you have beer, you have money. To show why this is true, it is necessary to elaborate several themes. First, I demonstrate why beer is crucial in Lisala's political and economic configuration. Attention is also paid to the question of beer distribution and supply, both to and in the town of Lisala. Third, I examine the politics of price control as it pertains to the bars and *buvettes* in Lisala, emphasizing the interactions between commercial and political sectors. Finally, the Mobutu government's attempt to harness the tax revenue generated from beer consumption to develop the nation's economic infrastructure is studied.

Although these questions relate directly to beer, they have wider significance in terms of the operation of local commercial and political systems. An examination of the political economy of beer ought to be taken as a case study of the way things tend to occur in the political-economic sphere in Zaire, because many of the analyses set forth here, particularly those concerning the politics of price control, are equally applicable to other commodities. Since bottled beer has rarely been deemed a subject meriting sustained attention by social scientists, it is necessary to describe the importance of this product in both the national and the local economies.[3]

Beer: National and Local Perspectives

While today Zaire boasts fifteen breweries and is Africa's largest producer of beer, this was not always so.[4] The first major breweries in Zaire were constructed in Kinshasa in 1923 and in Lubumbashi in 1925. The aim, at least initially, was to provide beer for the largely Belgian expatriate community living in the colony. At that time importation of European beer was not considered feasible because the degree of fermentation did not permit its transfer to tropical regions. This factor, coupled with high import duties, encouraged the substitution of local beer. The world economic crisis of the 1930s effectively halted the expansion of this industry, but production and consumption picked up following World War II, as noted in table 21.[5]

Although impressive in the African context, when compared with beer production and consumption in most of the Western world, Zairian figures represent a mere drop in the barrel.[6] On the other hand, an argument can be sustained that relatively speaking, domestic beer consumption has a far

TABLE 21
BEER PRODUCTION AND PER CAPITA CONSUMPTION IN ZAIRE, 1946–74

Year	Population	Beer Production (1000 ha)	Per Capita Consumption (b)
1946	10,667,087	182	1.70
1947	10,761,353	201	1.86
1948	10,914,208	212	1.94
1949	11,073,311	299	2.70
1950	11,331,793	369	3.25
1951	11,593,494	478	4.12
1952	11,778,711	649	5.50
1953	12,026,159	739	6.14
1954	12,317,326	882	7.16
1955	12,562,630	1,082	8.61
1956	12,843,574	1,229	9.56
1957	13,174,883	1,382	10.48
1958	13,559,000	1,190	8.77
1959	13,821,000	1,286	9.30
1960	14,150,000	1,425	10.07
1961	14,464,000	1,685	11.64
1962	14,797,000	2,109	14.25
1963	15,007,000	2,141	14.26
1964	15,300,000	1,921	12.55
1965	15,570,000	2,017	11.47
1966	18,350,000	2,240	12.20
1967	19,150,000	2,230	11.64
1968	20,000,000	2,233	11.16
1969	20,880,000	2,706	12.95
1970	21,690,000	3,394	15.64
1971	22,300,000	3,803	17.05
1972	22,910,000	4,136	18.05
1973	23,560,000	4,727	20.06
1974	24,220,000	5,723	23.62

SOURCE: *Rapport annuel sur l'administration de la Colonie du Congo belge,* 1946–57; United Nations, *Statistical Yearbook,* 1959–65, 1976; United Nations, *Demographic Yearbook 1976,* p. 138; and Lacroix, *Industrielisation au Congo,* p. 316.

aHectoliters
bLiters.

greater impact upon the Zairian economy than on any European or North American economy. In 1974 the per capita beer consumption figure for Zaire was 23.62 liters. Since beer is sold in 0.72-liter bottles, this is the equivalent of thirty-three bottles of beer per person per year. At the official government price of 20k per bottle, this works out to an expenditure of Z6.60 per year for beer. The average per capita *income* for Zaire is, at most, Z50 ($100).

While of course it cannot be said that Z6.60 of every Z50 will be spent on beer, the importance of beer in the Zairian economy should still be manifest.[7]

More specifically, the significance of expenditure for beer in the Lisala household budget is, to a certain extent, demonstrable. I calculated that in the eighteen-month period between January 1974 and June 1975 the average monthly beer sale in Lisala was 72,637 bottles.[8] Lisala's population is roughly 27,000, but is is incorrect to assume that beer consumption is distributed equally among all these people—women and children included. An educated guess is that perhaps 85 percent of the consumption is accounted for by a group I shall the hard-core drinkers (HCDs). These men and women are usually salaried and include workers, state employees, merchants, fishermen, and prostitutes, groups that number approximately 3,900 people.[9] If we assume they account for 85 percent of the average monthly beer sales in the city, each one drinks about sixteen bottles of beer per month at the cost of Z3.20. (The officially imposed price of 20k per bottle is understood.) If, as state employees, they average salaries between Z15 and Z35 per month, it becomes apparent that beer could account for 10 to 20 percent of their monthly household expenditure.[10] In purely economic terms, therefore, it makes sense to study the political economy of beer in the local arena.

The bar trade in Lisala is a lively one, and those with commercial instincts have found it rewarding. The number of bars has expanded over the years for several key reasons. First, as might be expected, beer is a popular product. Considered a first-necessity item by the authorities, the demand for beer is virtually insatiable. It is restricted only by the vagaries of the distributive system, the limited financial capacities of the wholesalers in the interior of the country, and, most important, the limited purchasing power of the clientele. Second, because the demand is so large, the product can be turned over quickly; the bar owner therefore does not have to keep vast amounts of capital tied up for extended periods. Third, not much money is required to begin operations. All one needs is the price of one *case* of beer and an empty backyard. More than one of Lisala's important bar owners began in just this fashion. Finally, the profits can be immense. The legally allowed retail profit margin on each bottle of beer sold is 21 percent. As becomes evident later, though, official prices are rarely enforced and the profit is actually much higher.

Bars in Lisala are important in another fundamental economic way. Many local merchants and small plantation owners derived their working capital from the profits of bars they had previously established. In the words of one local entrepreneur:

> As soon as the construction was finished, I opened a bar. At that time, I had decided to build a plantation in my native village, sixty-five kilometers from Lisala. . . . In 1965 I began with the receipts from the bar and I was able to hire workers. They were paid by the bar. It [the plantation] has eighty hectares.[11]

Since 1970 most of the ten or so really important bar owners in Lisala have diversified their interests. In an obvious way this has aided the local economy because Lisala now has shops and plantations that would not have been developed had it not been for the commercial and financial foothold afforded by the bar trade. Not every subsidiary investment has proved profitable, and bars are still responsible for keeping many afloat. Beer may thus be seen as one of the foundations of the local commercial system. When bars are forced to close, other enterprises suffer as well. Moreover, Lacroix notes that beer "often created the first ties between the subsistence economy and the market economy," and when commercial disorganization followed the political and financial chaos of the early years of Zairian independence, the desire to buy beer was often the only factor holding village farmers to even a tangential involvement with the market economy.[12]

Of political significance as well, territorial commissioners in Lisala and elsewhere spend a great deal of time trying to maintain an adequate supply of beer. Their attempts to better the situation spring from a desire to avoid political unrest. An ample supply of inexpensively priced beer contributes to political quiescence. A holiday in Lisala without beer for the population to drink is cause for political alarm on the part of the authorities. One informant well placed in collectivity administration told me that there was considerable grumbling when the eighth anniversary of the MPR rolled around and there was no beer in town. In previous years it had been the custom to allocate party funds to the collectivity and locality chiefs so that they might stand some of their people to a round or two of beer. When, in May 1975, this was not done, people were quite annoyed with the local authorities.[13]

In more everyday terms, there is usually a feeling that workers would be upset at the regime's political representatives if the supply of beer were not maintained at a price that, if not exactly equitable, was within their reach. Keeping the workers drinking may thus be considered a political plus for the regime in power, and Lisala's politico-administrative authorities are well aware that beer is as essential to their well-being as it is to the population's. At one point the subregional commissioner was moved to instruct his subordinates that the

> stability of these [beer] prices ensures the confidence of the population in the Father of the Nation through you who are validly placed in the Zones to execute these social measures proclaimed by our Enlightened Guide with the aim of protecting the purchasing power of his people.[14]

Political legitimacy and stable beer prices would thus seem to go hand in hand. Price stability depends, at least in part, on the existence of a steady supply and regular distribution of beer. But such a distribution has not been maintained.

Distribution

On 6 October 1975 a high-ranking official in the National Economy Ministry told me that the policy of the government of Zaire is to assure a "rational" distribution of beer throughout the Republic.[15] This policy, at least as far as Lisala is concerned, has proved to be singularly ineffective. The two main sources of beer for the Lisala market are the Bralima and Unibra breweries in Mbandaka and Kisangani, respectively. Table 22 gives an idea of the amount of beer from each of these suppliers.

TABLE 22

TOTAL BEER CONSUMPTION IN LISALA,
JANUARY 1974–JUNE 1975, IN BOTTLES

Source	1974	1975 (six months)
Unibra-Kisangani	236,717	391,980
Bralima-Mbandaka	323,688	355,080
Total	560,405	747,060
18-month total	1,307,465[a]	
Monthly average January 1974–June 1975	72,637	

SOURCE: Production statistics, Bralima, Mbandaka; Unibra, Kinshasa.

[a]The total does not take into account traders who arrive from the interior of the zone to buy beer in Lisala and then resell it elsewhere. Nor does it account for Lisala merchants who buy beer either at the twice-weekly ONATRA boat or in Bumba. There is no way to pin down these figures precisely; most likely the data above are underestimates.

The monthly average of 72,637 bottles indicated in table 22 is far below what can be considered Lisala's *potential* absorption capacity. An informant in one of the wholesale houses that handles much of the beer trade maintains that the town is capable of consuming 300,000 bottles per month without difficulty. In April 1975, for example, he was able to sell 264,000 bottles in three weeks.[16] As a result of the gap between potential capacity and actual supply, the population's demand for beer is rarely satisfied. What shipments do arrive—be they from Mbandaka or Kisangani—are sold out almost immediately. Furthermore, since a steady supply of beer is not assured, Lisala is plunged into frequent and recurring beer crises. During these crises acute shortages of beer occur; the few cases that trickle in are sold at exorbitant prices.

Why does this situation exist? The answer does not lie in the productive capacity of the breweries. For instance, Bralima-Mbandaka has never had to refuse anyone beer on the grounds that there was not enough in stock.[17] But an important problem emerges concerning the transportation of beer from the brewery to Lisala. Many local merchants and bar owners were quick to blame ONATRA, the national river transportation agency, for the irregularity of the beer flow. In 1974 one of the wealthiest and, politically, most well-connected merchants thought seriously about entering the beer trade as a depositor-wholesaler. He was unable to continue his initial venture because he found that beer was not profitable as an enterprise. The problems, he asserted, were caused by ONATRA's personnel.

> There were breakages and thefts at ONATRA. Sometimes I would receive only 800 cases. If I sent back 800 cases of empties only 600 of them would arrive at the brewery. I started it but it did not pay. Consumption is very high but with ONATRA it did not work. It's the personnel of ONATRA who do all that.[18]

This merchant is in many ways typical of the would-be wholesaler in Lisala. Losses incurred because of ONATRA's deficiencies tend to evaporate any profit that might be made, and the alternative—private transportation—is far too expensive to permit the sale of beer at a reasonable, yet profitable, price.

There is another important reason for Lisala's recurrent beer crises. Many people attributed at least part of the cause to the fact that the town did not have a viable beer depot or a wholesale house willing to serve in that capacity. Although the question of a depot is a crucial one, there is in fact much confusion about official policy, and the lack of clarity is by no means restricted to government circles.

While the stated government policy is to assure a "rational" distribution of beer throughout the Republic, much ambiguity exists as to how to effect this policy. Administrators in the National Economy Ministry maintain that the state has decided to leave the task of wholesaling to the major breweries themselves.[19] Officials at Bralima asserted they have been instructed by the relevant powers that in the future they will have to establish depots of their own in the interior. These decentralized and brewery-owned depots will enable the brewery to sell beer at factory prices directly to retailers in the more removed corners of the country. In this way the middlemen (individual wholesalers) would be eliminated and the price would be stabilized. The brewery would also be responsible for the transportation of beer from the factory to the depot. At Unibra, on the other hand, there is a different perception of government policy. Here officials asserted that the government had changed directions and abandoned plans for each brewery to set up depots in the interior. Since June 1975, therefore, they have been under the impression that the government wishes them to revert to the system of dealing with individual wholesalers and private depots.[20] If the government has a consistent policy, which is doubtful, brewery officials are not at all sure what it is. As a result, local officials in Lisala and other similarly affected areas must cope with beer crises as they emerge, on a strictly ad hoc basis.

The depot issue has plagued Lisala's political authorities for a number of years. They have tried, as a short-term measure, to encourage wealthier merchants and bar owners to become interested in the problem so that they might remedy it. Although the results have thus far been nil, this approach at least has the advantage of trying to anticipate events. Other parts of their strategy are more reactive. In general, when a beer shortage is in the offing, the authorities will call a series of meetings with the bar owners and attempt to pressure them into going to a neighboring town to replenish their stock. The results of such procedures are mixed, and at most they provide a short-term solution to a long-term problem.[21]

The capacity of the subregional, zonal, and collectivity authorities to resolve a problem like this is limited. Although they can, and occasionally do, come up with chewing-gum and rubber-band remedies, the problem is merely postponed until it resurfaces six to eight weeks later. Moreover, while the chewing gum is being applied, the problem is kicked upstairs to the next highest administrative level. In the issue of Lisala's beer depot, the buck landed at the top of the political system. In May 1975 President Mobutu appeared in Lisala on an impromptu visit. While there he met with members of the Subregional Committee of the MPR. They placed the beer supply problem before him in the hope that he would take decisive action where others had failed. Mobutu suggested that a retired Zairian army colonel, who was an old buddy, take command of a new beer depot in Lisala. Because the colonel had no resources of his own, the president said he would personally advance him the money necessary for this undertaking. At the same time he instructed the delegate-general of Bralima to open a depot in Lisala.[22] When I left Lisala in August 1975, these beer depots were concepts that still belonged to the future.

What might be called the "case of the disappearing depot" illustrates aspects of the decision-making process in Zaire. Government policy, which was expressed in platitudes, was poorly understood. Only minimal ad hoc measures were taken to implement it at the local level. More important, one may wonder why the president of the Republic should be the one to decide how best the bar owners and beer drinkers of a small town in Equateur might be accommodated. In most nations of the world, beer supply for 27,000 people is not usually a source of presidential decision making. Because vast power has been accumulated by the president, many lower-level authorities are afraid to take initiatives in either problem solving or policy making. The "implementation mentality" is rife throughout the bureaucracy as well as among politico-administrative officers. The inevitable result is a tendency to react to problems defensively rather than an attempt to prevent their occurrence. This is characteristic of the entire Zairian polity, not just of this specific case. The problem of beer distribution is by no means restricted to Lisala. The Tshuapa, Equateur, and Ubangi subregions suffer from the same difficulty.[23]

To this point our examination of beer distribution has been limited to the question of how beer gets to Lisala, when it does. Difficulties notwithstanding, some beer gets through, so that we can now consider the equally important matter of how beer is distributed among various bar owners in the city. To be sure, the recurrent beer crises and the problems inherent in establishing a functioning distributive system create a pervasive scarcity that conditions the way in which beer is divided among the town's bar owners. To begin, though, who owns the bars?

By Lisala's standards virtually all bar owners are extremely wealthy. Many own cars and trucks, obvious symbols of wealth, and have often been able to expand into other commercial ventures. In terms of ethnic origin, of the twenty-five bars in town I would estimate that at least ten are owned by Ngombe and another ten are held by members of other Equateur ethnic groups. Significantly, the remaining five bars are owned by Kongo from either Bas-Zaire or Angola. Other bars are controlled by corporate groups that often include state agents of no little importance as participating members. In two cases of which I am aware, the state agents involved are accountants, and it would be a reasonable assumption that official monies are channeled into these private enterprises. Although illegal, such behavior is widespread.

When beer arrives in Lisala, it is usually distributed through two of the local wholesale houses. The house that handles beer from Kisangani is part of a larger firm based in Gemena. The managing director is an Angolan who has lived and worked in Zaire for many years. The wholesale house that distributes the intermittent supply of beer from Mbandaka is owned by a firm whose main offices are in Karawa. This commercial house is managed by a Portuguese. Beer sales from these wholesale houses to retailers in the city is not based on an equitable or monitored distributive quota. The Angolan manager who dispenses the Kisangani beer often favors his Bakongo kinsmen at the expense of merchants of local origin. Similarly, the Portuguese manager favors the Bakongo because they speak his language. These sales are usually clandestine and the other bar owners resent it.[24] During periods of extended beer crisis (shortage), if any bar in town had something to offer, it would usually be one owned by an Angolan or a Bas-Zairian.

What we have, then, is a Kongo combine. In periods of beer shortage Bakongo bar owners and managers were usually able to dominate the bar trade because they controlled the two local sources. Other bar owners in Lisala would protest vigorously to the economic affairs agent, but there was not much that he could—or would—do. The major reason for his lack of zeal in ensuring a more equitable distribution of beer and his failure to eliminate secret sales was the involvement of a number of Lisala's most important administrative figures in the operation of the Kongo combine. One bar, which was almost always supplied with beer, was run by a group of bureaucrats. Those involved were the budget officer, the *ordonnateur-délégué*, the director of the water and electricity parastatal, and the state accountant for the subregion. The first three were from Bas-Zaire. The fourth, a Mossakata from Bandundu Region, was viewed by most people in town as a Bas-Zairian. The zone commissioner, the subregional commissioner, and the chief prosecutor were also Bakongo from Bas-Zaire. Although these three officials were not directly involved in the management or ownership of this bar, it is probable that they knew about the situation and might have at least been willing to look the other way. In addition, the heavy involvement of the subregion's financial officers probably guaranteed that any protests would fall upon deaf ears. No funds could leave the state coffers without the signatures of the budget officer, the *ordonnateur-délégué*, and the state accountant.

Beer distribution within the town of Lisala might best be conceived as a form of intraclass conflict. The salient axis of conflict was not between farmer and functionary, or between worker and farmer, but among merchants and bar owners. The ethnic dimension seems to be of crucial importance; I found no other reason why Angolan and Bas-Zairian merchants were favored. The involvement of local officialdom is also noteworthy. Quite a few administrators and politico-administrative officials have used their influence and control over state funds to gain access to the commercial sector. In Lisala this usually means the bars. State agents have consistently acted to preserve, protect, and defend their financial interests. The benevolence of high officials effectively shielded the members of the Kongo combine from the protests of disadvantaged bar owners. The quasi-legal involvement of political and administrative authorities in the mechanics of the bar trade is not restricted to Lisala; similar phenomena can be observed in Bumba and Gemena as well.[25]

Price Control

Like everything else, the price of beer in Lisala has risen over the years. Nonetheless, there is a set formula for establishing the official price of beer throughout the Republic. Wholesalers and retailers are given precise instructions on the way they are to calculate the price of a case of beer, as well as the cost of each bottle. A profit margin of 12 percent for the depositor (wholesaler) is built into the price structure. The bar owner, or retailer, is permitted a legal markup of 21 percent on the sale of every bottle of beer that comes his way. Transportation costs, however, vary from one location to another.[26]

Not unexpectedly, the economic affairs officer in Lisala spends a good deal of his time calculating the price of beer for all the zones in Mongala Subregion. But most of his work comes to naught. The official prices are predicated upon the assumption that there is an ample and uninterrupted flow of beer into the area in question, even though conditions of scarcity obtain more often than not in Lisala. In theory, when there is no beer in Lisala, merchants are permitted to add 1k to the price of each bottle they acquire elsewhere. This is to reimburse them for the time, effort, and costs incurred traveling to other locations in search of beer. In practice, bar owners do not abide by the official prices. Even if they are allowed an extra 1k per bottle, the actual retail price of beer usually far exceeds the official price. The political authorities are well aware of this situation but tend to wink at it.[27]

Calculation of an official rice is but one method by which the authorities may attempt to control the price of beer. Official pressure can also be brought upon bar owners to keep prices in line. According to law, beer prices must be posted where all can see them. The penalties for noncompliance are a Z25 fine or fifteen days in jail. Although the administrative archives are filled with threatening letters from territorial and legal authorities to bar owners, compliance is minimal. During my time in Lisala I recall only two bars in which the prices were posted for the clientele. If they are not posted, the customer has no way of knowing the legal price of beer and can be charged according to the barkeeper's whim—a circumstance by no means rare.[28]

Price-control measures are usually ineffective. To understand why, we must, in addition to keeping the problems of supply in mind, once again ask who owns the bars. The important points to be stressed here are that most bar owners are wealthy by Lisala's standards and that many are involved in politics. If they are not active themselves, they often have relatives who are extremely influential. One of the prime offenders is the president of the Association of Women Merchants in Lisala. Owner of a large, popular bar in one of the quarters of the *Cité*, she has repeatedly flouted the law by raising the price of beer. In July 1975 she again came under the scrutiny of the authorities. She was warned that the official price of Unibra beer was 22k a bottle and that she was to cease selling it at 27k.[29] Although she has received repeated warnings about her illegal gimmicks for raising prices, the local commissioners have not been able to get her to obey the law. The reason for their impotence is not hard to discover. She is a mother-in-law of Citizen Litho. Litho, cousin of President Mobutu and a former minister, was then the delegate-general of Bralima, one of Zaire's major breweries. It is probable that a territorial commissioner who somehow managed to arouse Litho's wrath would soon find himself out of a job. Thus, although numerous letters are sent to the recalcitrant bar owner, there is little or no effort to carry out any of the enforcement penalties provided by law. This solution keeps everyone happy but the consumer. The bar owner knows, threatening letters notwithstanding, that she will be able to carry on as in the past. The competent authorities, for their part, do not zealously try to change her behavior. Should their superiors accuse them of failing to act, they can always point to the barrage of letters they have sent to the offending party.

This particular case has been discussed because there is ample documentation for it. It is not an unusual example. Other frequent offenders include two commissioners of the people and a collectivity chief who rank among the most important bar owners in Lisala. Their political importance should not be underestimated. A word or two from them might make or break the career of a politico-administrative agent. Territorial commissioners are thus wont to think twice before doing something precipitate that could alienate one or more of these influential persons. Instead, most commissioners make a determined effort to cultivate the friendship and goodwill of the more important tavern owners.

It is not difficult to see who drinks with whom in Lisala. The same officials who regularly castigate Citizen Litho's mother-in-law can often be seen drinking with her in the *buvette* behind her house. Moreover, once there, they are content to pay the illegal prices she charges. One well-placed observer of subregional administration in Lisala put it this way:

> The official prices are not respected. The merchants are permitted to sell as they please. They add 10k or 15k. They are not controlled. The authorities drink together with the bar owners. They have not got time to apply the law.[30]

There is also a question of relative wealth. Although Lisala's political authorities are well paid by national standards, many bar owners are much wealthier, and the bureaucrats responsible for price control may not always be immune to the financial blandishments these merchants can offer.

It might be said that the political and economic standing of those who are supposed to be controlled militate against the serious application of price-control measures. I would also argue that the real victims of this kind of political-commercial interpenetration are the less wealthy people of Lisala who do not have much money to spend. To them the difference between a beer priced at 20k and one priced at 25k is enormous. Although the official policy is to keep the price of beer within the financial reach of the least wealthy strata of Zairian society, the interpenetration of commercial and political sectors acts to defeat this aim.

Development

Yet another side to the multifaceted phenomenon of beer in Zaire is the government's attempt to harness the tax revenue generated by beer consumption to the task of national development. In principle, all citizens should benefit from this initiative. Predictably, however, this has not been the way things have worked. Given the amount of beer consumed in Zaire, the beer tax has proved to be a lucrative source of revenue. To be sure, in Lisala it was one of the main financial pillars of collectivity administration. In 1973 the beer consumption tax generated the sum of Z1,876.97, which accounted for 20.63 percent of the collectivity's non-CPM revenue. It was the third leading income producer for the local administration; only the CPM and the tax on land proved to be more productive. The beer tax constituted 8.5 percent of the *Cité*'s total receipts.[31] A common situation throughout the Republic, these proportions are likely to be much higher for towns and cities where there is a brewery in operation. Nzongola's data on local administration in Kananga are eloquent on this point. In 1972 the city's total receipts were Z216,397.65. Of this sum, Z83,189.32, or 38.44 percent, were furnished by the beer consumption tax.[32] Kinshasa has long been aware of this revenue source, and there have been recent efforts to exercise direct control over these funds.

In 1970 official policy was to leave the field of beer taxation open to the financially autonomous cities and collectivities. The national government wanted the tax uniformly applied throughout the Republic with no double taxation. To this end, it was decided that the minimum tax would be 1k on each bottle of beer produced in Zaire. This was ultimately to be charged to the consumer, but no real directive relating to tax collection methods was issued.[33] Almost immediately a series of administrative disputes arose over who was to collect the tax. This was especially true in areas without a brewery. If beer arrived from other regions, for example, it might already have been taxed in the city where it was produced. This would preclude, at least in theory, a second tax in the area where it was consumed. It was finally decided that beer produced in Mbandaka for consumption in Mbandaka would be taxed at the brewery. Beer destined for other parts of the region would be taxed in those localities, and the funds would be collected from wholesalers by agents of the city or collectivity. In short, the tax would be applied at the point of consumption.

In the field, confusion reigned. A new policy was enunciated in October 1972. After 15 October 1972, all beer tax revenues of 1k per bottle would be collected only at the level of the region.[34] Other centralization measures were being implemented at that time, and such a move was neither startling nor outside the logic of the political evolution of the Mobutu regime. Furthermore, such a move would have the advantage of ending the administrative difficulties relating to tax collection. The new policy was clear enough; it just did not last very long. For reasons I could not determine, an almost complete reversal occurred one month later. The regional commissioner revoked his decision of 15 October, and the fruits of the beer consumption tax were restored to the financially autonomous administrative entities. Shortly before this decision was made, the tax was reduced by 70 percent to 30 sengi per bottle.[35]

Throughout 1973 the local units of government were responsible for the collection of the beer tax and benefited from the revenue it produced. Another change occurred in early 1974, however. On 26 February the regional commissioner informed all his politico-administrative subordinates that the beer tax would be centralized as of 1 March 1974. It was to be collected by the region, directly from the brewery, so that, as before, the collectivities would be eliminated as beneficiaries. The letter mentioned that the funds provided by this tax would be devoted to rural development. There were plans to repair rest houses; build and repair schools and dispensaries; open and maintain roads; and construct soccer fields and certain buildings of public utility. Funds generated by the beer tax were to be distributed three times a year, but it was not made clear who would receive them. It was clear, though, that Mbandaka would be doing the distributing. Parenthetically, although rural development projects were the stated reason for this change, there is some reason to believe that this money was being used to finance purely political expenditures such as cheerleading festivals, propaganda, and presidential visits.[36]

This time, too, there was an almost immediate change in the announced policy. On 20 March 1974 the political affairs commissioner informed the regional commissioners that the tax on beer would indeed be centralized, but not at their level. Perhaps Mobutu had realized that the beer revenue was too substantial to be controlled by the regions. In any event, regional commissioners were instructed that the resources generated by the beer consumption tax would be used for community service development plans, and each zone was requested to submit a list of its priority development projects. The national government would then make appropriations for each project approved. Funds would have to be accounted for specifically; each project would have its own budget.[37] Plans were submitted to the political affairs commissioner, but in October 1974 he rejected them, noting disapprovingly that all the projects pertained to subregional and zonal headquarters. Regional and subregional commissioners were reminded that territorial administration was really the administration of the collectivities, or baseline units. As a result, the political affairs commissioner demanded that they submit development projects centering on the collectivities. He especially wished territorial commissioners to be aware of collectivities that needed dispensaries, roads of local interest, and office equipment.[38]

Mongala Subregion submitted its revised proposals to the regional commissioner in November 1974. The cover letter noted that many data provided by the zones had been reviewed and corrected, often with an eye toward their "reduction to more realistic and reasonable proportions."[39] The proposals make interesting reading. In the first place, speaking only in financial terms, it is difficult to agree that they are reasonable and realistic. Each collectivity in the subregion is represented in the list of proposed projects. The total estimated cost for all projects in all twenty-three of the collectivities comes to Z333,130. In 1974 the Bralima brewery in Mbandaka produced 29,106,396 bottles. Since the beer consumption tax was a mere 30 sengi per bottle, the brewery's total beer production would have generated tax revenues of Z87,319. On these grounds alone, the costs involved are scarcely realistic. Presumably, the proposed development projects in the five other subregions in Equateur were equally grandiose.

Second, although the proposals are not in toto financially feasible, they nonetheless provide some insight into both how Zairian politico-administrative officials perceive development and how the system works. Space limitations do not permit the reproduction of the proposed projects for all twenty-three collectivities, but representative illustrations are furnished by the projects for three collectivities in table 23.

The "priority" development projects prompt two observations. First, although beer tax revenues were officially targeted for infrastructural development, that is not how most of the revenue will be spent. Only a small percentage of the funds proposed for these projects is earmarked for this kind of development. Instead, a study of the projects shows a numerically restricted minority appropriating most of the resources to provide itself with certain amenities. The three collectivities cited in table 23 are not extreme; their proposals are typical. It will be noted that many, if not most, of the projects have to do with activities like building the chief a new house,

TABLE 23
PRIORITY DEVELOPMENT PROJECTS TO BE FUNDED
FROM BEER CONSUMPTION TAX, MONGALA SUBREGION, 1974

Project	Cost
Collectivity A	
Install 4 public water fountains	Z2,500
Hire 20 roadworkers	4,000
Buy 100 shovels	150
Buy 100 machetes	100
Buy 100 coup-coup [grass-cutting tools]	100
Buy 100 picks	350
Buy 20 wheelbarrows	500
Repair public market and build stands around it	3,000
Enlarge collectivity office	2,000
Buy 2 typewriters	370
Construct and furnish house for collectivity chief	5,000
Total	Z18,070
Collectivity B	
Construct collectivity office	Z3,500
Construct house for chief	4,000
Construct well	1,200
Maintain avenues and streets	1,000
Buy office machines	300
Buy equipment	370
Total	Z10,370
Collectivity C	
Construct collectivity office	Z3,500
Construct house for chief	4,000
Construct 40 houses for collectivity personnel	4,000
Construct guest houses	2,000
Repair two stopover houses	500
Furnish above houses	1,500
Total	Z15,500

SOURCE: Archives, Mongala Subregion, Political Affairs Department, Lisala. "Besoins pour les travaux prioritaires des collectivités," 12 November 1974.

providing him with electricity, rebuilding the guest houses that territorial commissioners use on inspection tours, building new homes for those who are employed by the collectivity, and constructing new offices for the collectivity. Collectivity C proposals are especially significant in this light. This collectivity is in an area that has only one secondary school, no books, no blackboards, and no desks; if the students wish to sit down during their lessons, they must bring chairs and stools from home. The second observation is that the fairly widespread nature of beer consumption throughout Zaire and the regressive beer tax structure work to ensure that resources will be transferred from those at the poorer end of the scale to those at the wealthier end.

Conclusions and Contradictions

If a systemic perspective is adopted, it may be said that beer is of political and economic importance.[40] We have seen that an ample supply of beer helps to ensure political tranquility. Furthermore, its economic significance is impressive. It provides a durable link between the cash and subsistence economies. In a more specifically local context, beer is a major pillar of Lisala's commercial system and is the financial base for many enterprises in the area. Because it is a scarce resource, it has also become a source of intraclass conflict in the town. Close attention to the politics of beer also serves to highlight the interpenetration of Lisala's commercial and political sectors.

An examination of the political economy of beer in Lisala is of wider interest because it points to several contradictions that seem to exist in the Zairian polity. First, although government policy is to keep the price of beer down so that the majority of the population will be able to buy it, it has not hesitated to impose a beer consumption tax that is charged directly to the consumer. In the words of a former political affairs commissioner:

> Local beer is the drink of the mass of workers and economically weak people and any modification in its price weighs heavily on the budget of small wage earners. ... It is the role of the State to assure that the price of this drink remains accessible to all incomes.
>
> On the other hand, no consideration of a social nature militates in favor of limiting taxes to imported beers and alcoholic drinks other than local beer.[41]

The regressive tax on beer consumption is supposed to be used to promote local development. This goal notwithstanding, a small coterie of relatively privileged politico-administrative officials have chosen to define development primarily in terms of their personal needs and comforts. It beggars the imagination to understand how the mass of Zairian people might benefit from new houses for collectivity chiefs and new offices for collectivity administrations. This singularly class-oriented definition of development is the second contradiction that might be observed.

The third contradiction concerns the distributive system. Since those who are politically and economically powerful own the bars, they have most to gain from an uninterrupted supply of beer. Although they have used their considerable influence to bring the problem before the president of the Republic, no permanent, long-range ameliorative action has yet been taken. This may be because of certain characteristics of the Zairian political system. As previously mentioned, Kinshasa's stated policy of assuring a "rational" distribution of beer is so confused that each of the two major breweries has a different idea of what that policy is. Territorial commissioners are equally baffled about this matter. In a highly centralized system, policy ambiguity at higher levels makes creative policy implementation at lower levels a chimera. Most officials hesitate to take any action without clear and direct instructions from their superiors. In addition to policy vagueness, officials must also contend with frequent and, at times, dramatic policy reversals, as attention to the beer tax has shown.

Finally, aspects of national policy may not be enforced because it is not in the interests of the enforcers to do so. The politics of price control in Lisala provides a case in point. Although national policy is to ensure that prices are kept low, the very character of political-commercial interaction precludes this eventuality. If a territorial official owns a bar, or if his wife has a *buvette*, he has little interest in seeing that the legal profit margins are maintained. Further disincentives are provided by the obvious wealth and political influence of some of the bar owners. The safest and most politically prudent strategy is to treat these people with circumspection, even deference. Words whispered in high circles can destroy careers and no career is worth risking over the price of a bottle of beer.

CHAPTER 6
The MPR: Political Mobility and Social Closure

The MPR presents itself as a large family to which all Zairians without exception belong. All Zairians are born equal members of the MPR. Each has the chance to realize his destiny and to assume any responsibility provided that he furnishes the proof of his competencies and his talents. . . .

Its power does not serve to found the dictatorship of an historical class but to assure national cohesion on the strict basis of fraternal relations.

—Citizen Engulu, State Commissioner
for Political Affairs and Permanent
Member of the Political Bureau[1]

Inspiring words, misleading words. It will be argued in the following pages that the leaders of the Mouvement Populaire de la Révolution (MPR) have consciously used the party to increase life and mobility chances for a tiny group of already-privileged citizens. Because access to high political office remains restricted, only a few Zairians can attain their "destinies" within the party structure. Most people find this mobility route barred to them because of the economic yardsticks employed by the MPR. The intention here is double-edged: first, to show how the MPR functions as an avenue of political mobility and to discuss how it has contributed—and is still contributing—to the formation of a class system in Zaire. A close analysis of the 1970 legislative elections in Mongala Subregion will call attention to the criteria on which advancement in the party is based. Second, an examination of political mobility and social closure will again stress the interpenetration of the commercial and political sectors.[2]

The MPR: An Overview[3]

Almost immediately after seizing power in November 1965, President Mobutu realized the necessity of institutionalizing his rule. Initially this was to be accomplished by a protopolitical organization known as the Corps des Volontaires de la République (CVR). Founded in January 1966, the CVR was not envisaged as a political party. Its functions were to assure the flow of communication between the political powers in Kinshasa and the people in the countryside. In addition it was to organize "vigilance" in favor of the new regime and its new leader. The CVR was a short-lived experiment. Whatever the reasons behind its failure, it gave way to the MPR in April 1967, when it was made clear that the CVR would not be the embryo of a new party. On 20 May 1967 the MPR received an official send-off with the publication of the *Manifeste de la N'Sélé*, an extremely vague attempt to create a party ideology. Structurally it was announced that at the national level there would be a Congress presided over by President Mobutu, a Political Bureau charged with the tasks of policy conception and general orientation, and a National Executive Committee, which was to run the party on a day-to-day basis. In the lower reaches of the hierarchy there would also be committees at regional, subregional, and zonal levels. Below that there were to be other committees.[4] Although the 1967 constitution allowed for the existence of two political parties, it was almost immediately apparent that the MPR would, in fact, evolve into a governmental single party.[5]

Important organizational changes were made in October 1967 and again in March and September 1968. The reforms of 13 October 1967 proved particularly significant. It was announced that the regional commissioner, subregional commissioner, and zonal commissioner would become presidents of the MPR at their respective levels. This had the effect of halting the overt conflict between party and administrative officials at each level of government. It also provided the first example of what would be a continuing trend in the evolution of the MPR: the interpenetration of party and state. At this time, too, the importance of the National Executive Committee was substantially reduced by making it subordinate to the Political Bureau. In March 1968 Zairian leaders gave further thought to the structure and organization of the party at its lower levels and decided to adopt a delegate system. Regional committees would be composed of delegates from the subregions; subregional committees would be made up of delegates from the zones; and representatives of the collectivities would be on the zone committees. Village committees would be under the auspices and control of the zone committees. Additional elaboration was provided in September 1968, when members of the Political Bureau decided that those named as vice-presidents of the MPR at their respective levels would become second vice-presidents. Thus, at the subregional level, for example, the commissioner would be president of the party; his assistant would become first vice-president; and the party official who had previously occupied this post would become second vice-president in charge of party affairs. This was also the pattern for regions and zones.

Much of 1969 was spent preparing the groundwork for the upcoming legislative and presidential elections. This meant increasing the presence of the MPR in the countryside and making contact with the bulk of the population. In May 1970 the First Extraordinary Congress of the MPR was held at N'Sélé. At its conclusion the Congress passed three resolutions. First, President Mobutu would be the only candidate for the presidency. Second, legislative elections would take place with only a single list of party candidates from which to choose. Third, it was declared that the MPR was the only political party in Zaire, as well as the nation's supreme political institution. The legislative elections, held in November, are the subject of extended discussion below. By the end of 1970 the major structures of the MPR were in place and functioning with varying degrees of efficiency.

In 1971 no major changes were made in the party's structure, but the following year saw several important modifications. The National Executive Committee was abolished, its functions having become increasingly redundant in light of the Political Bureau's preeminence. The Council of Ministers was replaced by a National Executive Council, which performed the same functions but under the aegis of the party. The composition of the MPR committees at the lower levels of the hierarchy was substantially altered. The delegate system that had previously operated was scrapped for one that favored different state institutions present in the area. At the subregional level the members were the subregional president (subregional commissioner), the first subregional vice-president (assistant subregional commissioner), the second subregional vice-president (assistant subregional commissioner), the subregional secretary of the JMPR, the presiding magistrate of the tribunal, the chief prosecutor, the army commandant, and the secretary of the Union Nationale des Travailleurs Zairois (UNTZa), the sole trade union.[6]

All the changes were designed to speed the fusion of the MPR with the state. According to the press, party publications, and speeches of various dignitaries, the party was the dominant element in this merger, and the MPR was said to have absorbed the state. While perhaps true at the policy-making level, the composition of party committees suggests that the reverse was true outside Kinshasa. A new constitution, approved in 1974, advanced the process. This document consecrated the MPR as the nation's only institution; all other previously existing institutions became organs of the party. In that same year the Political Bureau declared that henceforth the state administration no longer existed—it had now become the administration of the party.[7] Consequently, the few remaining vestiges of the party bureaucracy, such as subregional and zonal secretaries, were merged into the state's administrative apparatus. In practice the state had swallowed the party bureaucracy. In public it was widely proclaimed that the reverse had happened.

In this light it is difficult to argue with Thomas Callaghy's assessment of the relations between party and state.

> At the center, in the high levels of power, the MPR may well have absorbed the state in terms of decision-making power. But in terms of the implementation of policy even in the center, the state structure remained intact. In the periphery where the party has not become well institutionalized, the state administration clearly absorbed the party. The state remained and the state administrators took over all party functions.[8]

Equally relevant, in my opinion, is a passage drawn from Frantz Fanon's *Les Damnés de la terre*.

> After independence, the party sinks into a spectacular lethargy. The militants are only mobilized on the occasion of so-called popular manifestations, international conferences, or independence celebrations. The local party cadres are appointed to administrative posts, the party changes into an administration, and the militants return to the ranks and take the empty title of citizen.[9]

Problems and Activities in Mongala

Although a number of my respondents asserted that the implantation of the MPR in Mongala Subregion was carried off without great difficulty, the documentary evidence presents a far different picture.[10] First, there was the basic problem of establishing and maintaining the MPR in the farthest reaches of the subregion. A difficult task under the best of circumstances, the problem in Mongala was complicated by the lack of an adequate road system. Indeed, territorial officials in that part of the country were usually unable to get out into the countryside. Party officials were obviously faced with the same obstacles. It was not until October 1968, fully eighteen months after the party's inception, that the subregion's second vice-president was able to visit the zones of Businga, Bumba, and Mobayi-Mbongo. During this period there was almost no direct supervision of party activities in these locales. After touring Equateur Region in 1970, the regional commissioner castigated all his subregional and zonal commissioners because, in his words, "inspection never occurs."[11]

Transportation difficulties posed another, and perhaps more serious, problem for the young party. It will be remembered that through 1971 the party committees at each level were composed largely of delegates from the tier immediately beneath it. It was thus difficult for, say, the delegate from Businga or Mobayi-Mbongo to appear in Lisala for the monthly meeting of the subregional committee. One 1969 report noted that because of this problem, committee meetings were no longer held. From 1967 to 1970 there were few party committee meetings at any level in Mongala Subregion.[12]

Money, or rather the lack of it, was also an obstacle. There were not enough funds to provide party officials with automobiles. This was another reason for the lack of inspection tours and direct supervision by those in authority. MPR officials in the bush were often left to their own devices; as a result, party activity became lethargic at best and nonexistent at worst. Moreover, funds were not always sufficient to assure the purchase and distribution of party propaganda materials. Items like party cards rarely found their way to the people. In 1970, for example, three thousand MPR membership cards were found abandoned in a locked trunk in a collectivity office in Bongandanga. Last, there was the ever-present question of salaries for the "permanent" staff of the party in each of its locations. Throughout the early years of the MPR's existence, the absence of regular salaries created difficulties. The secretaries and staff who were responsible for the maintenance of the party's office [*permanence*] would go unpaid for long periods, and their militancy and devotion to the cause of spreading the MPR's gospel among the uninitiated suffered accordingly. When party funds did arrive in an area, the local president (who was also an administrative official) would often appropriate them for some administrative chore deemed more pressing. The overall picture presented by the documents is one of apathy and enervation. The MPR's effective presence in the hinterland was, at best, intermittent. Although the party's importance was stressed by the national authorities in Kinshasa, it seems clear that at least until the 1970 elections MPR presidents at most levels were content to devote most of their time to their administrative responsibilities. This emphasis on administrative rather than political functions was undoubtedly one cause of the usual tension between MPR presidents and second vice-presidents in most areas of the subregion.[13]

Despite the reams of favorable propaganda that poured out of Kinshasa, most people in Mongala soon became profoundly indifferent to party activities. Because *Salongo* has already been discussed, here I am primarily concerned with party demonstrations and cheerleading rallies. Most bureaucrats, perhaps sensing the irrelevance of these activities to their own lives, were generally less than enthusiastic about participating. In July 1970, shortly after the Party Congress, the subregional commissioner wrote a scathing letter on the subject to all subregional service chiefs, noting that "the majority of Service Chiefs display an indifference with regard to the Party and do not make the effort to answer the requisitions or the meetings or the demonstrations of the party." Consequently, from that day forward each service chief was ordered to appear at rallies and mass meetings accompanied by all his subordinates. The commissioner also informed them that attendance would be taken.[14]

The mobilization of bureaucrats has remained an unsolved problem. In my informal discussions with many of Lisala's administrators it was evident that they were unhappy about aspects of party life. More than one, in private, expressed outrage at the indignity of having to dance at party meetings. Even a member of the MPR Subregional Committee indicated his displeasure with such "revolutionary imperatives." Lower-level clerks complied with these directives only because they knew that if they did not they would lose their jobs. It should be pointed out that yearly fitness reports judge each bureaucrat, regardless of level, partly on the basis of militancy. For the most part, militancy translates into regular attendance at popular meetings, marches, and *Salongo*.[15] Since the legal fiction is that all bureaucrats are functionaries of the MPR and there are no longer party cell meetings within the administration, presence at such functions is really the only way in which militancy can be assessed.[16]

Salongo, marches, and rallies aside, it is not always easy to ascertain exactly what the party does. In 1972 the subregional commissioner must have been equally puzzled because he wrote to his second vice-president, asking him precisely that question. He had noted that during a one-week period the party offices had not even opened.[17] When various MPR committees sporadically meet, their reports are rarely furnished to the higher party authorities on time, and instructions passed down the line from one party committee to those immediately below are often ignored.[18] Bureaucrats also wonder about the MPR's activities in Mongala. One lower-level clerk observed that

> it is impossible for me to say anything. Since the appearance of the movement I only see that the situation has remained like that. Expenses are only inflated. And the assistant zone commissioner in charge of political affairs . . . What exactly does he do?[19]

Others in the administration shared this curiosity.[20] It is not always easy to discern what the assistant commissioners in charge of political affairs accomplish or, for that matter, are supposed to accomplish. Perhaps some idea of their duties can be gained, however, by noting the following job description of the assistant subregional commissioner for political affairs:

> Mobilization, cheerleading, payment of the politico-administrative cadres. Periodic updating of the subregion's repertoire of revolutionary songs. Organization of seminars, educational chats, mass rallies at the subregional and zonal levels. Organization of the monthly meetings of the Subregional Committee of the MPR.[21]

These are not weighty responsibilities.

When reading the minutes of the various MPR committee meetings, I was often struck by the apolitical nature of the discussions. In general most subjects inscribed on the agenda dealt with purely bureaucratic affairs. Road conditions, inability to get crops to market, and payment of collectivity personnel were perennial topics. These subjects should not have been ignored, but they could easily have been discussed at a meeting of field administrators with no connection whatever to the MPR. When people were asked about the MPR, they would respond that the party directs everything, that it surveys all aspects of life in Zaire. True enough. But when a party bureaucrat was questioned specifically on what the MPR does to aid the economy, he replied that

> nothing can be done outside the MPR. The economy depends on the sons of this country. Then, it is very normal that given that the sons of this country, being members of the MPR, that the MPR can take care of the economy.[22]

Such logic is reminiscent of the Mad Hatter's tea party.

It was mentioned earlier that the administrative preoccupations of subregional and zonal commissioners created tensions between these officials and their respective second vice-presidents. But administrative priorities were not the only source of difficulty, for MPR presidents were usually outsiders brought in from other parts of the country. This was in keeping with President Mobutu's plan for national integration. This policy was implemented quite slowly, however, and with much thought. In the early years of the MPR, Zairian leaders perceived that the people's identification with the new party would substantially be accelerated if there were not too brusque a break with the old familiar and popular figures. A former minister of the interior described the policy this way:

> Representative people were chosen. They had the feelings of the masses. They were made use of. We had to reverse the process. At the start of the new regime all power came from the interior. Federalism was ill-conceived and started badly. Instead of taking all of the particular interests to make a general interest of them, it was believed that the particular interests themselves were the general interests. That put the interests of each before the interests of everyone. The authorities began to eliminate the elements that were dividing. They wanted to reinforce the authority of the central power. That was done by associating the central authority with local men who had the confidence of the masses.[23]

Thus, the second vice-presidents—those officials with direct and daily responsibility for the smooth functioning of the MPR at its various levels—were almost always native sons, well-known individuals, and former First Republic politicians who had rallied to the new regime.[24] Many had power bases and understood local conditions more acutely than did their immediate party superiors. This was certainly true in Lisala.

The second vice-president at the subregion from 1968 to 1974 had made his mark in both Equateur and Moyen-Congo *provincette* politics. An administrative clerk for twenty years before independence, in 1960 he requested detachment from the civil service and immediately began an active political career in Jean Bolikango's Parti de l'Unité Nationale (PUNA). He was elected a provincial counselor in 1960, and before the dissolution of the province he served as minister of economic affairs and the middle class. A native of Lisala, he returned home during the *provincettes* to become minister of information, interprovincial relations, and health for the government of Moyen-Congo. His political responsibilities during these years were not so great as to prevent his devoting at least some time to starting a plantation and a cattle ranch in the Lisala area. Genuinely popular around Lisala, he became second vice-president in January 1968.

His counterpart at the Zone of Lisala was also a figure of some local importance. Between 1943 and 1959 he had worked at a variety of jobs for the state and private corporations. An early and active militant in Kinshasa's Bangala associations, he worked in the capital for the radio station that broadcast in Lingala. He was a well-known and visible member of PUNA and returned to Lisala in 1963, when that party took over the government of Moyen-Congo. From 1963 to 1967 he occupied a series of responsible positions in the governmental apparatus of the *provincette*. In 1968 he was designated second vice-president of the MPR for the Zone of Lisala.[25]

One of the prices paid for this policy, though, were tense and insecure relations between MPR presidents and their second vice-presidents. Because second vice-presidents were old politicians, the new leaders, particularly in the early years of the regime, could not be absolutely certain of their loyalty. In Lisala there was much cause for alarm on this point. In November 1968 both second vice-presidents were arrested on charges of breaching state security. They were apprehended by agents of the *sûreté* while having a clandestine meeting with other former members of PUNA. Several traditional chiefs were also present. They were accused of trying to overthrow the new territorial commissioners and were flown immediately to Mbandaka. Eventually, both men were released and returned to their positions. Perhaps the meeting was harmless; perhaps not. It did take place, though, and after that relations between the imported commissioners and the two Lisala natives responsible for political affairs were usually strained.[26]

The denouement of the episode also indicated that the new regime did not feel strong enough at that point to forego the symbolic representation and legitimacy these men incarnated. Succeeding subregional and zonal commissioners were thus faced with the task of balancing the sometimes conflicting demands of administrative responsibilities against the political pressures of their second vice-presidents. Tension between them would be diminished only in 1973, when a new statute was passed clearly placing all territorial authorities under a five-year mandate that was revocable at any time.[27] The new law may have increased the political zeal of some of the more administratively oriented commissioners, but it was only in the following year that the central authorities felt themselves strong enough, and their system of control sufficiently elaborated, to rotate the assistant commissioners in charge of political affairs (the former second vice-presidents). Once removed from their own bailiwicks and placed more firmly under the control of their immediate superiors, they found these tensions dissipated.

The 1970 Legislative Elections

Although the MPR is beset by apathy and personnel problems and is less than successful in mobilizing the masses, it functions—for some—as an avenue of upward mobility. It will be recalled that in its early years the MPR suffered from acute financial difficulties, causing problems over the payment of party bureaucrats and officials at various levels. The leadership in Kinshasa was well aware of this and sought to alleviate it. By mid-1968 a set of detailed instructions had been issued to the regional presidents of the MPR concerning the staffing of the party at all levels:

> All your collaborators must be convinced that the only advantage they have to gain from their militancy in the Party is the social promotion of our society . . . the satisfaction of a duty well done.
>
> A militant of the MPR must not be waiting at all moments for material remunerations.
>
> That is why around the Provincial President, the District President, the Territorial President, and the Circumscription President it is only forseen that

there be members representing the different administrative entities who will not be reimbursed by the Party. These different members must therefore be chosen among those who have the means to live decently on their own.

On the other hand, it is necessary to avoid giving these members functions which would prevent them from devoting themselves to their own activities.[28]

These directives are clear. Members of the party committees at all levels were to be chosen from those in society who would not need to be paid by the MPR in order to live decently. In practice this meant that posts in the JMPR and MPR administration, as well as positions on the party committees, tended to go to the wealthier members of the community. Few, if any, village farmers had the means to assure themselves a "decent"living. As a result most party work was done by merchants, bar owners, plantation owners, bureaucrats, and others who had regular sources of income and support. Inevitably the party mandarins tended to perceive these wealthier elements as the true militants of the country. A good militant came to be defined as someone who served the MPR without being paid; as someone who donated his bar (and beer) so that party meetings could be held; as someone with many economic interests and resources who could lend his car or truck to the MPR authorities if needed.

The importance of wealth as a necessary, but not sufficient, condition of militancy—and thus of upward political mobility—became apparent during the 1970 legislative elections, which took place throughout the country in mid-November. Since there was a single slate of candidates approved by the party, this was very much a pro forma exercise in mass mobilization. The real decisions as to who would become commissioners of the people were made in party committees at all levels of the hierarchy, with the final word reserved for President Mobutu and the Political Bureau.

Procedurally, each prospective candidate had to file his candidacy papers with the territorial authorities at the zone. Among the documents required were a curriculum vitae and a certificate of good conduct from the local judicial authorities. In addition, each future commissioner of the people had to submit a Z100 deposit to show that the candidacy was serious, in theory at least, to be returned to unsuccessful candidates.[29] By both national and Mongala standards, Z100 is a large amount of money, so the deposit had the effect of screening out all but the wealthiest members of society. Once the dossiers were complete and the funds received, the MPR Zone Committee offered its evaluations on each of the would-be legislators. When this process was completed, the dossiers and the committee evaluations were passed up the line to the subregion. At this level (at least in Mongala), a special committee meeting was called. Its participants were the regular members of the subregional party committee and the presidents and second vice-presidents from each of the five constituent zones. This combined committee judged each candidate and sent its own evaluations to the regional committee at Mbandaka. At that level the process was similar, and the regional recommendations were forwarded to the Political Bureau in Kinshasa for final disposition.

During the course of my research I was fortunate enough to gain access to the subregional files on the 1970 elections. They consisted of the curricula vitae of all sixty-four candidates and the evaluations of the MPR committee that screened their applications. Each candidate was judged on the basis of his position in the party hierarchy, if any, and on the basis of his economic standing in the community—that is, whether the candidate had any significant economic activities in Mongala. Plantations, stores, other businesses, and bars were all considered. Some attention was also paid to the candidate's degree of militancy. After these factors were weighed, the committee gave each candidate an overall rating. Ranging from elite to zero, the ratings are discussed below. In general it may be said that the emphasis on party position and economic activity continued the recruitment policy in effect since at least 1968. As seen in the 1968 party instructions cited above, and as seen in the analysis of the candidacies presented below, wealth was a crucial precondition of political advancement.

An overview of the kinds of people who submitted their candidacies in Mongala provided in table 24. It should be noted that the categorization of

TABLE 24

1970 LEGISLATIVE ELECTIONS IN MONGALA SUBREGION: TOTAL AND SUCCESSFUL CANDIDATES, BY OCCUPATION

Occupation	Total Candidates	%	Successful Candidates	%	Alternates
1. Merchants, bar owners, plantation owners	25	39	2	13	0
2. Company employees	7	9	1	7	0
3. First Republic politicians	15	23	8	53	3
4. Bureaucrats	10[a]	16	3	20	1
5. Chiefs	1	2	0	0	0
6. Teachers	2	3	0	0	0
7. Trade unionists	2	3	0	0	0
8. University administrators	1	2	1	7	0
9. Unknown	1	2	0	0	0
Total (N)	64	99	15	100	4

SOURCE: 1970 Election File.

[a]Of the bureaucrats listed, four were lower-level clerks, three were important Kinshasa officials (e.g., directors-general), and one was a Mbandaka bureaucrat. The other two were an assistant subregional commissioner and a subregional magistrate.

occupations is arbitrary. Many First Republic politicians could just as easily have been classified as bureaucrats. At the time of the elections two were ministers in Kinshasa, and there were also several second vice-presidents.

Furthermore, many of the politicians could have been classified also as merchants, plantation owners, or bar owners. Most had used their tenure in office during the First Republic to set themselves up in business ventures on the side, and this was also true of some of those who are here classed as bureaucrats. Such overlaps exist between other occupational categories as well. Merchants, politicians, and bureaucrats accounted for the majority of the candidacies, a fact that can probably be explained by the nature of the selection process as well as by the requirement of a Z100 deposit. Politicians garnered over fifty percent of the seats in Mongala. The overall success of the First Republic politicians in the selection process is evaluated more fully later, but for the moment let us state that this occurrence is probably explicable in terms of both social class and patrimonial models of the political process.

One of the criteria for ranking candidates was their economic importance in the subregion. To appreciate this factor some notion of the kinds of evaluations that were made is necessary. A selection of those pertaining to wealth (or lack of it) is provided in table 25.

TABLE 25
CANDIDATE EVALUATIONS AND ECONOMIC ACTIVITY

Occupational Classification	Evaluations and Ratings[a]
Merchant (no. 4)[b]	Secretary of party subsection. Works for nothing. Good militant. Rating: very good. He buys and sells agricultural products at Yakoma and is also a bar owner. He has a truck.
Bureaucrat (no. 6)	Director of JMPR subsection. Convinced militant. Rating: very good. He has agreed to work without pay for the party.
Politician (no. 17)	Elite militant of the MPR. Rating: elite. Owner of several plantations and other activities in Mongala.
Chief (no. 20)	Subsection MPR president without serious activities in the party. Rating: fair.
Politician (no. 22)	Convinced militant by his quality as member of the MPR and by his acts as part of the governmental team and among the population of Mongala. Rating: elite. Many economic activities in the region.
Merchant (no. 30)	Cell president of the MPR who has devoted himself by working without charge for the party since its installation. Very good militant. A plantation owner and bar owner whose bar was pillaged for the cause of the party.[c]
Merchant (no. 31)	Very active member of the section committee. Excellent militant who brings many militants to the party. Rating: excellent. Merchant.
Merchant (no. 36)	Adherent without any activity in the MPR. Rating: opportunist.

TABLE 25 (continued)

Occupational Classification	Evaluations and Ratings[a]
Politician (no. 42)	Second vice-president of Mongala Subregion whose [pro-MPR] activities are incontestable. Thanks to him the MPR has been implanted in Mongala since 1968. Rating: elite. Independent plantation owner and rancher.
Employee (no. 48)	Militant adherent having no activity in the MPR; endowed with opportunistic sentiments. Rating: zero. Salesman.
Merchant (no. 49)	Very good militant who spontaneously donates his equipment (amplifiers, microphones, etc.) to the party for popular meetings and who answers all party requisitions. Rating: very good. Merchant and bar owner.
Merchant (no. 62)	Subsection president of the MPR. Devoted militant and very active. Rating: very good. Industrial merchant and bar owner.

SOURCE: 1970 Election File.

[a]A more detailed view of specific ratings is presented in table 28.

[b]Numbers in parentheses refer to those in 1970 Election File.

[c]The incident occurred when the merchant was given forty pieces of women's cloth to distribute to the *militantes* of his quarter in the city. Word spread quickly, and over two thousand women appeared to claim them. When they discovered there would not be nearly enough for everyone, they became angry and destroyed his bar. (Interview, Lisala, 26 June 1975, no. 67, p. 1.)

As the evaluations made clear, many merchants were able to parlay their advantaged economic standing in the community into positions of political importance within the MPR. Clearly, at least in Mongala the 1968 party-staffing instructions were applied. Merchants, particularly wealthier ones, had the means to live "decently" and were able to devote much time and energy to party affairs. They were thus absorbed at the lower levels of the party hierarchy. When the 1970 elections rolled around, it was normal that those in high positions of authority would view this activity as proof of their militancy and try to reward them. This combination of factors again points to the pervasive interpenetration of the commercial and the political sectors in Zaire.

It is important to emphasize, however, that though wealth was an important and necessary condition of party militancy, it was not a sufficient one; other criteria were invoked to evaluate prospective commissioners of the people. In addition to economic resources, attendance at party rallies, marches, and meetings was required. Even if wealthy, many of those who applied for legislative positions were eliminated because they rarely attended such functions. Table 26 illustrates the importance of these criteria in the evaluative process.

The first two evaluations in table 26 also make it clear that not all

TABLE 26
CANDIDATE EVALUATIONS AND ATTENDANCE AT PARTY FUNCTIONS

Occupational Classification	Evaluations and Ratings
Merchant (no. 8)[a]	Adherent who responds to no party call, who is waking up because he wants a political post. Rating: zero. Big merchant and plantation owner; bar owner and hotel owner.
Merchant (no. 12)	Ex-permanent secretary who no longer attends rallies since he was replaced. Rating: mediocre. Big merchant.
Trade unionist (no. 38)	Member of JMPR section committee who participates in many party rallies. Good militant.
Bureaucrat (no. 43)	First vice-president of the MPR in Mongala Subregion. As for his militancy, he has always been punctual at all the party requisitions [sic] even before he became first vice-president. Rating: elite. Functionary and assistant subregional commissioner.
Bureaucrat (no. 44)	Very remarkable cell president who responds to all party gatherings and requisitions. President of the Tribunal of Mongala. Rating: elite.
Bureaucrat (no. 50)	Militant who often attends party rallies. Seen at all party requisitions even though he has just arrived. Good militant. State agent.

SOURCE: 1970 Election File.

[a]Numbers in parentheses refer to those in 1970 Election File.

businessmen meet this criterion of militancy. Many Mongala traders are indifferent to both the lure of elective office and the numerous calls and activities of the MPR. Even after the 1970 elections the mobilization of some segments of the business community has remained a thorn in the side of party authorities. In 1971, for example, Bumba's JMPR secretary was annoyed enough to report to his superiors about this matter. On the eve of the nation's eleventh anniversary of independence, all bar owners were asked to close their establishments so that the people would come to a torchlight parade planned in honor of the event. Although compliance had previously been requested, the bars in Bumba remained open. Several days later the secretary wrote:

> To our great astonishment, our vigilance service reports that all bars and *buvettes* were functioning. This did not permit the people to come in great numbers to the march.[30]

This was not an isolated incident; there is ample administrative correspondence on the subject.[31] For instance, in April 1975 at a meeting of Lisala's merchants, they were criticized because many of them did not participate in *Salongo*, attend mass rallies, or donate cars and trucks when territorial commissioners needed them.[32]

The two criteria of militancy and political mobility have been dealt with in detail because they are the most important. But there are other ways of being perceived as a true party militant in Zaire. One method is denouncing the enemies of the revolution. In 1970, for example, one would-be legislator from Mongala was evaluated as follows:

> Convinced militant propagandist. Rating: elite. His devotion has gone so far as denouncing party reactionaries at Abumobazi. Independent plantation owner, transporter, and bar owner.[33]

Of course, this method has its dangers, not the least of which is that it tends to make one unpopular with fellow citizens. Nonetheless, this phenomenon (often called *vigilance*) is widespread and contributes to the political insecurity that many Zairians feel.

Concerning the relationship between electoral success and position in the party hierarchy, table 27 indicates that the distribution of candidates among the levels of the MPR hierarchy closely resembles a normal curve; there were

TABLE 27

1970 LEGISLATIVE ELECTIONS IN MONGALA SUBREGION:
TOTAL AND SUCCESSFUL CANDIDATES, BY PARTY POSITION

Level of Party Position	Total Candidates	%	Successful Candidates	Alternates
1. Nation 2 ministers 1 political bureau member	3	10	3	0
2. Region 1 regional committee member	1	3	0	1
3. Subregion 1 JMPR director-secretary 1 second vice-president 1 first vice-president	3	10	0	2
4. Section 1 section president 5 second vice-presidents 1 section committee secretary 1 JMPR committee assistant secretary 5 section committee members 1 JMPR committee member	14	47	4	1
5. Subsection 2 subsection presidents 1 subsection secretary 1 director JMPR	4	13	0	0

TABLE 27 (continued)

Level of Party Position	Total Candidates	%	Successful Candidates	Alternates
6. Cell				
4 cell presidents	4	13	1	0
7. Subcell				
1 subcell president	1	3	0	0
Total	30[a]	99	8[b]	4

SOURCE: 1970 Election File.

[a] All Zairians are members of MPR. Only thirty of sixty-four candidates had a formal position or title within the party structure. Fourteen of the sixty-four dossiers were incomplete because the candidate did not reside in the subregion. The mention on each of these dossiers is "Refer to the competent political authority." No information was available for these fourteen.

[b] There was no information on four successful candidates. Three others had no positions in the party other than that of militant. Of these, one was a bureaucrat, one a merchant, one a company employee.

very few candidates from either the upper reaches or lower extremes of the party structure. The middle level—the section—provided almost half the candidates, partly because at this level many of those active in party affairs probably believed themselves important enough to risk submitting their candidacies. Significantly, for the *successful* candidates, the same distribution does not obtain. Although it is true that four of the eight future commissioners came from the section level, here we can see the importance attached to high party position, particularly at the national level. All three candidates with positions at the highest levels were successful in their bids to become commissioners of the people.[34] There is nothing surprising in this. It seems clear that those with great power in Kinshasa used it on behalf of their own candidacies, a trend that—as shown in the next chapter—would recur when economic resources were distributed in the immediate aftermath of the nationalization of commercial houses and plantations. Indeed, of all the candidates for whom information is available, only one with a position in the party below the section level was ultimately successful.

The Subregional MPR Committee was responsible for rating each prospective candidate. These evaluations ranged from elite to zero. A summary may be found in table 28, which shows that almost 60 percent of the candidates received ratings of either elite or very good. Almost all successful candidates (10 of 11) were rated either elite or very good by the committee. Not surprisingly, while the committee ratings could not guarantee a candidate success, they could significantly reduce his chances if they were less than very good. The party's higher echelons, however, did accept one candidate who received a mediocre rating by the subregional committee.[35]

TABLE 28

1970 LEGISLATIVE ELECTIONS IN MONGALA SUBREGION:
TOTAL AND SUCCESSFUL CANDIDATES, BY RATING

Rating[a]	Total Candidates	%	Successful Candidates	Alternates
1. Elite-excellent	14	28	4	4
2. Very good	15	30	6	0
3. Good	3	6	0	0
4. Fair	5	10	0	0
5. Mediocre	5	10	1[b]	0
6. Zero-opportunist	8	16	0	0
Total	50[c]	100	11[c]	4

SOURCE: 1970 Election File.

[a]Ratings were attributed by the Subregional MPR Committee with the participation of all five zone commissioners and their respective assistants in charge of party affairs (second vice-presidents). A *cote,* or rating, was attributed wherever possible.

[b]This candidate was given the rather bizarre rating of "adherent."

[c]The committee did not evaluate fourteen of the sixty-four dossiers because the candidates did not live in the subregion and were not known to the members of the committee. These dossiers were referred to the competent political authority in other areas.

The committee ratings may also be broken down by occupational category to show how each grouping fared in the general evaluative process. On the basis of the evidence presented in table 29, it seems that, in general, First Republic politicians were given good ratings. Nine out of ten received

TABLE 29

1970 LEGISLATIVE ELECTIONS IN MONGALA SUBREGION:
OCCUPATIONAL CATEGORIES, BY RATING

	Rating						
Occupation	Elite	Very Good	Good	Fair	Mediocre	Zero	Total
1. Merchants	4	7 (2CP)[a]	1	2	3	4	21
2. Company employees	0	1	0	2	2 (1CP)	2	7
3. First Republic politicians	7 (4CP) (3A)	2	0	0	0	1	10
4. Bureaucrats	3 (1A)	3 (2CP)	1	0	0	0	7

TABLE 29 (continued)

		Rating					
Occupation	Elite	Very Good	Good	Fair	Mediocre	Zero	Total
5. Chiefs	0	0	0	1	0	0	1
6. Teachers	0	1	0	0	0	1	2
7. Trade unionists	0	0	1	0	0	0	1
8. University administrators	0	1 (1CP)	0	0	0	0	1
Total	14 (4CP) (4A)	15 (5CP)	3	5	5 (1CP)	8	50

SOURCE: 1970 Election File.
aNotations in parentheses refer to people in this category who were chosen either as commissioners of the people (CP) or as alternates (A).

evaluations of very good or elite. This was undoubtedly part of the reason for the overall success of candidates in this category, and all seven politicians who received elite ratings became either commissioners or alternates. Bureaucrats, too, tended to receive favorable evaluations. The subregional committee gave ratings of very good or better to six of the seven candidates in this occupational category. The only small surprise in table 29 is that merchants did not fare so well as either their bureaucratic or political competitors. Although eleven candidates received ratings of very good or elite, twenty-one merchants presented their candidacies. The committee, then, seemed more likely to assign poorer evaluations to merchants than to the other two numerically important categories, no doubt because some traders attended party demonstrations, marches, and rallies less than faithfully.

The election data on Mongala candidacies also indicate the occupational groupings more likely to be serving at certain levels of the MPR. As shown in table 30, the distribution of the three numerically most important occupational categories across the levels of the MPR hierarchy is of some importance. Bureaucrats are evenly distributed, with one at each party level from the region through the cell. The distribution of First Republic politicians is of note because these candidates make their appearance at the section and then rise through sub-regional and national levels. Not one is found below the section, which would indicate that many old politicians were able to convert their high political status in the First Republic into corresponding positions in the Second Republic. Finally, it should be observed that there are no

TABLE 30

1970 LEGISLATIVE ELECTIONS IN MONGALA SUBREGION:
CANDIDATES' PARTY POSITIONS BY OCCUPATION

Level of Party Position	Occupation[a]								
	M	E	P	B	C	T	TU	UA	Total
1. Nation	0	0	3 (3CP)	0	0	0	0	0	3
2. Region	0	0	0	1 (1A)	0	0	0	0	1
3. Subregion	0	0	2 (2A)	1	0	0	0	0	3
4. Section	6	1	3 (2CP) (1A)	1 (1CP)	0	1	1	1 (1CP)	14
5. Subsection	2	0	0	1	1	0	0	0	4
6. Cell	2 (1CP)	1	0	1	0	0	0	0	4
7. Subcell	0	1	0	0	0	0	0	0	1
Total	10 (1CP)	3	8 (5CP) (3A)	5 (1CP) (1A)	1	1	1	1 (1CP)	30

SOURCE: 1970 Election File.

[a]The following abbreviations are used: M, merchant; E, company employee; P, First Republic politician; B, bureaucrat; C, chief; T, teacher; TU, trade unionist; and UA, university administrator.

merchants in the hierarchy above the section level. The reasonable conclusion here is that the lower levels may have been the most amenable to penetration by those merchants who either developed or maintained an active interest in political office under the new regime. In large measure, this is probably due to the application of the 1968 staffing instructions regarding independent income.

The Elections and Political Mobility

Writing a year after the conclusion of the 1970 elections, an observer noted:

> The technical or administrative meaning is doubtlessly the most important. By that we mean that the new regime proved, on these occasions, its penetration of the interior of the country, its organization, and its mean of control.[36]

With the benefit of hindsight it can now be argued that while the organizational capabilities of the MPR received an important boost from the electoral mobilization, the party soon reverted to its apathetic ways. Most of the problems MPR officials had struggled to overcome during the party's first four years resurfaced after the legislative elections. It is difficult to believe that the organizational stimulus the elections provided was anything other than transitory. Many businessmen, most bureaucrats, and the majority of ordinary citizens in Mongala soon lapsed into their normal pattern of behavior vis-à-vis the party: They ignored it whenever possible. The *étatisation* of the MPR since that time has also contributed to this apathy. As noted previously, many people living in Lisala today have difficulty distinguishing the party from the state. They find it hard to identify just what the party contributes to their lives and well-being. The few party activities such as *Salongo*, meetings, and marches that can be identified by almost everyone leave most people resolutely uninterested. Although the MPR still enjoys a small residue of good will because of its role in halting the ethnic strife of the First Republic, it is questionable how much longer this will last.

It does not seem fruitful to conceive the 1970 elections as a long-term organizational triumph. Nor does it make sense to treat the MPR itself as an agency of mass mobilization. Instead, the significance of the 1970 legislative elections, and indeed comprehension of the MPR, should be sought by focusing on the party as an avenue of upward political mobility for a favored few.

To recapitulate, the candidate selection process was multilevel. Recommendations and evaluations were passed up the party hierarchy; the final decisions and nominations were handed down by the Political Bureau. In retrospect, it is difficult to say with certainty how much influence the recommendations of the Subregional MPR Committee had on the final selection of candidates in Mongala. Three of the fifteen successful candidates were either in the Council of Ministers or on the Political Bureau. To each the subregional committee attributed superlative ratings. These candidates would probably have succeeded even if the committee had been less generous—though there was little chance of that happening. Four other candidates were not evaluated by the committee in Mongala, and these would-be legislators were doubtless championed by the party elite in Kinshasa. There were eight other successful candidates, then, whose chances may have been significantly increased by the ratings they received. But the final decisions were made in Kinshasa. The function of the MPR committees at each level was to provide national decision makers with a group of eligible candidates. In this light the key task of the subregional committee was to certify the economic and ideological acceptability of the pool of potential legislators. Of course, throughout this process almost all candidates were campaigning for themselves wherever they thought it would do the most good. This pattern would be repeated in 1973 after the nationalization of European-owned economic activities.

Perhaps the most important aspect of the 1970 election results was the relative success of the group I have labeled First Republic politicians. In Mongala these candidates gained eight of the fifteen seats, as well as three of the four alternate slots. More generally, this pattern seems to have been largely replicated in other areas of the country. Why was this the case? First, the new regime's leaders made a definite effort to co-opt politicians who were relatively untainted by their activities in the First Republic and who still retained some popularity with the masses. This was particularly true for second vice-presidents of the MPR at zonal and subregional levels. Even in 1970, five years after the birth of the Second Republic, there may still have been a feeling that it would be best to incorporate some comfortably familiar personalities into the new legislature. While many members of the Political Bureau ran for office outside their home areas, the bulk of those elected were still representative of their native subregions.

A second reason also merits serious consideration. The stunning electoral victory of many who had been active politicians in the period before Mobutu's takeover is certainly consistent with a general patrimonial explanation of the political process in Zaire. It is easy to view the 1970 elections as an attempt by Mobutu to create or renew bonds of personal loyalty by dispensing over four hundred legislative positions. To put the matter more starkly in terms of patrimonial pork barrel politics, there were unconfirmed rumors among some candidates in Mongala that Jean Bolikango (former PUNA leader and at that time still considered an important regional suzerain) was given a veto over candidacies from this area.

President Mobutu may also have believed it would be in his political interest to keep all these former politicians active, thus precluding any trouble. Perhaps on the theory that busy hands are happy hands, Mobutu may have believed it would be safer to keep the new legislators occupied making money. It should be stressed that election to the National Legislative Council did not imply either an increase in political power or the creation of great political opportunity. It was clear from the beginning that the legislature would be used as a legitimizing rubber stamp to the policies the president and the Political Bureau had already decided to follow. If this aspect is considered, the main advantage of election is that membership in the National Legislative Council quickly became a means of increasing personal wealth. Legal and extralegal opportunities for some intensive—but primitive—capital accumulation were made available to most of those fortunate enough to be selected. The seats in the legislature themselves, therefore, ought properly to be thought of as much in economic as in political terms.

While such explanations may be persuasive, the patrimonial game itself must be understood as a product of its parameters. In the example of the MPR and the 1970 elections, these boundaries were largely defined by social-class considerations. The 1968 party instructions set the tone for the staffing decisions made at all levels of the hierarchy since then. These directives, coupled with the use of specifically economic criteria in selecting candidates in 1970, may be seen as a class action that restricted mobility chances to the wealthier segments of society. In addition, these procedures obviously facilitated the interpenetration of the commercial and the political sectors. The Mongala election dossiers have illuminated the interdependence of commerce and politics. It will be remembered that most of those classified as First Republic politicians had, somewhere along the line, accumulated enough money to begin their own businesses, bars, or plantations. Since all the candidates were rated on the basis of their economic well-being, the financially dominant strata of the population were clearly not at a disadvantage in the competition for political office and, with it, further economic advantages. The MPR might therefore be perceived as a vehicle for political advancement in which economic considerations played, and are continuing to play, a crucial role. In a society characterized by economic scarcity, such considerations also serve to close off political mobility opportunities for most of the population.

In some respects the 1970 elections should be viewed not as a watershed, but as an event that continued a basic policy orientation. Already relatively wealthy when they arrived in the legislature, most commissioners of the people were able to use their mandate to accumulate additional economic resources. In this, they were actively aided and encouraged by the higher political authorities of the Mobutu regime. Making money has always been the cornerstone of Zairian legislative activity. Citizen Bo-Boliko, President of the National Legislative Council, struck the following note when opening the October 1971 legislative session:

> We wish to obtain three objectives:
>
> First, unlike a Deputy in the old regime, we want, in addition to his parliamentary mandate, the Deputy of the new regime to have an occupation which can assure him most of his means of subsistence.
>
> Second, by inviting the deputies to agricultural work, we want to invite them to create new jobs in the rural areas.
>
> Third, by assuring a lucrative activity to each of the Deputies, we mean to give them the occasion to lead a normal life after their mandate.[37]

Support for this kind of legislative activity was more than merely moral. The following year, in May 1972, Bo-Boliko became agitated because many people thought the legislators had somehow received funds and material without cost from the state. Denouncing the counterrevolutionaries who had spread this tale, he explained that

> steps were undertaken to influence the Government, the Bank of Zaire, and the commercial banks in the area. . . The result of multiple negotiations which lasted more than a year was that a *bank credit* was obtained by each Deputy under the guarantee of the National Assembly which will make monthly withholdings on the parliamentary indemnities for the repayment of this debt. These withholdings, on the order of 60% of the parliamentary indemnities, are repaid monthly to the lending banks. . . .
>
> It is therefore a *bank credit* and not a gift that the Deputies have received.[38]

Even if the funds in question were bank loans, the significant fact remains that legislators were able to obtain commercial credit solely on the basis of their political position at a time when such funds were extremely scarce. The possibility still exists that the counterrevolutionaries were correct and the controversial funds were gifts.

Over and above the advantages to be had at the national level, commissioners of the people were periodically requested to return to their home areas. When there, legislators could enter into mutually profitable arrangements with local territorial commissioners. This often took the form of exclusive buying rights in coffee- and rice-growing areas, but other agreements could be worked out as well. In return, territorial commissioners would create contacts with commissioners of the people, which might stand them in good stead professionally—in addition to any lucrative financial understanding that might be devised. Often, particularly in the Lisala area, genuine friendships arose between territorial commissioners and legislators. In the words of one assistant subregional commissioner, "We are comfortable with the commissioners of the people and the merchants."[39]

Finally, the 1970 elections may be considered an important intermediate step in the commercial consolidation of the politically dominant elements in Zairian society. The elections were instrumental in placing certain individuals in positions in Kinshasa, where they would be able to benefit from economic opportunities that happened to come along. As we shall see, the commissioners of the people did extremely well for themselves when President Mobutu decided it was time for Zairians to take economic destiny into their own hands.

CHAPTER 7
Economic Independence: 30 November and the Politics of Class Formation

Some people's belly is like the earth. It is never so full that it will not take another corpse.

—Chinua Achebe[1]

Unbelievable things happened at the practical level.

—An acquirer[2]

On 30 November 1973 President Mobutu delivered his annual speech before the National Legislative Council. His discourse was intended to be a clarion call for the total economic independence of Zaire, and the decisions he announced touched virtually every important sector of the economy. In brief, he stated that since all land belonged to the state, henceforth all plantations, ranches, farms, and quarries would be returned to Zairians. Declaring that an equitable indemnity would be paid to the former owners over a ten-year period, he called for the progressive but rapid Zairianization of the economy's entire commercial sector.

The speech was a broad statement of national policy; it did not detail specific measures of implementation and application. Only the vaguest references were made to the Zairians who would take over the European properties and thus become acquirers. Although there were some indications that Mobutu intended to favor his immediate collaborators with these newly nationalized enterprises, he assured his audience that the replacement of foreigners with nationals would neither favor a minority of citizens nor create a national bourgeoisie. Indeed, in his concluding summary of the decisions the president was content to say only that he had given instructions to the state commerce commissioner that Zairianization would take place without fail.[3]

Although many observers of the Zairian scene were surprised by the sweeping nature of the new policy, the nationalization of foreign-owned economic activities had been an important part of the political landscape in the underdeveloped world since at least 1956. Other African nations—Nigeria most notably—had recently undertaken similar policies.[4] In Zaire, too, there had been reasonably clear indications that European ownership and control of the economy would not be permitted to continue indefinitely.[5]

Although an extended discussion of Mobutu's motives would take us well beyond our intended scope, it should be said that the president is a sincere and thoroughgoing nationalist. Sharing his nationalism, many highly placed

Zairians believed that the presence of small European merchants constituted an obstacle to the country's further economic development. In addition, there was a pervasive feeling that Zairians were fully capable of taking the nation's economic reins into their own hands. Such feelings may well have been encouraged by the then favorable economic conjuncture and the high price of copper on the international market. But President Mobutu might also have wanted to assert his claim to a respected place in Third World and African circles. Mobutu was long perceived, rightly or wrongly, as a puppet of foreign political and economic interests; his slightly tarnished image needed polishing. On 4 October 1973, before the United Nations in New York, he delivered a speech that was critical of multinational corporations and of certain kinds of international assistance, which aid the donor more than the recipient. The speech was widely acclaimed, and the favorable reaction may have heightened his resolve to deal with the question of foreign-owned commerce and plantations in a swift and highly dramatic manner.

However laudable the initial motivations, the acquirer cited above is correct; unbelievable things did happen at the practical level. This chapter focuses on questions of policy implementation and application. Sustained attention to the subject helps to underscore both the political dynamics of class formation and the way decisions are generally executed in the Zairian polity. Particular stress is given to measures concerning commerce and agriculture because they had an enormous impact on life in Lisala. In addition, I draw attention to the class-oriented aspects of policy implementation, the fluidity of class boundaries in Zaire, and the new dimension of economic insecurity that appeared in the aftermath of the 30 November proclamation. Finally, the economic, social, and political consequences of the nationalization effort are examined.

Implementation: Who Gets What and Why?

It became clear almost immediately that if the policy makers in Kinshasa had been considering the idea of Zairianization for some time, they had devoted painfully little thought to concrete measures of implementation, which would be necessary to bring the policy to fruition. To place the process of selecting acquirers in its historical context, a brief comment is needed on the social atmosphere created as a result of the 30 November speech. The often conflicting series of "clarifications" that soon began to pour out of Kinshasa must also be noted.

One early and continuing concern of capital's leadership was the fear of economic subversion by European merchants and planters who were being relieved of their holdings. On the same day as the speech, Citizen Kithima, then state commissioner for political affairs, alerted regional commissioners to possible attempts to subvert the economy.[6] In general, the authorities were afraid that stores and plantations would cease to function because the former owners would lose interest, try to repatriate funds, or stop restocking their shelves. These fears were not groundless. Many European shopkeepers and planters actively tried to smuggle their wealth out of the country. In the Lisala area, where controls were not applied, some new acquirers found that what had once been reasonably prosperous enterprises proved no more than empty stores and barren cash boxes with no records to indicate what business had once been like. At least part of the ensuing economic chaos, therefore, must be placed squarely on the shoulders of the departing foreign owners.

The Kinshasa leaders naturally wanted commerce to continue as normally as possible, and the territorial administration was counseled to avoid any zealousness in applying these decisions; stores were not to be looted and foreigners were not to be molested in any way. Zone commissioners were to instruct the population about the nationalization during political rallies.[7] In addition, a series of inventory controls was instituted.

Although bank accounts of foreign merchants were blocked, withdrawals were authorized for restocking goods and paying salaries. These required the signature of the former owner, a bank representative, and a territorial administration representative. In a general way, all business activities were to continue under the surveillance of the state.[8] In Lisala, however, because there was no bank, there was an immediate disruption in payment of workers' salaries. Moreover, there were not enough territorial administration representatives to warrant an even minimal surveillance of economic activites. Undaunted by administrative realities, decision makers in Kinshasa continued to send down instructions that were almost impossible to apply. On 4 December 1973, for example, the national economy commissioner issued an edict ordering regional commissioners to avoid the hasty liquidation of store merchandise. This was to be effected by weekly inventories of the shelf goods. Foreign merchants would then have to provide justifications for any unexplained variations in the inventory. In theory, this was a good idea; in practice, because there were insufficient administrative personnel to carry it out, the directive was ignored. Of Lisala's seven commercial houses, not one was subject to any sort of inventory control—let alone a weekly one—until the official takeover by a Zairian acquirer. There were not enough people to do the job.[9]

On 5 December 1973 the political affairs commissioner sent a long, detailed circular to regional commissioners, instructing the territorial administration to prepare an inventory of goods for each nationalized business that would be signed by the former owner and a representative of the state. The administration representative and the former owner would then jointly manage the business or plantation until the arrival of the new Zairian acquirer. According to a confidential memo attached to the circular, this was to be completed by 31 December 1973.[10] To the best of my knowledge this did not occur in Lisala, although a number of territorial commissioners paid inordinate attention to the cash boxes of the European merchants. A few even took it upon themselves to collect receipts, which somehow disappeared. By 14 December 1973 the situation had apparently reached disquieting proportions, because the political affairs commissioner dashed off a message to his regional representatives expressing stupefaction that bureaucrats were collecting business receipts. He told them, in effect, to maintain general surveillance, but to keep their hands off and let former owners operate their enterprises as they had in the past.[11]

To inhibit European subversion further, the Centre National de Documentation (CND), or secret police, issued instructions that neither Air Zaire nor ONATRA could handle the cargoes of European merchants and planters. Also, no foreigner was permitted to leave before his Zairian acquirer had completed the official inventory and takeover. This order, too, created confusion. In Boende, for example, the "forces of order" installed an illegal checkpoint at the airport.[12] Given the nature of the situation, and of the forces of order, it is doubtful that any seized contraband filtered into the state coffers.

More serious disruptions were brought about by spiteful Europeans. An official at Bumba reported that the managers of one of the large rice mills there had deliberately burned out the main motor.[13] It is difficult now to capture the mood of rumor, innuendo, and confusion in the Zairian countryside. The Bumba rice mill was sabotaged. Wild stories, however, circulated all over Mongala and few, if any, were factual. To cite one example: The last week in December 1973 an assistant zone commissioner was dispatched to the plantation at Binga to check the rumor of white mercenaries, which had been heard in Lisala. He found that although the whites were demoralized by the presidential decisions, there were no mercenaries, and the rumor had started when a couple of plantation managers had decided to spend an afternoon shooting pigeons.[14]

In general, the greater the distance between Kinshasa and the countryside, the greater the chances for confusion and misguided interpretations of administrative directives. This was caused, first, by a poor communications infrastructure. Although Mbandaka is linked to its subregional centers by telegraph and radio, communications between the subregion and the zones is often chaotic even under the best of circumstances. In Mongala, for example, it could take weeks before policy directives would arrive at zone headquarters like Businga, Mobayi-Mbongo, and Bongandanga. Communication between the zones and their collectivities was even slower. Thus, although implementation directives were being formulated with great haste in the capital, their arrival in the farthest reaches of the country was often delayed by at least thirty days. Second, because of this communications lag, zone commissioners and collectivity chiefs were often left on their own. They had to figure out what to do and how to implement presidential policy. (Radios are used everywhere, so people would quickly have been aware of the 30 November speech.) On the border with the Central African Empire and well off the beaten path, events in the Yakoma Collectivity of Mobayi-Mbongo Zone illustrate this phenomenon. The local JMPR leader, infused with party zeal but lacking instructions to the contrary, prevented white merchants from continuing normal activities on the grounds that the president had forbidden it in his 30 November speech. Commerce in Yakoma came to a halt and the population was unable to buy necessary items. Again, because of the poor communications system, the subregional authorities in Lisala did not become aware of the problem until mid-January 1974.[15] It is only within the context of delay, confusion, and fluidity in the hinterland that the process of selecting acquirers can be understood.

The Official Policy

The assignment of European plantations and stores to Zairian acquirers took place at many levels and in many dimensions. The process was confusing, contradictory, and often impossible to comprehend. It is not clear that there was, in fact, any single policy, even at the formulation level. Nonetheless, to place what happened in Lisala and Equateur in a broader national perspective, events in the capital need to be detailed.

The first indication of the identity of the acquirers was obviously contained in the 30 November discourse. At that time President Mobutu encouraged his collaborators—specifically, the commissioners of the people—to have lucrative occupations in addition to their official functions. He specified that all of them would have to be busy in 1974 with the operation of business and agricultural activities in the countryside. The obvious implication was that the national legislators would be chosen to lead Zaire into the promised land of economic independence. Clarifications were not long in coming. The National Executive Council met on 3 December 1973; at the conclusion of the meeting the national orientation commissioner told the press that properties would not be given to insolvent citizens. On the other hand, he stated that these measures were not designed to create a bourgeois class to the detriment of the laboring masses.[16] The first written instructions concerning distribution seem to have been contained in the political affairs commissioner's previously cited circular of 5 December 1973. Here, Kithima advised regional commissioners that they could propose the names of militants believed to be financially capable of taking over foreign enterprises. Moreover, as for commerce, they were instructed to favor local notables and merchants. He also specified that until further notice no authority of the territorial administration could appropriate property titles to abandoned houses or plantations.[17] But the circular gave no hint as to who such "notables" might be. Another clarification was sent down the line on 14 December 1973. At this juncture, the political affairs commissioner asserted that no one could appropriate an enterprise, a farm, or a business merely by an arrangement with the regional authorities.[18]

The next official elaboration came on 26 December 1973, when the Tripartite met in Kinshasa under the chairmanship of President Mobutu. This body is composed of the Political Bureau of the MPR, the National Executive Council, and the officers of the Legislative Council. It is, military leaders excepted, a collection of most of the influential and important political leaders of the regime. The Tripartite decided that the state would take over large agro-industrial and commercial units, which were considered strategic. Ranches, plantations, and certain commercial houses would go to the president's closest collaborators—that is, the members of the Tripartite and the commissioners of the people. As for retail trade, it was declared that those who acquired it would have to live where the business was located. Members of the armed forces, judges, bureaucrats, ambassadors, territorial commissioners, collectivity chiefs, and locality chiefs could *not* take over European enterprises because the national interest required that these guardians of the smooth functioning of the state retain their independence vis-à-vis all business.[19]

The 26 December meeting of the Tripartite was an obvious attempt by the most powerful politico-administrative leaders to appropriate for themselves the immense wealth the Europeans were turning over. As such, it represented the continuation of a prevalent pattern in Zairian politics since 30 June 1960: the conversion of political power and position into economic wealth for the benefit of the few at the expense of the many. Indeed, it might be said that the Tripartite's decision was a class action by the politically dominant elements in Zairian society. This aspect of the Tripartite's action was immediately apparent to almost everyone, and an outcry ensued. But much of this protest, one suspects, may have been generated by those politico-administrative officials who had been specifically excluded from the benefits of Zairianization, many of whom, as will be seen, eventually became acquirers.

On 30 December 1973 the political affairs commissioner held a mass meeting in Kinshasa, at which he declared that President Mobutu's immediate collaborators would merely be communal managers of this wealth and would be required to present balance sheets at the end of each year.[20] Two days later Mobutu began to backpedal furiously. His New Year's speech noted that the Tripartite's decision insufficiently translated the legitimate aspirations of the Zairian people. He announced that therefore all economic activities affected by the measures of 30 November would be taken over by the state. Included were large commercial units, plantations, farms, and agro-industrial enterprises. An exception was made of retail trade, which was to be taken over by Zairians who had "the means and the vocation." Those who wished to acquire a plantation or a farm would have to pay the state for it, and the appropriate ministry would determine the conditions and methods by which the cession could be accomplished. Mobutu reiterated that he would not tolerate the existence of a category of privileged citizens.[21] President Mobutu's decision that the state would take over the major units of production was not carried out for almost a year. But his speech of 1 January 1974 certainly foreshadowed the measures of radicalization that were announced on 30 December 1974.

The public outcry against the Tripartite's decision continued unabated. The editor-in-chief of *Salongo* published an extraordinarily critical commentary on the way these measures were being implemented. He noted that the choice fell on the president's close collaborators because of their "honorability and with an eye towards the sound management of these goods." Even so, the people were upset about this decision, and with good reason. After all, were not the people as honorable as their leaders? He even questioned the business ability of some of the nation's legislators. Many had been allocated important sums of money by the president and, despite this largesse, had failed to establish thriving enterprises. In conclusion he noted that the members of the Tripartite, contrary to the MPR motto, had served themselves instead of the nation.[22]

The *Salongo* article appeared on 2 January 1974. A period then followed during which no major policy statement was made concerning the implementation of the Zairianization measures. On 13 March 1974 Citizen Nguza, the permanent secretary of the Political Bureau, broke the silence and announced that President Mobutu would reexamine the dossiers on the application of the Zairianization measures to discover and remedy any irregularities that might have cropped up during the distribution process. He again mentioned that these decisions had been made to reinforce the country's economic independence and not to enrich any particular group of individuals. The European enterprises would have to revert, according to the firm criteria initially defined, to any citizen who had "the means and the vocation."[23] It is questionable whether any list of firm criteria ever existed.

By the time Nguza's statement was published, numerous irregularities had become readily apparent. Another article appeared in the Kinshasa press about this time that cataloged some of the more flagrant abuses. First, a complete list of acquirers, although promised, had never been made public. In addition, quite a few *citoyennes*—apparently wives and concubines of high government officials—had obtained an impressive numer of boutiques and stores. In some stores, moreover, acquirers were pocketing the daily proceeds to cover their personal expenses. The article went on to report that import houses were not making new orders, and that some city-dwelling citizens had acquired stores in the interior and therefore could not supervise them properly.[24]

On 22 March 1974 the National Executive Council met under the chairmanship of President Mobutu. At the termination of this meeting a spokesman announced that a high-level Request Committee would be formed under the direction of the political affairs commissioner, which would include as regular members the state commissioners for agriculture, national economy, commerce, and justice. The committee would be asked to gather the complaints of all Zairians and foreigners who believed themselves wronged in any way by the application of the 30 November decisions. It was yet again proclaimed that economic independence must benefit all Zairian people and that in creating this committee, President Mobutu was guided by a desire to see that the application of the 30 November measures was not contrary to the spirit of his speech.[25]

The next day the political affairs commissioner chaired a working meeting of all regional commissioners in Kinshasa. Also present were the director-general of the Political Affairs Department, the political affairs commissioner's cabinet director, and the coordinating secretary in charge of MPR *encadrement*. The minutes of this meeting indicate that the highest echelons of Zairian leadership were aware of, and concerned about, the way the population perceived the implementation process. Explicitly, the state commissioner was worried about safeguarding the good reputation of national and regional leaders. He was concerned that those who exercised power in the party would be seen as having violated the MPR motto, *servir et non se servir*, by siphoning off most of the European wealth. He told the regional commissioners that President Mobutu had decided that his immediate civilian and military associates could not benefit from these stores and plantations. Specifically, this meant political commissioners, state commissioners, territorial commissioners, bureaucrats, those who work in department cabinets and for parastatal organisms, and soldiers. Everyone in these categories had to renounce any goods already acquired. Expatriate wealth would have to be left to those who, as usual, had the means and the vocation. Nor could the wives of these officials acquire anything. Their relatives could come into expatriate wealth only if they carried out the necessary steps themselves. Commissioners of the people, however, were not affected by this decision. From the printed minutes it is difficult to gauge the reaction to this presidential ukase. It may be assumed, however, that there was at least some resistance. At one point the chairman had to remind the participants that they should always have confidence in the "Guide" [Mobutu]. The recording secretary noted that this reminder was imparted rather energetically.[26]

Such an interpretation is at least partially borne out by the minutes of a second meeting held three days later. Withdrawing from his previous stand, the political affairs commissioner announced to the participants that President Mobutu had changed his mind. They could now retain one item among the mass of things they had obtained as a result of Zairianization. The commissioner told them to choose judiciously among the items they had acquired and gave them a relatively important, but unspecified, period in which to decide what to relinquish. When this decision was announced, the recording secretary noted, perhaps wryly, that the regional commissioners applauded with great satisfaction.[27]

On 27 March 1974 President Mobutu extended to all acquirers the decision he had imposed on regional commissioners and other high-level cadres. At the end of a Political Bureau meeting, the permanent secretary declared that the president was waiting for the final report of the Request Committee. After the president had seen the report and the complete list of Zairians who felt slighted in the distribution process, all acquirers who had taken over several businesses would be asked to retain only one. The remainder would revert to the state via the Commerce Department, which would reassign them to Zairians whose complaints were found to be valid. It was also announced that most of the Zairianized enterprises were already working smoothly, this to the great satisfaction of the president.[28] This, though, was a most optimistic assessment of the situation.

Since a decision made in the capital does not necessarily ensure that territorial authorities in the hinterland will know about it, it was not until almost one full month had passed that the regional commissioner in Mbandaka asked his subordinates to furnish a list of unassigned stores as well as the names of Zairians who had received more than one business per family.[29]

By mid-August even President Mobutu had recognized that Zairianization had not gone according to schedule and had produced a series of unintended consequences. Before the high party cadres at the opening session of the Makanda Kabobi Institute, the MPR school, he reflected that "with a few rare exceptions—and I insist on the word rare—the manner in which the assignments and takeovers occurred is a veritable shame for most of the cadres of the MPR."[30] At a mass meeting in Kinshasa on 25 November Mobutu asked the crowd whether they wanted to become a nation of nouveaux riches. Commenting on the rise of this category of people since the 30 November measures, the president reiterated that he would like to have done with this group in Zaire and had therefore banned the importation of Mercedes automobiles into the country. He urged Zairians to abandon useless luxury and devote themselves to development expenditures.[31] Finally, on 30 December, Citizen Nguza announced that the president and the Political Bureau had decided to "radicalize" the Zairian revolution. He enumerated ten scourges plaguing Zairian life as well as the measures designed to deal with them. While it is beyond our scope to analyze these decisions in detail here, two of the ten are worthy of attention in this discussion. Scourge number eight was social injustice. As of 1 January 1975 the state would take over all major units of production and distribution. The tenth scourge, egoism and individualism, was highly relevant to the distribution of Zairianized goods. It was announced that all cadres of the MPR would have to abandon what they had acquired as a result of 30 November, as well as those commercial activities they had in their own right before that time. Henceforth, they would have to concentrate only on agricultural activities.[32]

The radicalization of 30 December 1974 thus marks at least a partial admission that the general policy of Zairianization had failed. The implementation of these later measures would itself make an intriguing study, but for the moment attention is focused on the thirteen months between Mobutu's speech before the Legislative Council and the radicalization of the revolution. Now that the broad outlines of policy have been sketched, it is appropriate to examine the patterns and processes of distribution that occurred, official policy notwithstanding.

Cui Bono?

Like every other aspect of the 30 November episode, the actual process in which acquirers were selected is confusing and muddled. Very early the National Executive Council declared that a census would be conducted and a definitive list compiled of all commercial houses, plantations, farms, ranches, and agro-industrial enterprises that would fall under the measures. This accomplished, the relevant ministries would be responsible for the registration of the candidacies of those who would like to become acquirers.[33] The census question is a murky one. It is not clear whether a census actually took place, but in the course of inquiries at different levels of government I discovered that no one had a precise idea of how many items were to be taken over. Lists of Zairianized enterprises existed at every level, but they were often vastly different and contradictory. For example, *Salongo* reported that there were only fifty-one plantations in Equateur affected by the measures. The 30 March 1974 issue of *Mambenga* (the weekly newspaper of Equateur Region), however, produced a list of 609 plantations in the region that fell under the Zairianization decisions.[34] To complicate the task further, the lists of Zairianized items at each level often differed substantially in their accounts of exactly what had been given to whom. While an honest attempt has been made to present an accurate picture of both the selection process and the distribution pattern, the reader is nevertheless cautioned that, Lisala and Bumba excepted, much of what follows must be considered highly tentative.

On 7 December 1973 the Executive Council decided that all potential acquirers, without exception, had to present their dossiers to the relevant departments.[35] In practice, though, the territorial administration had to compile the dossiers and register the candidate acquirers in the interior. Beginning at the zone level, candidates submitted their papers. These were then judged by zone commissioners and passed on to the subregion, where they were also examined and rated. The same process then took place at the region before the dossiers were sent to the Executive Council in Kinshasa. Thus the selection process, at least in Equateur, was multilevel. In many significant respects it resembled the process by which the 1970 MPR legislative candidates were selected; there was a filtering of potential acquirers at each level of the politico-administrative hierarchy. We have already examined the 1970 candidate selection process, and it is apparent that the same criteria—wealth, militancy, position in the party—were used in judging the dossiers of potential acquirers. The result, naturally, was that the same categories of people, and often the very same individuals, benefited from the selection process.[36]

What happened in Lisala? By any standards Lisala is not a thriving commercial center. On the eve of 30 November 1973 there were perhaps fifteen or twenty Zairian merchants inscribed on the commercial register. Most of them owned bars, *buvettes*, or the small boutiques that lined the two markets of the town. There was only one Zairian merchant who had succeeded in establishing a cement-built store before Zairianization. In the town's trading center there were seven commercial houses run by Portuguese merchants. Six of them dealt primarily in general commerce and trade goods such as tinned margarine, sardines, enamel basins, buckets, jerry cans, machetes, cigarettes, matches, cloth for women, some kinds of men's clothing, and school supplies. One of the European firms dealt in wholesale goods and occasionally acted as Lisala's beer distributor.

The first point to emphasize is that the selection of acquirers was purely political and not technical. The subregional economic affairs and agriculture service chiefs were not consulted in the decision-making process. The MPR committees at each level considered the dossiers, and it seems unlikely that any technical criteria such as successful past performance were considered.[37] The two party committees did, however, pare to twenty the number of candidates who wished to acquire commercial establishments. Eliminated in this first evaluation were an impressive number of small shopkeepers and itinerant merchants. The twenty remaining candidates included two collectivity chiefs, one locality chief, the wife of a Portuguese merchant, the wife of the assistant subregional commissioner for political affairs, four bar owners, one planter, and eleven traders.[38] Of these twenty, three were ultimately given commercial houses in Lisala and one received a store in Bumba. As in the 1970 elections, not all the candidates put forth by the lower administrative levels were accepted, and potential acquirers operating at the national and regional levels succeeded in gaining access to stores and plantations in Lisala. The prescribed process and the lower levels of the hierarchy were bypassed.

Initially there were thus twenty serious candidates to acquire seven stores. The selection process is illuminated if we examine how these stores were distributed among those who requested them. For analytic convenience these seven stores are grouped into four categories, or case studies.

Case 1: The Ethnic Link. The sole Zairian merchant who had established a cement-built store of his own before the 30 November measures had originally come from Kasai. A Muluba, he had been in commerce ever since he could remember. When a student, he had earned enough money to finance his studies by selling peanuts, bananas, and bread to other students. During the postindependence chaos he had been interned in a United Nations refugee camp in Kasai, where he had been able to set up a small commerce in foodstuffs. He gained his initial stake while trading on the Zaire riverboat from 1964 to 1969, and established himself as a shopkeeper in Lisala's small market in 1969. After one year he accumulated enough money to open the first Zairian-owned store in town. Although viewed as an outsider by the local people (he is the only Luba trader), he was widely respected. Indeed, he was elected vice-president of the local chapter of the Association Nationale des Entreprises Zairoises (ANEZA).

When the president announced the Zairianization measures, he was one of the first to file his papers with the zonal authorities. At least outwardly, he respected the procedure prescribed by the national authorities. On other levels, however, he immediately began to lobby intensively for his candidacy.

At this time the wife of the subregional commissioner was also a Kasai-Luba, a merchant and president of the Association of Women Merchants in Lisala. A number of informants well-versed in subregional politics believe that the commissioner's wife was active in supporting his candidacy with her husband, himself from Bandundu. Rumors indicate that money changed hands. As vice-president of ANEZA, the Luba trader chaired the Mongala delegation that went to Mbandaka to promote the candidacies of Lisala merchants (that is, their own). In Mbandaka the divisional chief of the Economic Affairs Bureau was instrumental in presenting recommendations to the regional party committee. There is good, though inconclusive, evidence that this bureaucrat, also from Kasai, actively supported the candidacy of his fellow Kasaian from Lisala. Lisala's one Luba trader became the acquirer of a commercial house with several stores in Lisala and Binga valued at ± Z30,000.

Long friendly with another local shopkeeper, the Luba merchant effectively promoted his friend's candidacy through this own ethnic links. His friend, a Ngombe trader from Binga, piggybacked his own request to that of his colleague because he knew the Luba had influential support in both the region and the subregion. For example, his Luba friend included him in the ANEZA delegation from Lisala even though he was not an officer of the association. Thus, although his dossier had been submitted at the zonal level, his success was due to ethnic influence, even if it was not from members of his own group.[39]

Case 2: The Close Collaborators.   Two of the seven commercial houses in Lisala were assigned to commissioners of the people. As close collaborators of President Mobutu, these gentlemen were clearly given preference in the selection process. Although the Executive Council had declared that all candidate acquirers would have to submit their dossiers to the relevant ministries, the commissioners of the people were exceptions. Nor, it should be said, were they required to file their candidacies with representatives of the territorial administration. The bureau and officers of the National Legislative Council greatly facilitated matters for them. All they had to do was to leave their demands at the bureau of the legislature, and the rest was taken care of. There was no need to run around to various ministries promoting their virtues as potential acquirers. It was assumed that since the president wished to try this experiment with his closest associates, their requests would be honored. They were. Everywhere.

One of the commissioners came late to politics. He had been a small merchant and bar owner in Lisala for a number of years, but had been accepted as a candidate in the 1970 elections because his militancy and economic activities were deemed sufficient. He acquired a commercial establishment, a plantation, and a bakery. The bakery no longer operates, however, and the plantation was later reassigned to a *citoyenne* whose background I was not able to trace. He was thus left with the commercial house, which takes in Z6,000 to Z7,000 per month. Though a commissioner, he has no real political influence at either the national or the local level.

The same cannot be said of Lisala's other commissioner of the people. Long a politician, he had been active in First Republic politics as a member of PUNA and had once been provincial governor of Moyen-Congo. He had successfully made the transition to politics under the new regime, and from 1966 to 1970 he filled a number of responsible positions. After a short stint as political affairs minister, he fell from grace in 1970 and retained only his position as a national legislator. Still an important regional figure, he was given a commercial house in Lisala, which grosses Z26,000 per month. He also acquired two agro-industrial plantation complexes in the Zone of Bongandanga, across the river from Lisala, and an electrical appliance store in the Memling Hotel in Kinshasa. He may have come into even more European wealth, but these are the only items I was able to confirm.[40]

Case 3: The First Family. One wholesale house in Lisala was hit by the 30 November measures. It is a branch office of a firm based in Gemena, which also has outlets in Libenge, Businga, and Bumba. The Lisala branch dealt in most of the currently demanded first-necessity articles and serviced merchants in the town and its environs. It specialized, however, in the beer trade and was the usual distributor of Kisangani beer before Zairianization. This branch had monthly sales of Z66,000 before the takeover.

Soon after Zairianization measures were announced, the firm was ceded to the Office National des Fibres Textiles (ONAFITEX). But in July 1974 it was acquired by a *citoyenne* living in Gemena. Married to a European trader, she was a competent merchant and had a number of small but profitable businesses on the eve of 30 November 1973. Informants in Lisala were unable to provide precise information, but there was a consensus that this firm's acquirer was selected at the highest level in Kinshasa. The acquirer is Mongwandi and thought to be a blood relation of President Mobutu.[41]

Case 4: Holy Matrimony. Two retail shops in Lisala were given to Zairian wives of former Portuguese owners. It had been decided fairly early that foreign merchants with Zairian wives could cede their enterprises to their spouses and children.[42] One Portuguese trader in Lisala had been legally married to a Zairian for a number of years. As soon as the measures were announced, he ceded all his holdings to his wife by means of a legal gift— which some cynics suspect was preceded by a liberal consideration to a local magistrate. His wife submitted her credentials at zone headquarters, but the Portuguese immediately dispatched her to Mbandaka to see what could be done at the regional level. In the regional capital she was told that this matter had to be taken care of at the Ministry of Commerce in Kinshasa. After spending several months knocking on doors in the capital, she finally obtained a letter that ceded her the store. Her husband continues to run the business as in the past. I was told that her store takes in Z3,000 per month, perhaps an underestimate.[43]

Another Portuguese merchant, long established in the town, had been living with a Zairian woman for many years, but the legal status of their relationship was moot. In late January 1974 his store was handed over to one of the local trade union officers. The official takeover completed, the unionist found no money in the bank account and little merchandise on the shelves. A receipt book and relevant papers appeared to have been "lost." The Portuguese merchant then made a legal gift of all he owned to the children he and his companion had produced. In this instance, too, there is some indication that the legal act was antedated so as to bear a date prior to 30 November 1973. The woman went to Mbandaka to plead her case to the regional commissioner. She, too, was referred to Kinshasa, where she apparently had little difficulty in getting the original assignment annulled. The commerce commissioner reassigned the store in early March 1974; thus the initial acquirer was in place for only about six weeks. On the second takeover, however, a deficit of Z4,000 was discovered. Clearly, the trade unionist had not been idle and had made the most of his time as manager of the enterprise. The new acquirer's husband continues to run the store as before and the business takes in about Z9,000 per month.[44]

In summary, the attribution process for the stores in Lisala was multilevel. Only three eventual acquirers went through the motions of filing their candidacies at the zonal office. Depending upon the personal situation of each candidate, pressure was brought to bear where it might do the most good. The Luba trader made use of his ethnic connections at the subregion and in Mbandaka. The commissioners used the political leverage they had accumulated over time and worked through the institutional facilities of the Legislative Council. The acquirer of the wholesale house probably relied on her family relationship with President Mobutu. The two Portuguese merchants operated both locally and in the capital. They procured antedated documents in Lisala and then dispatched their Zairian wives to obtain the other necessary papers in Kinshasa.

The political manipulations that affected the distribution of goods in Lisala were also multidimensional, and a number of useful trumps were played in the 30 November card game. First, the ethnic dimension was unquestionably important. Lisala's lone Luba storekeeper was able to parlay his ethnic ties into the possession of a rather lucrative business. Similarly, the acquirer of the wholesale firm successfully exploited her ties with the president. It should be pointed out, however, that the ethnic dimension of this process seems to have been played out within a set of fluid and imprecise class boundaries. It seems unlikely that either of these two acquirers would have been accommodated by their ethnic kinsmen had they been perceived as obviously unsuited. Both, it will be remembered, were already active merchants, and they are undoubtedly two of the more dynamic elements to have come into property taken over from the Europeans.

In a related vein, I am unaware of any lower-level bureaucrats, primary or secondary school teachers, or low-ranking military personnel who became acquirers. One reason for the exclusion of these occupational categories was the requirement that potential acquirers have money in the bank.[45] Although relatively wealthy, their incomes do not permit ample opportunities for saving. Second, a class bias was especially evident in the distribution of businesses to the commissioners of the people. They were given European enterprises because of their positions in the national hierarchy and their political connections. Last, the example of the two Zairians with Portuguese husbands conforms to neither the class nor the ethnicity model. This pattern may, however, constitute the holding action of a group of expatriates whose days of influence and importance are perhaps numbered.

Although it is both difficult and dangerous to generalize on the basis of events in one small town in the hinterland of Equateur, one might hypothesize from the Lisala experience that positions in the politico-administrative hiearchy will be used to appropriate spoils when the rules of the game have not been clearly elaborated or are not being enforced. Personal connections become a factor when the resource seeker himself has no position of authority. A small degree of confirmation for this hypothesis is provided by the town of Bumba. Unlike Lisala, Bumba is known throughout the area as a lively commercial center. In general the commercial firms in Bumba are far more lucrative and desirable than those in Lisala. If we omit wholesale houses with branches in Bumba, such as Sapro, Sedec, Scibe-Zaire, and Socomu, there were twelve enterprises that fell under the presidential measures of 30 November. Of these twelve, nine of the new acquirers could be identified.

The distribution pattern in Bumba, shown in table 31, would seem to bear out my contention that position in the politico-administrative hierarchy is a key variable in determining who gets what. The striking feature of the allocation of stores in Bumba is the number of party bureaucrats who got into the act. Seven of the nine identified acquirers had some position with the party. Of the remaining two, one was an army general who later became a member of the MPR Political Bureau, and the othe was a well-connected Kinshasa merchant who originally came from the Bumba area.

In Equateur Region there were two sides to the coin of 30 November: commerce and agriculture. Because of time constraints and resource limitations, I was unable to devote the same detailed attention to unraveling the acquisition process in the agricultural sphere. Nonetheless, a few reasonable deductions can be made on the basis of distributions in this sector. In the Zone of Lisala, for example, six agro-industrial activities fell under Zairianization measures. The immense Binga and Bangala plantations went straight to the president of the Republic. Another large plantation was given to a commissioner of the people from Kinshasa. A much smaller plantation was turned over to one of the local legislators, and two sawmills were given to Zaire's ambassador to Belgium and an army general, respectively.[46] The

TABLE 31
ZAIRIANIZATION IN BUMBA

Type of Commerce	Acquirer
1. General commerce, rice mill, sawmill, gas station	Commissioner of the people
2. General commerce	Commissioner of the people (alternate)
3. General commerce and food store	Commissioner of the people
4. General commerce and coffee factory	Kinshasa merchant
5. General commerce and radio repair shop	Unknown
6. General commerce	Assistant regional cheerleader[a]
7. General commerce and agricultural trade	Unknown
8. Garage and butcher shop	JMPR leader
9. General commerce	Collectivity chief
10. General commerce	Unknown
11. General commerce and food store	Party bureaucrat
12. General commerce	Army general

SOURCE: Archives, Equateur Region, Economic Affairs Department, Mbandaka. Administrative correspondence, 3 September 1975.

[a]MPR cheerleaders are responsible for developing and perfecting party chants and songs. The regional cheerleader has the rank and salary of a subregional commissioner.

selection process went on exclusively at Kinshasa. One might speculate that the more valuable the enterprise to be attributed, the more likely that (1) the decision would be made in Kinshasa and (2) the decision would favor someone with a very high politico-administrative position.

Equateur is primarily an agricultural region. Whatever real wealth exists in this part of Zaire is tied to the plantation economy. The most important members of the national leadership, many of whom come from this region, were well aware of this fact. A more detailed analysis of some acquisitions of two important figures, President Mobutu and State Commissioner Engulu, may therefore prove enlightening.

In Equateur Region President Mobutu[47] acquired the large Elubangi ranch (which does not concern us in this analysis) as well as four major plantations in the northern part of the region. The plantation surface area under cultivation is presented in table 32.

State Commissioner Engulu's acquisitions after 30 November were equally impressive. He acquired the agro-industrial firms of Cequa, Cie

TABLE 32
MOBUTU'S EQUATEUR ACQUISITIONS
(by Crop, in Hectares[a])

Plantation	Coffee	Cocoa	Rubber	Palm	Total
SCZ Binga	728	1,199	2,538	7,156	11,621
SCZ Bosondjo	309	—	—	12,958	13,267
Bangala-Lisala	1,248	1,901	4,266	—	7,415
Bangala-Gemena	764	295	—	—	1,059
Total	3,049	3,395	6,804	20,114	33,362

SOURCE: Région de l'Equateur, Division Régionale de l'Agriculture, *Rapport annuel 1974*, pp. 132–138.

[a]One hectare = 2.47 acres.

Hevea, Busira Lomami, Sobol, Schoofs, Macodibe, Maurice, Verbuyt, and Socobe. These nine firms account for thirty-six plantations in the southern half of the region. They are spread throughout the zones of Bikoro, Boende, Bokungu, Befale, Monkoto, Djolu, and Ikela. Table 33 gives the totals for the thirty-five plantations on which data were available.

TABLE 33
ENGULU'S EQUATEUR ACQUISITIONS
(by Crop, in Hectares)

Plantation	Coffee	Cocoa	Rubber	Palm	Total
35 plantations	2,132	887	20,026	12,682	35,727

SOURCE: Région de l'Equateur, Division Régionale de l'Agriculture, *Rapport annuel 1974*, pp. 132–138.

If we combine the total acquisitions of President Mobutu and Commissioner Engulu and calculate the percentage of land under cultivation that their holdings represent, we arrive at some eloquent figures. The data are presented in table 34.

Although production figures are difficult to obtain for individual plantations, the data are available for SCZ Binga and SCZ Bosondjo plantations, which the president acquired. By combining the totals for these two enterprises, it is possible to determine what percentage of total regional output they represent. The totals for these two plantations can then be added to the production figures for Entriac, one of the major enterprises taken over by

TABLE 34
COMBINED EQUATEUR ACQUISITIONS, 1974
(by Crop, in Hectares, and as % of Total Crop Area)

	Coffee	Cocoa	Rubber	Palm
Mobutu	3,049	3,395	6,804	20,114
Engulu	2,132	887	20,026	12,682
Total	5,181	4,282	26,830	32,796
Total Equateur area	79,749	27,489	81,964	114,826
Mobutu and Engulu holdings as % of total Equateur area	6%	16%	33%	29%

SOURCE: Région de l'Equateur, Division Régionale de l'Agriculture, *Rapport annuel 1974,* pp. 84–89, 132–138.

Commissioner Engulu. This figure will permit us to calculate a combined percentage of the total regional production. These figures, presented in table 35, are remarkable, to say the least.

The Zairianized acquisitions of President Mobutu and Commissioner Engulu account for 7 percent of the coffee and 3 percent of the cocoa production in Equateur in 1974. Furthermore, they account for 32 percent of the rubber tonnage, 60 percent of the palm oil tonnage, and 41 percent of the cabbage palm production for the entire Equateur Region. Mobutu's holdings alone account for 67 percent of the region's palm fruit production, even though only two of the president's four plantations are represented in these calculations. Similarly, not all of Engulu's acquisitions are part of Entriac. The percentages must therefore be taken as significant *underestimates* of the productive capacity of the agro-industrial enterprises these two important politicians acquired. One other word of caution: The data set forth in tables 32, 33, 34, and 35 should be treated as tentative. Data collection in Zaire, particularly when carried out by the agricultural service, leaves much to be desired. Although these data can provide us with general indications and perhaps an aggregate picture, they are not amenable to sophisticated statistical manipulation.

As should by now be apparent, the distribution pattern that emerged from the Zairianization policy favored the most important officials in the land. Why? The patrimonial explanation of Zairian politics put forth by Jean-Claude Willame merits serious attention.[48] Was Mobutu, as a patrimonial ruler, hoping to increase the number of fiefs at his command? And with these new resources, was he trying to bring more and more people into a direct dependence on his authority for economic as well as political favors?

Given the still rudimentary state of our knowledge concerning the dynamics of the 30 November phenomenon, I cannot pretend to answer these questions definitively. Additionally, and perhaps fortunately, political

TABLE 35
TOTAL PRODUCTION OF MOBUTU AND ENGULU ACQUISITIONS, 1974
(As % of Total Equateur Production, by Crop, in Tons)

	Coffee	Cocoa	Rubber	Palm Fruit	Palm Oil	Cabbage Palm
Mobutu	1,584	278	2,647	105,006	28,942	5,831
Equateur total tons	34,816	15,338	39,859	155,892	70,091	19,941
Mobutu percentage	5%	2%	7%	67%	41%	29%
Engulu	686	179	10,272	—	13,450	2,421
Mobutu and Engulu totals	2,270	457	12,919	—	42,392	8,252
Combined percentage	7%	3%	32%	67%	60%	41%

SOURCE: Région de l'Equateur, Division Régionale de l'Agriculture, *Rapport annuel 1974*, pp. 84–85, 87, 88, 89, 107; *Mambenga*, 5 July 1975, p. 15.

science methodology has not yet evolved to the point where reading the minds of men in power is feasible. Nonetheless, one can make certain deductions and draw a number of inferences based on the pattern and process of distribution. It does not now seem plausible to argue that 30 November was an attempt to bring more people into a direct political and economic dependence on the polity's central power source. A striking impression retained from an examination of the distribution of Zairianized acquisitions in Equateur is that, on the whole, very few *new* people were brought into President Mobutu's dependency network. High politico-administrative cadres who were already dependent on the president for their jobs in the hierarchy, and for the concomitant quasi-legal opportunities for capital accumulation, received most of the European wealth. On the other hand, if patrimonialism is conceived as an ongoing dynamic process, it makes sense to suppose that Mobutu might have felt the need to reaffirm the dependency of his bureaucratic and political retainers by letting them acquire even more personal wealth and general economic control. In either case, European plantations, like collectivity budget revenues, might also be seen as the "spoils" of the political game.[49]

Other preliminary conclusions emerge from this examination of the distribution of acquisitions. Official policy enunciated in Kinshasa concerning who was to acquire European possessions was never followed. Although it was announced that Zairians could acquire only one business, farm, or plantation, many politico-administrative leaders did not respect this policy and came into possession of several items. In addition, the pious statements pouring out of the highest Zairian decision-making bodies on the subject of 30 November lost all credibility after a short time. It is not believable that these measures were taken to promote the happiness and well-being of the entire population, as was often claimed by Kinshasa officials. One confirmation of this is provided by President Mobutu's acquisition of the immense plantation at Binga, in the Zone of Lisala. Before the presidential decisions, the plantation paid its thousands of unskilled workers a monthly salary of Z3–5. Although they were housed by the company and could make use of the well-stocked company stores, this was still well below the legal minimum.[50] After President Mobutu acquired the plantation, there was no change in the salary scale.

It might be objected that because Mobutu is a busy man, he could not have known of this injustice. Although possible, there is evidence suggesting that the president took an active interest in his acquisitions and was probably well aware of what was going on at these plantations. In April 1974, for example, he visited the Binga plantation. Two months later there was a meeting in Kinshasa of all the former owners and directors of the agro-industrial firms that had been acquired by the "presidency." Moreover, the telegram calling the directors to Kinshasa was signed by Citizen Bisengimana, Mobutu's chief of staff.[51] This, too, is an indication that the president was indeed aware of, interested in, and probably well informed about his acquisitions. As for the general pattern of distribution, it is reasonable to suppose that Mobutu knew what was happening. On 15 April 1974 he spoke to a mass rally in Bumba, where he defended the way things were being done. This defense is worth citing at some length:

> Here is the message that I have to communicate to you. You must know that we did not Zairianize our economy with the aim of distributing enterprises to every citizen, but rather to better our living conditions. Even had we wanted to, we would have been handicapped by material considerations. For how could we have succeeded in dividing the 2,920 coffee plantations among the 22 million *zairois* and *zairoises* that we are? It can therefore happen that some citizens who are more enterprising than others manage to get themselves assigned some businesses; which could incite those who have nothing to cry injustice. In the precise context of Bumba, you are thousands of inhabitants for about twenty stores. And it could be possible that a particularly enterprising citizen living in Kinshasa could manage to get himself a business to the detriment of the inhabitants of the places, which sets off whining and complaints.[52]

The implication of the phrase "even had we wanted to" seems clear. There was no desire ar attempt to assure anything even remotely resembling an equal distribution.

These facts and patterns indicate that while a partial patrimonial explanation fits the known data, the 30 November experiment is also interpretable in terms of social class. On the basis of the evidence, I am prepared to argue that however exemplary the initial motives may have been, Zairianization constituted a class action by the highest levels of the Zairian leadership. The extraordinary pronouncements of the Tripartite after its 26 December 1973 meeting support this interpretation. Their aim was surely to increase their own access to the immense wealth of the Europeans while, at the same time, denying it to other Zairians. Additional substantiation may be found in the frank discussion among the regional commissioners on 23 and 26 March 1974, to which I have already referred. The nationalization of the commercial and agricultural sectors of the economy represented, for the most part, the substitution of indigenous politicians for expatriate planters and traders. Over the years the Zairian politico-administrative leaders had accumulated enough power to permit the translation of their political authority into control over the nation's economic wealth. In short, political analysts who underestimate the importance of collective cupidity as a wellspring of political motivation do so at their own risk.

Finally, though written in a different context, Marx's analysis of mid-nineteenth-century France remains apposite.

> Driven on by the contradictory demands of his situation, Bonaparte [read Mobutu], like a conjuror, has to keep the eyes of the public fixed on himself, as Napoleon's substitute, by means of constant surprises, that is to say by

performing a coup d'etat in miniature every day. He thereby brings the whole bourgeois economy into confusion, . . . creates anarchy itself in the name of order, and at the same time strips the halo from the state machine, profaning it and making it both disgusting and ridiculous.[53]

Effects and Consequences

The effects of the 30 November decrees did bring "the whole bourgeois economy into confusion"; commercial supply and distribution networks were, and have remained, completely disrupted. The best demonstration is the always lively commerce in beer. As we have seen, before 30 November 1973 Lisala's beer supply was intermittent under the best conditions. There was, however, an arrangement between a local wholesale house and a Kisangani-based Greek merchant who owned a boat suitable for transporting large quantities of beer. The Greek had originally financed his boat through an agreement and credit arrangement with the Unibra-Kisangani brewery. Each month he would make two rounds trips between Lisala and Kisangani, depositing 10,000 cases in Lisala on each voyage. In this way he was gradually able to work off his debt to the brewery and acquire complete ownership of the boat and of the lucrative transport commerce in beer between the brewery and Lisala. Although it required that he spend most of his time on the boat, the trade was financially rewarding and each round trip was worth approximately Z10,000.

The effect of Zairianization on the magnitude of this trade is shown in table 36. The transport commerce and boat of the Greek merchant were

TABLE 36
KISANGANI BEER TO LISALA AND BUMBA

Year	Quantity
1972	27,077 hl[a]
1973	31,035 hl
1974	5,676 hl

SOURCE: Interview with Unibra official, Kinshasa, 25 September 1975.
[a]Hectoliters.

acquired by the head of Sonas Immobilier, the state housing insurance agency, in Kisangani. Because the citizen had acquired a diverse panoply of items, he could not maintain individual control over all of them and still perform his official functions adequately. He therefore confided the management of the Lisala beer trade to one of his "little brothers." Unfortunately, the little brother had never been a success in any endeavor and had been living off the largesse of the insurance director for some time. At the end of his first trip to Lisala the wholesale house paid him the customary fee of Z10,000. This was more money than he had ever seen in his life, and he promptly decided there was no longer any need to work regularly at the beer transportation business. Money in hand, instead of returning to Kisangani with the empties to load up for a new trip, he and his secretary took off down the river on a scenic pleasure cruise that lasted about six months. The cruise ended when his cash did, and he then returned to make another trip. Table 36 tells the story of his escapades. In fairness, it should be mentioned that the acquirer eventually realized that his little brother's behavior was hurting him financially. Consequently, in May 1975 he gave him a new way to keep himself busy and turned over the beer barge to someone else. Still, this unhappy situation had not been rectified as of my departure from Lisala in August 1975; beer was still in very short supply and prices were high.[54]

The disruption in the flow of beer had wider effects on the local economy. As noted in the discussion of the political economy of beer, merchants depend on their bars and *buvettes* to finance a wide range of other economic enterprises. Receipts from beer sales are often used to finance plantations and small stores. When this income evaporated in the wake of the 30 November measures, these other commercial activities inevitably suffered.

Important political effects also resulted from the haphazard beer supply. As noted earlier, the territorial commissioners find it politically prudent to ensure that their respective administrative entities are kept afloat. Beer drought is cause for alarm since this provokes grumbling and discontent among the people. By way of illustration, events in Lisala during the week immediately preceding 24 November 1974 are germane. At that juncture Lisala was bone-dry, and the subregional commissioner was very concerned lest nothing arrive before the anniversary of the new regime. On 19 November 1974 he sent a wire to a beer depositor in Bumba to inform him that one of his boats had "broken down" in Lisala. The barge was loaded with 10,000 cases of beer from the brewery in Mbandaka. The commissioner asked the Bumba depositor to make "a revolutionary contribution" and authorize the sale of 4,000 to 5,000 cases in Lisala so that the national holiday could successfully be feted. Because the response from Bumba was negative, the subregional commissioner decided to exert a bit of pressure on Bumba's zone commissioner. The next day he sent a telegram to the commissioner in Bumba asking him "to intervene energetically" with the recalcitrant beer depositor so that 4,000 cases could legally be sold in Lisala. In this wire Bumba's zone commissioner was informed that the barge in question was being "detained" in Lisala until he could produce a "revolutionary" answer. That night the barge slipped away from Lisala without having sold any beer. The subregional commissioner was furious and immediately penned an angry message to his subordinate in Bumba, telling him that he was dispatching Lisala's owners in trucks so that they might purchase the beer in Bumba itself. He was ordered to see that they were sold

3,500 cases and that they had enough time to return to Lisala before the beginning of the national holiday.[55] All went well, but such occurrences are not at all unusual.

A second result of the application of the presidential decisions was the widespread turmoil and confusion over the fate of those Zairian employees who had worked for the former European owners. Although given strict instructions that there were to be no changes in personnel, the first act of many acquirers was to dismiss the clerks, salesmen, and manual laborers who had been employed by their European predecessors. In Lisala and many other locations, the hiring and firing often followed ethnic lines closely. A prime example was the Luba acquirer who has already been noted (Case 1). Perhaps because he did not know or trust the workmen he inherited, perhaps because he was pressured by the felt responsibility to provide jobs for as many members of his family as possible—whatever the reasons, shortly after completing the official inventory and takeover, he released a number of unskilled workers who had been hired by the Portuguese merchant. One of these employees wrote to the zone commissioner asking for redress. "Being the father of nine children," he wrote, "realizing the cost of living, the Citizen acquirer must not hardly make me live [sic] tribal segregation which our Guide has just banished from the Republic of Zaire."[56] To the best of my knowledge, no actions were taken either by the territorial administration or by the trade union in this or any other, analogous case.

If unskilled workers were let go with impunity and quickly replaced by ethnic kinsmen or family, the process was less direct and more subtle for the salesmen (*capita-vendeurs*). The salesmen usually work on a commission, receiving a set percentage of the daily sales. Some of them are fairly wealthy by Lisala standards and own *buvettes* on the side. Firing them openly, therefore, would have presented certain political problems since many are well connected with the local bureaucrats who often drink in their establishments. To replace the salesmen, then, called for a slower and more complex strategy. The Luba trader initially left them in place as *capita-vendeurs*. He had inherited a commercial house with six or seven stores, so he had a good deal of latitude in determining which shops he would stock with the most popular and fastest-selling merchandise. He then began to channel systematically the best articles into certain stores while ignoring others. This resulted in a drastic decline in total sales for some of the salesmen; several were forced to resign because they could no longer make ends meet. In a letter of resignation one salesman bitterly noted that he did not deserve this fate because he had worked blamelessly for the European since 1957. Continuing, he remarked:

> Now that the whites have left and their firms have been given to you, our Zairian brothers, with the idea that we will be well treated, more than the whites [sic] but it is the contrary. A Zairian treats his Zairian brother completely like a slave.
> You always want to give merchandise only to the three stores which are run by your brothers and brother-in-law and if I want to make a requisition for

merchandise which has arrived you always create a quarrel. . . . Go see the three stores run by your brothers are always filled with merchandise; come to my place and my brother's and there is a big difference.[57]

The salesman's bitterness at this treatment was probably all the more pronounced because he had been an unsuccessful candidate to acquire the same commercial house.

Most of the letters of resignation written to this acquirer stressed the same motives: a perception of lack of justice concerning the distribution of merchandise and an unwillingness to work with those engaged by the former owner. One disgruntled employee told the Luba acquirer:

Upon receiving the firm of Mr. X you predicted that you were not going to retain the people who had worked with him. According to your word, there are already five workers who have been fired, that is to say you do not need to work with the rest of us.[58]

Although this section has emphasized the closure mechanisms employed by the Luba acquirer, similar wheelings and dealings occurred everywhere in Lisala; most of the other acquirers were guilty of the same maneuvers. It should be clear from the letters cited above that those who were discharged or forced out generally believed themselves to be victims of ethnic discrimination; when the acquirer was a member of a local ethnic group, however, this motif was more muted.

Another problem arose from these personnel changes. As mentioned, the *capita-vendeurs* worked on a percentage basis of the total daily sales. One of the areas of contention between the salesmen and the acquirers was the money owed them by the former owners. Many of the acquirers, despite official instructions, refused to honor the debts incurred by their predecessors. One salesman complained to the trade union secretary that when the official inventory and takeover had been accomplished in early March 1974, he had accounted for a total sale of Z16,140.80, for which he was due a commission of 3 percent, or Z484.22. Moreover, he had a credit with the firm of Z149.69. In sum, he was owed Z633.91, which the new acquirer had steadfastly refused to pay because he maintained that he was not responsible for the debts of the former owner. To make matters worse, this *capita-vendeur* had not received his commissions or family allotments since the takeover. In concluding his letter to the official, the salesman wrote: "The difficulties that the acquirer is provoking with regard to me stem from his bad intention to fire all those who used to work with the European and replace them with his own brothers."[59] To present both sides of the story, it must be noted that some acquirers had a great deal of trouble meeting their payrolls because they found nothing but an empty cash box on the date of their official takeover. Most of the complaints launched against the acquirers, however, and especially those cited above, were well-founded.

A third unintended consequence of Zairianization was a drastic decline in the state's revenues since many acquirers have refused to pay their taxes. As a general rule, European merchants and planters regularly paid their taxes to the appropriate state agency. Indeed, there was rarely any question of this and there were not many cases calling for coercion. This situation changed after 30 November 1973. There are now numerous difficulties and problems involved in getting the acquirers to pay up. As one official put it, "When they are summoned, they do not come." Their standard reply is, "I am not going to pay because I am the brother of so-and-so." Frequently they retort that they are not going to pay because they are a minister, a legislator, or a party official. I was told on good authority that the worst recalcitrants in Lisala were the commissioners of the people. Ironically, the acquirers who seem to honor their financial obligations to the state are the wives of the Portuguese merchants. Their husbands are still effectively running the businesses and their taxes are still being paid.[60] Nevertheless, one result of the 30 November experience has been a precipitous decline in tax revenues. In a period of generalized economic crisis caused by falling copper prices and successive increases in petroleum prices, the reluctance of the acquirers to pay their taxes has scarcely eased the financial burdens of the state.

A fourth result of Zairianization was a dramatic rise in prices throughout Equateur Region. Although the inflation was in part attributable to the vagaries of the international market, implementation of the 30 November measures was nonetheless one cause. The months immediately following 30 November were characterized by intense commercial activity, partially ascribed to the increased purchasing power of those who had acquired European businesses.[61] As often as not, however, this new source of liquid assets in circulation was translated into various kinds of conspicuous consumption. The beer baron referred to above is but one case in point. Another example of this generalized phenomenon is demonstrated by brewery sales for the city of Mbandaka. By restricting our attention to sales made within the city itself, it is possible to control for the shortcomings of the distributive system. The average monthly sale for 1973 was 713,116 bottles. The increase following Zairianization can be found in table 37. An examination of the table 37 figures shows an almost immediate upswing in the

TABLE 37
MBANDAKA BEER SALES

Month	Sales[a]
October 1973	750,816
November 1973	724,992
December 1973	929,916
January 1974	766,224
February 1974	624,420[b]
March 1974	1,475,820
April 1974	1,434,552
May 1974	1,445,832

TABLE 37 (continued)

Month	Sales[a]
June 1974	1,326,228
July 1974	1,660,068
August 1974	1,574,772
September 1974	1,454,124
October 1974	1,621,656
November 1974	1,418,628
December 1974	1,739,016

SOURCE: Figures provided by Bralima, Mbandaka.

[a]In bottles.

[b]The decline in Mbandaka beer sales during January and February 1974 may partially be accounted for by a corresponding increase in sales in other parts of the region.

amount of beer purchased in Mbandaka. The real upsurge, however, was a long-term one. The 1974 monthly sales average jumped from 713,116 bottles to 1,378,450 bottles. Although it cannot be claimed that the increase in beer sales was solely due to the marked consumption of the Mbandaka acquirers, this was undoubtedly one of the contributing factors; the correlation is illuminating.

The wave of conspicuous consumption ignited by Zairianization was also reflected in the sharp increase in the importation of Mercedes Benz automobiles. On 25 November 1974, almost one year to the day after his speech before the Legislative Council, President Mobutu publicly denounced the nouveaux riches in Zaire. He told a Kinshasa rally that less than six months after the announcement of the presidential decisions a report had arrived from Germany indicating that Zaire had broken a record for the number of Mercedes in circulation. Consequently, the president declared that in 1975 no more Mercedes would be imported. It is apparent where the acquirers were getting the funds necessary to import these cars and to improve their life-style in other ways. Many, but not all, were using the daily receipts of their acquired firms and plantations to cover their personal needs rather than leaving the money where it belonged, in the enterprises.[62]

The dishonesty of many acquirers is also worth mentioning under the rubric of inflation. Immediately after taking over, and for no apparent economic reason, certain acquirers raised the prices of merchandise they found on the shelves. For example, acquirers in Mobayi-Mbongo were selling packets of sugar at Z5–7, when they had been obtained in Bumba at Z1.70. In addition, all articles left on the shelves by the departing European traders underwent immediate increases of 10 to 20k per item. Acquirers were, according to one critic, making the population suffer, and people were beginning to compare them unfavorably with their European predecessors. Similar events were occurring all over Mongala. While summing up the economic trends and events for 1974, one technician attributed at least part of the inflation throughout the area to the actions of dishonest acquirers.[63] This question was further complicated because administrative efforts to control prices failed dismally. *Elima* reported that price controllers often had to struggle against very powerful individuals who "send them to the devil. These characters who call themselves untouchable are at the base of the vertiginous rise in the price of merchandise." As was true for beer, efforts made to regulate prices were not taken seriously because most acquirers were well placed.[64]

A fifth effect of the presidential measures was the end of what little commercial credit there had once been in the Zairian economic system. A repeated complaint of all Lisala merchants was that Zairianization had resulted in the termination of the thirty-, sixty-, and ninety-day buying, which had once been possible. This practice had greatly facilitated commerce because it permitted a merchant to increase the amount of stock he was able to handle without tying up his capital. In the words of one old, established Lisala trader who did not become an acquirer:

> In the past there was everything. You almost didn't have to move. The suppliers withdrew their confidence. All businesses were taken away from the Europeans. To enjoy some credit you must have a good reputation. After the measures everyone saw that the acquirers had gotten their goods because they were the little brother of someone "big." They did not necessarily have a good reputation. Thus the wholesalers said that we must buy everything with cash. Nothing on credit. That is beginning to change a little bit in places where there is a bank. A little bit of credit has been given to merchants in these places. Everything you see in my stores I've bought for cash.[65]

The new necessity to purchase from wholesale houses with cash rather than credit has obviously been one of the factors responsible for the rise in prices. Because cash payments are required, small merchants do not have the capacity to keep their stores stocked the way they could in the period before 30 November 1973. In consequence they may well be ultimately forced out of business. A smaller quantity of merchandise in circulation has also made many articles scarcer and thus more expensive.

While discussing the inflation that resulted in part from implementation of the 30 November decisions, another, perhaps banal, observation can be made. The operations required to manage a business enterprise successfully are not intuitively obvious to the layman. A fund of specialized knowledge is required to convert a store with empty shelves into a going business venture. As already demonstrated, most of the wealth left by the Europeans was acquired either by Kinshasa political figures or by individuals with good political contacts. Some of these acquirers were merchants and traders in their own right; most were not, and an effective career in politics does not necessarily prepare one for a successful life in commerce. Even when the acquirer was honest and wished to run his enterprises in light of sound business principles and in accordance with the law, abysmal ignorance of standard commercial procedures often precluded this possibility. One observer of Lisala commerce noted that many acquirers could not grasp the complexities of applying the legally established profit margins. Moreover, out of sheer ignorance many acquirers provisioned their shops from other retail outlets instead of from a wholesale house. This factor, as well as the others already mentioned, contributed to the increase in prices.[66]

Conclusion

By way of partial summation it might be said that Zairianization threw virtually the whole economy of Equateur Region out of joint. Furthermore, all the consequences and problems resulting from the 30 November measures were compounded by the multiple distribution that plagued the region's commerce and agriculture. Three ministries were involved in granting letters of acquisition to prospective acquirers. The Commerce Ministry took care of the commercial sector; the Agriculture Ministry handled farms, ranches, and plantations; and the National Economy Ministry was responsible for doling out the plantation factories known as "agro-industrial enterprises." In theory the lines of demarcation were clearly drawn so that jurisdictional disputes would be avoided. In practice there were numerous instances of multiple distribution, particularly of moderately large plantations, which also maintained commercial outlets for their workers and factories to refine or convert the raw materials before shipping them. In some instances the commerce commissioner attributed the store to Acquirer A, the agricultural commissioner gave the plantation to Acquirer B, and the national economy commissioner handed over the factory and industrial complex to Acquirer C. The result was complete confusion.

One example is the fate of an agro-industrial enterprise in the Zone of Bongandanga. A moderately large operation, in 1974 it had 200 hectares of palm trees under cultivation and its total production was 820 tons of palm fruit, 170 tons of palm oil, and 48 tons of cabbage palm.[67] The establishment was known by a number of different names, but all were run by the same Portuguese planter. In addition to two palm plantations, there were a rice mill, a soap factory, an oil works, a bakery, and several retail outlets for the workers. The first wave of selections saw this agro-industrial complex given to a commissioner of the people from the Zone of Bongandanga. By the end of March 1974, however, it was decided that the commissioner could not acquire the enterprise because of the firm's industrial character; it would have to be taken over by one of the appropriate parastatal organisms. Consequently, the blockage imposed on the firm's bank account in Kinshasa was lifted and the commissioner was asked to cease the official inventory then under way.[68] When this occurred, he began pulling strings to see if he could get this order quashed at the highest levels. His manuevers were apparently to no avail, because by the end of June 1974 the enterprise had been reassigned. But instead of a parastatal organism, the new acquirer was the state commissioner for transportation, a well-known figure in Lisala.[69]

By August 1974 total confusion existed concerning the acquisition of this enterprise. The subregional commissioner had been presented with three seemingly valid letters of attribution. Part of the enterprise had been given to the state commissioner, a second part to the commissioner of the people, and a third portion to an unidentified individual. Unclear about the appropriate course of action, the subregional commissioner passed the buck. He asked the regional commissioner to intervene at the national level to annul all the conflicting designations because the enterprise could not be divided in such a manner and still function effectively.[70] What forms of political infighting took place in Kinshasa over this enterprise are unknown, but the issue was decided by December 1974, when the commissioner of the people finally prevailed.[71] Much of his success in this matter may be ascribed to the transportation commissioner's fall from grace at approximately that time. He was stripped of honorifics, excluded from the government, and eventually imprisoned for corruption; it appears likely that the loss of this lucrative enterprise was one of the penalties incurred for arousing the presidential displeasure.

The commissioner of the people who finally inherited this agro-industrial enterprise had little or no commercial ability. The deputies had obtained bank loans before Zairianization, and were dispatched to the interior to begin businesses of their own. After some time as a fish merchant in Bongandanga, the legislator discovered that he was operating at a loss and could not continue without aid. He therefore asked the economic affairs service chief for assistance in establishing prices. He also requested that the bureaucrat intervene on his behalf with one of the large plantations in the zone so that they might come to his aid with moral as well as material support. (He was probably more interested in the latter than the former.) As of December 1974 this acquirer had not been able to make a go of it.[72]

Even when only one ministry was involved, there was often serial distribution. A sawmill on the outskirts of Lisala, for example, was given to the new Office National du Bois (ONB) after the presidential decisions. In June 1974 it was reassigned to an army general then serving as Zaire's ambassador to Togo. Since his high functions would not have permitted him to oversee the workings of the mill in detail, he appointed one of his nephews as delegate-administrator. The operation went from bad to worse, and the normal degree of confusion inherent in the transfer of any business enterprise was compounded. The delegate-administrator insisted that the mill's clients deposit their payments directly in his personal account rather than in the firm's. One result was that the mill's workers went for months without receiving any regular wages. The manager, who had been held over from the previous parastatal acquirer, received practically nothing for his efforts to keep the firm going; in fact, the new delegate-administrator sued him for an alleged deficit of Z1,500 and fired him as well. When the courts finally got the case, they found that the deficit was only Z38 and that the manager had taken this sum because he had not been paid in months. The manager, originally from Bandundu, believes that he was the victim of ethnic prejudice on the part of the delegate-administrator, who is from Equateur. Be that as it may, what remains incontestable is that because of the serial distribution of the saw mill, approximately 200 of Lisala's workers had to go without salaries for some time.[73]

This problem, evident all over Equateur, was particularly acute in the subregional center of Basankusu. In that town only one of the five Zairianized stores has not undergone a change in acquirer. This one house was given to the Zairian widow of a Belgian merchant. Another store has gone through a succession of four Zairian acquirers within the space of a year, a Kinshasa editor-in-chief and a commissioner of the people among them. The three other stores have each had two acquirers since the measures were announced. Such circumstances can only lead to speculation on the part of each incoming acquirer, totally disorganized sales, and, perhaps most important, exorbitant prices.[74]

Other results of multiple and serial distribution may not be readily apparent. In the first place, because these redistributions were fairly common, a widespread insecurity of economic tenure seems to have developed. On 30 November 1973 the rules of the game were suddenly and definitively altered. Where people previously were fairly secure in their tenure over goods and property, Zairianization radically changed this. First the Europeans were ousted—which was expected and normal under the circumstances—but then many of the first wave of Zairian acquirers were ousted, which was neither normal nor expected. In addition to producing a widespread insecurity in the economic domain, it has greatly increased the dynamic fluidity of class formation in Zaire. Acquirers rise and fall. It therefore seems plausible to maintain that those who are easily identifiable as wealthy merchants today might not be so tomorrow. This represents a radical departure from the pre-30 November 1973 situation, where if access to, and tenure in, political and administrative office were precarious and problematical, economic activities and position were protected and stable. Thus, in the wake of 30 November, a new variable has been introduced, and class fluidity and insecurity have become manifest in both the politico-administrative and the economic spheres. This fluidity and tenure insecurity result, at least on the level of identifiable phenomena, in a continuing dialectic of class formation and dissolution. Furthermore, the boundaries that divide classes at the upper end of the social hierarchy from those below are at best amorphous and protean.

In the second place, this extraordinary game of economic musical chairs naturally results in a lack of incentive to develop the acquired enterprise as a long-term venture. After all, why should someone begin to plow back resources into a business if there is more than a good chance that he or she will not be there to reap any possible future gains? This attitude seems to be prevalent among many acquirers and produces another reason to treat the enterprise's coffers as a source of petty cash on which one can draw to meet personal and current needs such as a case of beer, a new car, or a new wardrobe for one's spouse. Tenure insecurity has thus contributed to the tendency of many acquirers to loot systematically the businesses they have been given.

Finally, as an almost direct consequence of these effects, many of the more marginal businesses will never regain their former vigor. Gutted and destroyed, most will remain stores with empty shelves and plantations with unweeded coffee fields. One footnote to this story is that many fine Zairian traders correctly perceived the essentially political nature of the distribution process and decided to stay out of it completely. In Lisala two of the most effective and experienced merchants did not even submit their candidacies. One told me that he believed nine-tenths of the acquirers were incapable merchants. Since the key date of 30 November 1973 he has been offered no fewer than three commercial houses, which had been ceded to acquirers who had not the least notion of what they were doing. He refused the state's offers to take over these businesses because, in his estimation, they were already dead—ruined by the first acquirers. Had he been offered them earlier, he thinks he would seriously have considered accepting them.[75] One of the real tragedies of the whole Zairianization episode is that marginal and shaky businesses were more likely to be found in the rural areas and in small urban centers such as Lisala. Thus, while the valuable and well-managed affairs will eventually recover from all this turmoil, I am pessimistic about the fate of the small stores and plantations in the interior, on which the rural population depends for the few amenities and first-necessity items it can afford. The immediate losers in the 30 November sweepstakes were the Europeans. In the wider perspective, the real losers may be the rural population of Zaire, in whose name and for whose benefit these measures were originally and ostensibly promulgated. Acutely aware of this, citizens in the interior were not long deceived by official pronouncements concerning Zairianization. An analysis of their reactions is presented in chapter eight as part of a broader investigation of class consciousness in contemporary Zaire.

CHAPTER 8
Consciousness and Context

Do I contradict myself?
Very well then . . . . I contradict myself;
I am large . . . . I contain multitudes.
—Walt Whitman[1]

One of the elements contained in the definition of class put forth in chapter 2 was the process by which groups of actors become increasingly or decreasingly conscious of varying degrees of access to life and mobility chances. In addition it was suggested that such consciousness was contextual and likely to differ with the political, economic, and social conditions of the moment. In this chapter I further elaborate the Azikiwe paradox by delineating more precisely the contextual notion of class consciousness. In doing so I also examine some of the various manifestations of class consciousness that exist today in Zaire; explore more fully the impact of the economic reforms of 30 November 1973 on the formation of class consciousness; and discuss some of the difficulties presented in the study of so elusive a subject. By way of introduction it would be wise to cast our attention backward and examine the historical foundations of this consciousness during both the colonial and the First Republic eras.

Historical Evolution

Referring to the African labor force, Peter Gutkind reminds us that the history of colonialism might well be viewed as a history of "controlling and containing the very class consciousness which all too many observers insisted was lacking" in African workers.[2] While perhaps partially true in Zaire, the situation was generally more complex. Bogumil Jewsiewicki maintains that European employers in the cities would send unneeded workers back to their villages of origin. This circumstance, coupled with the generalized lack of social security for laborers in urban areas, had the effect of encouraging the workers to define their social relations as well as their search for security by their ethnic groups. The increased social salience of the ethnic community thus served as a brake on the process of proletarianization, and social identity among the workers came to be defined more in ethnic than in class terms.[3]

Until the last few years of colonialism, *évolués* seemed unwilling to provide any leadership for the masses of Zairian workers. As mentioned previously, this social category was more concerned with obtaining a social status distinct from that of the masses. Most *évolués* were acutely conscious of their elevated position in the social hierarchy and wanted the European colonial establishment to recognize it.[4] Such recognition, however, usually came with outward acceptance and approval by either the missionaries or the colonial administrators, and one condition of their blessing was a European life-style. Excessive association with the *"indigènes"* could thus easily jeopardize their precarious position as *évolué*. They could, and did, associate among themselves, however. Since the colonial administration would not permit either economic or political organizations, *évolué* associations necessarily took on a sociocultural aspect. Most of these organizations were founded with the intention of either furthering or preserving the ethnic culture of their members. In the decolonization period, when overt political activity was permitted for the first time, these ethnically exclusive cultural associations were the only well-known, accepted, and comfortable form of organization. As a result, many were transformed almost overnight into political parties. Ethnically divided, the *évolués* had few opportunities to work in organizations that spanned cultural differences. The new leaders thus had to seek political support from their respective ethnic kinsmen in thr rural areas of Zaire. Often, ethnic mobilization of one's own group entailed the denigration of someone else's, but this was the only means available by which the *évolués* could stake their claim to postindependence political power. Political conflict, and hence political identity, thus came to be defined along ethnic rather than class lines during the first few years of independence.[5]

It would be a mistake, however, to assume that most mobilization was done from the top. Substantial evidence now indicates that much of the impetus for the anticolonial political movements of the decolonization period came not from the *évolués* but from the rural masses. In his exceptionally fine study of the Parti Solidaire Africain in Kwango-Kwilu area, Herbert Weiss notes that spontaneous political protest in the rural areas antedated the existence of political parties. The political leaders were able to harness these movements, but the aims of the leaders and masses were not identical. On the one hand, the political leaders—the former *évolués*—wanted to Africanize the colonial apparatus; on the other, the masses desired its total destruction.[6] In Bas-Zaire, too, the long-suffering rural masses worked on their own to hasten the collapse of the colonial system. No intervention was needed from ABAKO cadres to sustain antiwhite protest. Indeed, in at least some locations, they had all they could do to contain the anticolonial virulence of the rural populations.[7]

The village farmers had long been victims of a vicious and exploitative system of colonial administration. They were well aware that crop requirements and colonial taxes were designed neither for their economic nor for their moral well-being. Forced labor rarely profited the farmers and they were conscious of this.[8] This lingering resentment toward the system erupted in a dramatic way during the decolonization period. The examples of rural radicalism presented above might well be seen as manifestations of a deep-seated rural hatred of colonial impositions and a keen desire for a different sociopolitical order. But these movements were ethnically fragmented, and there was little or no sense of solidarity that transcended ethnic lines. On the other hand, there appears to have been substantial agreement among the rural masses on who the enemy was, and the colonial order was perceived as the target of these mass protest activities and rebellions.

This pattern of weak solidarity coupled with a unified and widespread perception of the society's oppressive elements also characterized much of the First Republic period. The rural masses had developed a well-elaborated notion of "them," but "us" was still usually defined by ethnic categories rather than by some broader and more inclusive idea like class. This was certainly true during the rebellions that swept over much of the country from 1963 to 1965. These rebellions were partly overlapping, partly competing movements of social protest. They were without centralized direction and, with the possible exception of the Mulelist revolt in Kwilu, without an articulated revolutionary ideology.[9] Rebellions that had perhaps been sparked by widespread feelings of relative deprivation tended to degenerate into ethnic hostility or rural-urban conflict. Regardless of the outcome of these movements, almost all analysts who have studied them agree there were significant portions of the population who had somehow come to feel cheated by the turn events had taken since independence. In Kwilu, for example, people

> viewed themselves as worse off than they had been, and as worse off than they *should* have been compared both to what they had expected from Independence and to the way that they saw or imagined that certain privileged politicians, businessmen, clergy, and persons who had received a superior education were living.[10]

By the time President Mobutu seized power in 1965, the Zairian rural population had developed a skeptical, if not hostile, view of the better-educated and wealthier politicians, traders, and administrators who had dominated life under the First Republic. In many instances the agents of local collectivity administration—chiefs, tax collectors, and agricultural officers—bore the brunt of the villagers' hostility and resentment; generally speaking this has not changed under the Second Republic, although, as we shall see, the collectivity officials themselves are not immune to the sweep of social dynamics.

Consciousness and Context

The collectivity is crucially important; it forms the main point of contact between people and government and, as such, is the entity that directly administers the population. Chapter 4 described the way this level of administration functions and the role it plays in the system of rural exploitation. People in the rural areas regard the collectivity with loathing. They see it as an extractive agency, which exists to make their lives miserable. Most people in the Zairian countryside view these branches of local government—and the bureaucrats who staff them—as exploitative. But what of the agents who are employed by the collectivities? How do they perceive their own positions and functions in the system?

The answers to these questions are not simple. Let us take Lisala's collectivity chief as a first example. This official is quite aware of, and indulges frequently in, the budgetary manipulations necessary to ensure that there will be enough money in the coffers so that her *avantages* may be realized. As a result, Lisala's police, tax collectors, and roadworkers are not paid on time. On the days of political rallies and mass party meetings she can be seen coercing market women to attend these events by forcibly closing down their stalls and sending them, under police guard, to the site of the meeting. In these contexts the chief is an exploiter who is liked neither by her bureaucratic subordinates nor by the local population. And yet, that is only part of the picture. In other circumstances she is quite capable of feeling herself exploited by those above her in the hierarchy. When President Mobutu came to Lisala, there was a shortage of flour in the area. No bread had been available in the market for some weeks; in a gesture of presidential magnanimity, he gave 900 sacks of flour to the people of the town. Naturally, this gift was not distributed equally and the chief reacted in the following way:

> The president left 900 sacks of flour here. When the flour arrived, the population didn't even have a single sack. It was only the wives of the functionaries and the authorities who got it. I did not get a single sack of flour for the market women so that they could make their little cakes. It discourages me to work with such people.[11]

On the one hand, she forced the market women to attend rallies they found meaningless and taxed them mercilessly. On the other, she was genuinely discouraged and upset by their failure to receive part of the presidential largesse. In this instance her identification was with the populace, and it can be argued that she perceived herself to be exploited by those in the bureaucratic hierarchy with stations above her own.

A second example of this ambiguity comes from examining the perceptions of the collectivity's secretary. The collectivity secretary is really much more than that. As the chief's executive assistant, no aspect of administration escapes his attention. He is well aware of financial and other difficulties that beset the collectivity and participates in the procedures taken to remedy them. He is often responsible for supervising the work of the collectivity police and thus has some control over the most extractive arm of the local administration. Most people in Lisala have at least some notion of his role in the daily business of government; even though he is from the local area, he is not well liked. As an important part of the oppressive administrative machinery, he is widely perceived as one of "them." In this case, too, there are ambiguities. When asked if he was an acquirer, he replied:

> No. I did not even have the chance to become one of them. I did not even make a request. Priority was accorded to the better-placed people. Who among the villagers had this favor? Not one.[12]

His response is of interest for two reasons. In the context of the 30 November reforms he sees the acquirers as "them." They are viewed as a distinct social category. Second, and perhaps more important, in this instance he identifies with the villagers. But few villagers would be likely to feel a sense of solidarity with this bureaucrat because of the role he plays in the collectivity administration. Once again, the context seems to influence the class identification adopted by the actor. The same phenomenon is characteristic of the collectivity police. Exploiters in their relations with the village population, when asked, they are likely to affirm that they feel themselves maltreated by the collectivity chief, who does not pay their salaries regularly.

This ambivalence is common among many of the more thoughtful collectivity bureaucrats. In their more honest moments of self-evaluation they are probably aware of the role they play vis-à-vis the people in their jurisdiction. Nonetheless, they may maintain a residual sense of identification with the villagers, particularly when discussing broader social issues, which transcend everyday occurrences. One of Lisala's court clerks is another example that might be cited. Although the collectivity's court system is predominantly repressive, this official does not perceive himself as an exploitative agent. Indeed, when the scope of Zairian social dynamics as a whole is considered, the clerk is likely to identify with the more abused segments of society. When asked to speak generally about his problems, he answered:

Normally, my problem is that the superior authorities from the state commissioners up must understand that following the *Manifeste de la N'Sélé*, there are not big and little citizens in Zaire. Zaire is not for one sole Zairian. Why is there a difference and a distinction between salaries and lives? For my part, I see that one does not say that we should all have the same salary. We ask that if the state commissioner has Z1,000, it would be better if the simple citizen had even only, let's say, Z100. Because these state commissioners and their opportunities come from the contributions of everyone.

For my part, I see that this forms two categories of Zairians. The poor and the rich; the intellectuals and the nonintellectuals. At the Residence, yesterday, I learned that an augmentation [of salaries] is being spoken of but that there is no way to do it. They must also struggle against the rise in prices. For my part, I see that this is still insufficient. That cannot continue. We must have a reduction of the large salaries and an augmentation of the small salaries. If the large salaries remain as they are, there will be disorders in life. Then, in this connection, I ask that the government must think of the poor citizens who make the same sacrifices who must live well in Zaire as any other [citizen].

I would also like to ask the government not only to count on those who live in the cities, but to spend for those who are in the interior. Especially concerning building materials like metal roofs and other construction materials. We need to construct a modern Zaire but we lack the material. Because there, where there are large salaries, there are lower prices. There, where there are small salaries, there are truly exorbitant prices.

On the social plane, I see that normally the population will not have a good change because there is a very large difference between some and others; this is based on the president's passage that there are no big and little citizens. I very often converse with the population. This rancor does not end. We lack . . . There are some things understood [*sous-entendu*] between the population and the government. We know that the president has his decisions. The sabotage always comes from his entourage and I ask the entourage to conform to his options. If not, we see that they are there for themselves, but the president is there for the country.

The government must seriously try to look at the regions, subregions, and zones. Because we hear the decisions on the radio but we don't see the application of these decisions. If they were aware, we wouldn't be able to have the problems that we have now, but rather rapid change.[13]

The court clerk's statement is cited in its entirety because it expresses sentiments that are representative of Lisala's people. One has only to listen to conversations in bars, markets, or work locations to realize that many citizens are very concerned about the themes the clerk raised in his reply to my question. The respondent evoked several ideas that are central to his perception of the social order. First and foremost, he realizes there are two categories of citizens. One group is identified as "big," rich, and intellectual; the second is called "small," poor, and nonintellectual. He further maintains that there is too large a gap between the economic resources of the two categories, and that the current inflationary period seems to be hitting those in the latter group the hardest. In addition, he perceives that the urban areas are being favored at the expense of the countryside. There is not an equal distribution of construction materials, for example. He also notes that the authorities are not doing enough to bring this difficult period to a close. Decisions are made in the capital, which are not applied in the countryside. Some faith is retained in the stewardship of the president, but those around him are seen as saboteurs who are deliberately impeding reform. The strong implication is that they are doing this for their own benefit.

In many ways this is an eloquent statement of some of Zaire's socio-economic problems. There remains, however, the ambiguity of context. In the local context the court clerk is an exploiter; in the broader, national context there is little question that he identifies with the masses of the Zairian people in seeing himself the victim of those above him in the state hierarchy. To this point I have confined my elaboration of the contextual nature of class consciousness to the bureaucrats on the collectivity level. Often it is equally applicable to those who work either for the zone or for the subregion. At these higher state levels the feelings of the bureaucrats about their salaries are revealing. Well-paid by Zairian standards, they nonetheless believe that the higher authorities have not been fair with them.

One of Lisala's subregional service chiefs put it this way: "The director of the Political Bureau has Z12,000 per month. Why? It is not fair. And when it is proposed that the functionaries get an extra 50k, they say no."[14] One of the educational personnel discussed his salary in these terms: "The net salary is Z178 per month. . . . it is not enough . . . We cannot make ends meet. It is the misfortune of the administration that we are not well paid."[15] When asked about the sufficiency of his salary, a well-paid magistrate noted that "logically, yes [it is sufficient] because I am a young cadre. But if, for example, I have the desire to build a house, to have a car, to lead the life worthy of a judge, then it is not enough."[16] There is often a real reluctance on the part of these well-paid service chiefs to admit that they are better off than the majority of their compatriots. One of the agricultural officers told me that he could not live on his salary of Z56 per month. When I pointed out that most Zairians had to make do with considerably less, he said, "No, I tell you that most Zairians do not have less than that. Not the majority, I tell you."[17] It is inconceivable that an agricultural officer, who is in fairly close contact with the village population, does not have a reasonably accurate idea of what the average villager earns during the year. As we have seen, the *yearly* revenues of the village farmers are probably less than Z56. In this case, as in many others, there is some guilt. Moreover, most of these bureaucrats know that they form part of the more privileged sections of society.

In a formal interview one of the magistrates said that he made Z260 per month. Claiming that it was insufficient, he was unwilling to admit that perhaps 95 percent of the population had less money than that. In a totally informal situation one evening, this same judge confided that his father, a mason, had worked for thirty years and was earning only Z15 each month. He wondered aloud whether it was fair that he receive fifteen times as much as his father since, after all, he had been out of the university and working for only four years.[18] Complaints about insufficient salaries are quite common among Lisala's subregional service chiefs. They are bitter because they do not believe the higher authorities are paying them enough to live on, and they perceive themselves as disadvantaged and abused. But in another context, their relations with the rest of the population, I am sure that many perceive themselves as privileged members of society. This creates much inner tension—an attempt to ease the cognitive dissonance by denying their advantageous status and a great deal of ambivalence about the current Zairian social structure.

A contextual approach to class consciousness also has some explanatory power at the highest national levels. Indeed, its judicious application permits the clarification of some seemingly contradictory aspects of President Mobutu's behavior since his accession to power. We have already noted and evaluated Mobutu's performance in the 30 November debacle. In the domestic context he appropriated for himself many of the most valuable plantation lands in Equateur Region. In addition, on one of his large acquired plantations he failed to raise the salaries of the workers to the minimum legal levels. Official disclaimers to the contrary, there can be little doubt that he personally profited from the whole adventure while most Zairians were suffering the effects of a completely disrupted commercial system.

Some weeks before 30 November 1973, President Mobutu delivered a speech before the General Assembly of the United Nations in New York. Discussing the causes of poverty in much of the developing world, Mobutu asserted:

> The problem of the poor countries is a simple transposition, to the world scale, of the problems present at the national scale.
>
> It is thus that workers and peasants often revolt in the rich countries, and the leaders [*responsables*] of these countries find it normal. While our revolt, every bit as legitimate, is styled as without conscience, demagogic, and politically unstable.
>
> It is therefore completely erroneous to believe that the assistance of the rich countries consists of the poor of the rich countries enriching the rich of the poor countries. I believe that you conclude with me, after what I have just demonstrated, that it is the poor of the poor countries who enrich the rich of the rich countries.[19]

In the international context, therefore, Mobutu could wholeheartedly espouse the cause of the poor people in the underdeveloped world. The entire text of his speech proclaims his identification with the world's poor and sets forth his claim to act as a spokesman in their behalf.

How can this seeming paradox be explained? On one level, in the domestic context of the 30 November economic reforms, Mobutu identified with—and acted in the interests of—the highest segments of the politico-administrative hierarchy. But in the international context, on a different level, he set himself up as a defender of the poor people in the underdeveloped areas of the world. Many will believe that one possible explanation is hypocrisy, dishonesty, and amorality. While these factors can perhaps furnish part of the explanation, they still leave much unexplained. It would be more convincing to say that Mobutu's class consciousness, in certain cases, may be determined by the political, social, and economic contexts of the moment. In this respect his behavior is no different from that of Lisala's chief, the collectivity secretary, the local police, or the anguished court clerk, whose perceptions were previously examined.

Put another way, while structural characteristics such as income, occupation, and education level are important and ought to be considered, in and of themselves they are insufficient to determine who is exploiting whom. The answer to this question can only be given after attention is paid to the context and circumstances in which these social relations take place. An exploiter in one context might well have the tables turned on him in another. These general propositions find support in the recent pastoral letter of Monseigneur Kabanga, the Archbishop of Lubumbashi. This remarkably courageous document is worth citing at some length.

> The thirst of money thus transforms men into assassins. How many poor unemployed are condemned to misery along with their households, because they do not have the means to pay the one who is hiring? How many children or adults die without care, because they do not have the means to pay the nurse

who has to care for them? Why is there no longer medicine in the hospitals, when it can be found in the markets? How did it come there?

Why in our courts do people only obtain their rights by paying the judge liberally? Why do the prisoners live forgotten in the prisons? They do not have anyone who can pay the judge who has their dossiers at hand. Why in our offices of administration, like public services, are people required to return day after day to be able to obtain their due? If they do not pay the clerk, they will not be served. Why must parents go into debt at the beginning of the school year to pay the principal of the school? The children who cannot pay will not have school!

The merchants exaggerate either by hiding merchandise in order to make prices rise, or by fixing prices at random. Even the poor who sell in the market do not hesitate to exploit those who are poorer by exorbitant prices. How many heads of personnel do not require that young girls looking for work prostitute themselves with them to obtain a place? How many teachers and principals do not require their women students to prostitute themselves with them if they wish to be promoted? Are they still playing their role of educators at an hour when courses of religion are suppressed in the schools?

Whoever obtains a scrap of authority, or some means of pressure, profits from them to pressure and exploit people, particularly in the rural milieu. All methods are good to obtain money or to humiliate the human person.[20]

The Monseigneur's letter not only underlines the picture of Zairian life sketched in other chapters; it emphasizes that it is exceedingly difficult to isolate a class either of exploiters or of exploited in contemporary Zaire. Regardless of position in the socioeconomic hierarchy, those with scraps of authority tend to exploit them. The exploitative merchant who arbitrarily raises prices in the market might well find himself the victim of the exactions of the local school principal. Social context is crucial to our comprehension of the situation's political dynamics.

At this juncture it is once again possible to return to the Azikiwe paradox posited in chapter 2. Now it can be more fully appreciated that Azikiwe may not have felt any contradiction between his position as a banker, editor, and incarnation of the wealthy class, on the one hand, and his status as a symbol of hope for the farmers and working class, on the other. Although "objectively" a bourgeois, his class identification shifted according to the context of the moment. Like the collectivity chief, the court clerk, President Mobutu, and the Lubumbashi merchants, he is in large measure a creation of his context.

Popular Perceptions and Consciousness

In the historical overview presented above it was noted that the rural masses had developed a sense of "them"; a feeling that the bureaucrats and other wealthier elements were, in some respects, their adversaries. It should also be mentioned that the higher strata of the population believe they are in the grip of an adversary relationship with the villagers and other less-privileged sections of the society. The bureaucrats, too, have this sense of an adversary relationship. The feeling of opposition to the rest of the population can be demonstrated in a number of ways. When asked whom they like to drink with after hours, most of the service chiefs in Lisala responded that they usually associate with their social equals, or professional colleagues:

> Normally with those who work for the administration or in the private sector. We meet each other in the bars or at football matches. But with the natives, the villagers, I have no contact with them.
>
> I do not have contact with the people here.
>
> I do not go to bars very much. . . . Sometimes, however, I like to take a glass of beer with my colleagues, the other service chiefs.
>
> [A good administrative superior] . . . must have as companions people with more or less the same rank.
>
> Usually I share my glass of beer with those who are most often around me. Often they are the local authorities.[21]

In addition to these preferences, those with positions of authority often exhibit a certain scorn for their fellow citizens who are not so fortunate. One secondary school teacher, for example, was wont to complain about the kinds of clothing available in Lisala stores. He maintained that these garments were really not modern. Rather, he commented, they were more suited to the needs of the "*indigènes.*" One of the territorial commissioners in Lisala put a sign outside his door to aid people in finding their way around the offices. Although a fine gesture, his only comment was that it would be nice if the local people could read it.[22]

There is more to the authorities' perception of the people than mere scorn. There is also fear. All who command, all who are wealthy, and all who can influence policy have lived their country's recent history. They have only to think back to the examples of the early 1960s to know that armed insurrection can occur in Zaire. Furthermore, they are surely aware that the targets of the rebellions were usually those most closely associated with the abuses and exactions of the regime. It is only by understanding the fear that these tumultuous events might repeat themselves that the voluminous administrative correspondence on gun control becomes analytically intelligible. To cite only one example, in July 1973 the regional commissioner of Equateur ordered the military into the villages to confiscate all illegal firearms. So concerned are the national authorities about this situation that authorization for legal possession of guns can be issued only by the state commissioner for political affairs.[23]

There is little question that the territorial commissioners in Lisala are afraid of the people they administer. In 1972 one of the subregional commissioners asked the local gendarmes for a second policeman to guard his office. The reasons for this request were that, lately,

We give audiences to people who come to us with an indignant attitude which risks compromising our authority and, this occurring, they cry out in the office demanding an immediate solution to the problem evoked, even if it is a question for the lower authorities.

This manner of behavior causes a source of anarchy to appear which we can in no way tolerate.

In July 1973 the subregional commissioner once again addressed a letter to the commandant of the local gendarmes. It made the following points:

1. The Territorial Authority has become purely political and as such become more and more the enemy of everybody.

2. The situation of Lisala's Central Prison which sows so much worry among the population because of its defective state which facilitates the evasion of dangerous prisoners who terrorize the *Cité* and their threat to Authority *number one* of the Subregion. You have witnessed it yourself.

3. Lisala . . . has become a nest of armed bandits. . . . All the bandits and escapees aim only, in the first instance, at the Residence . . . [*ne visent au premier point que la Résidence*].

It is for the reasons evoked above that I ask you to please put back the guard at the Residence.[24]

The implications of these two letters are clear. Not only is there fear of the population, there is also something resembling a siege mentality. As primarily political officers, the territorial commissioners appear to believe that they are the most prominent targets for the wrath of the population; in this estimation, they may be correct.

It can be maintained, then, that those in positions of authority tend to perceive the villagers and ordinary folk as "them", as enemies against whom they have to be protected. It can also be argued that this category of people have developed an equally well articulated sense of "us." They are, in short, conscious of their elevated position in the social order, intent on defending it, and more than willing to accord each other the *avantages* and other courtesies that seem to go with their rank. Much of the evidence already presented bears this out. In the chapter on the political economy of beer the systematic cooperation of the bar owners and the politico-administrative authorities was noted. Mutual understanding through mutual profit is the order of the day. In the discussion of the politics of the economic decolonization, we saw how highly placed officials expropriated most of the European wealth for themselves. Indeed, this was done with an enthusiasm that might have made even Commodore Vanderbilt blush. A pervasive social symbiosis underlies the most flagrant manifestations of this consciousness. Perhaps this can best be described as a you-scratch-my-back-and-I'll-scratch-yours syndrome. One concrete example demonstrates the point. In 1973 one of Lisala's assistant subregional commissioners wrote to his superior on a matter he held close to his heart. He noted that the subregion had been allowed a budgetary credit of Z400 to buy material and office supplies and reminded the commissioner that it would cost only Z180 for a new refrigerator and Z30 for a new fan, which would make life much more pleasant for his whole family. Since the commissioner had firmly promised to consider his case when the new credits came, this would indeed be a golden opportunity. The assistant commissioner concluded his letter on an upbeat note. "Knowing your worry always to render life easier for your close collaborators, I am nourished with hope that satisfaction, certainly, will be given me."[25]

While it can thus be argued that those occupying advantageous positions in Zairian society manifest a sense of solidarity among themselves as well as a sense of distinction from, even opposition to, the rest of the population, the same cannot be said of those Zairians who are less fortunate. The villagers and other ordinary citizens tend to lack a sense of solidarity that crosscuts ethnic lines, although they continue to have a precise notion of who their adversaries are. Much of the evidence presented in chapter 4 supports this idea. It will be remembered, for example, that more and more villagers are beginning to vote with their feet. When tax collectors, police, and other local officials appear, the villagers leave for either the deep forest or the islands in the river. They know the purposes of the visits and are aware that no benefit will be forthcoming from them. They know, too, the way the local court system operates. As one respondent put it, "If you are before the prosecutor and you have a bit of money, it suffices to spend some of it and your business will be forgotten."[26] This official, a veterinarian, was bitter because the political authorities would not let him enforce the laws. In theory, domestic animals such as goats are not permitted to be left unattended. They may not wander around because they eat the crops in the local vegetable gardens. The veterinary officers are supposed to enforce these rules, but they find they cannot because almost all these animals belong to the political authorities. In one example an agent tried to pen a goat belonging to one of the JMPR leaders. This official became so incensed at the affront to his dignity that he ordered the members of the JMPR Disciplinary Brigade to beat up the agent. An official complaint was filed with the appropriate judicial authorities, but the case was dismissed. This incident bears out the bitter assertion of one lower-level clerk that the laws are enforced only on the poor; those who have money or connections are not touched.[27]

The villagers are also well aware of what happens to the monies collected from time to time for special projects. In Bumba, for example, when the chief informed the citizens that everyone—even little children—would have to purchase new identity cards, the people booed loudly. Equally unpopular are the bureaucrats who work for the ONC. When the new ONC chief was introduced to the people of Gemena, much vocal displeasure ensued.[28] ONC and its agents were certainly blamed for their inefficiency in getting coffee to market. At a popular rally in Binga in 1973 the microphone was grabbed by an angry citizen who cried:

Shut up JMPR, we have had enough of your slogans, your oyé, oyé, your Mobutu, your meetings, shut up! You have cars and your microphones for your meetings on your jeeps so why use the equipment of the company? You forget that your predecessors burned the cables of these microphones during your meetings and have you already paid for them? Even today do you want to make the same blunders against the company because of your Mobutu? I am Mongwandi [Mobutu's ethnic group], Mobutu is building things where he lives but what is he doing for the rest of you? What do you gain? You bring only your shouts and your lies. Get out and leave here.[29]

Such outbursts leave little doubt that most villagers do not perceive the government as a friend.

The frequent exactions described elsewhere have left the population with a profound sense of mistrust and fear. When the measures of radicalization were announced on 30 December 1974, it became government policy either to take over or to build nursery schools. Territorial authorities were informed that there had to be at least one nursery school in each collectivity. When some parents in Mongala heard this announcement, they refused to register their children for these schools because they were afraid it was merely a pretext on the part of the government to take their children from them.[30] Although this certainly was not the intention of the national authorities, it is nonetheless intriguing that the population would interpret these decisions in that way. But after all, they were used to having things taken from them by representatives of the state. This reaction to a government decree is indicative of an attitude pervasive in the rural areas. Simply put, people are afraid of the government and have come to despise it. They believe, with some reason, that agents of the security office—the CND—are everywhere, and they are afraid to speak openly about their feelings or about what is happening in the country. In Lisala the chief of the *Cité* even had her own information network, which consisted of ten "militant informers" for each quarter. On more than one occasion informants told me they would be glad to talk privately, but not if another person were present. One woman summed it up this way: "We are all afraid; everyone is afraid to say anything because if you do, they will come and kill you." "They," of course, are the state authorities.[31]

To a certain extent our perceptions of the social order are reflected in the language we use. In Zaire this is true of the term *Citizen*. Originally introduced by the Mobutu regime as part of its authenticity campaign, it was intended as a substitute for the then predominant European mode of polite address, *Monsieur* or *Madame*. People were instructed to substitute the new word for the old. Zairians were to call each other Citizen, but foreigners were still to be addressed as either *Monsieur* or *Madame.* Many adapted to this change with full awareness of the government's goal of authenticity. But among the poorer and less privileged people, the word Citizen acquired a different connotation. At the beginning of my stay in Lisala, I was surprised to find that people passing me on the street would call me Citizen instead of

Monsieur. At first it seemed this was simply an indication that they had not understood the sense of the reform, since it was obvious I was not Zairian and should therefore be addressed as *Monsieur*. After I had spent some time in the community, it became apparent that the popular view was that only people who had money were Citizens. As a white man, I therefore qualified. Two of Joseph Houyoux's respondents in Kinshasa expressed their feelings this way:

> Now I have understood that the true Citizens live in Kalina, that they travel in airplanes, in cars, but all those who walk are not real Citizens.

> We are not Citizens, we have to dig holes to have water.[32]

Rather than forging national identity and pride, as intended, the introduction of the term *Citizen* has come to stand for, and reflect, class distinctions among the Zairian people.

It should be remembered that the equation of Citizen and wealth in the popular consciousness is relative, contextual, and probably imprecise. In some areas one might be labeled Citizen for owning a motorbike or a new shirt. In others, it might be necessary to have a car before receiving this designation. Throughout this chapter the view is expressed that class consciousness is fluid and changes with the context of the moment. There are some signs, however, that elements of rigidity have begun to appear; it is with this in mind that I should once again like to examine the economic reforms of 30 November 1973.

30 November and Consciousness

Most people in Lisala correctly perceived the true nature of the distribution process. An agricultural officer described it in these terms:

> They asked anyone to introduce a request at the zone. Then the zone transmitted it to the subregion, to the region, and then to the central government in Kinshasa. Then the *grosses légumes* [big men] who are the closest collaborators of the *patron* introduced their requests to him.[33]

As we have seen, few people in Lisala submitted applications to acquire European stores or plantations. In general this was because there was an accurate perception that this would be a waste of time. When asked if he was an acquirer, one of the lower-level clerks told me:

> No, I am not. There were many conditions to become an acquirer. To have a bank account, it's a lot. The rest of us, we have nothing. It was useless to file our candidacies. One also had to be well known.[34]

Similarly, another clerk replied that he had not asked to become an acquirer because he knew this was going to be a favor restricted to the commissioners of the people and local businessmen. In the words of one collectivity employee, the whole thing was something "which happened like that, among the *grands*." Finally, one of the less important merchants informed me that he had not even submitted his candidacy because he was "a *petit*. I couldn't go and have myself entered in the business of the *grands*."[35] There was thus a belief that the distribution of European properties concerned only the wealthy and highly placed. Indeed, I suspect that many individuals in Lisala initially failed to perceive what this question had to do with their own lives. They were soon to find out.

The disastrous consequences of the economic reforms have already been detailed and need not be reiterated here. From the perspective of the village population, suffice it to say that perhaps the two most serious of these were the disruption of the commercial distributive network and an almost immediate rise in prices. Although before the implementation of these measures one could find first-necessity items in the interior, in the months that followed the takeover, goods such as agricultural implements, tinned foods, cloth, and enamel basins became increasingly scarce. In addition there was a series of across-the-board price hikes in almost every affected store in Equateur. Ordinary items that had once cost, say, 10k, were now sold at 15 or 20k. The significance of these two changes should not be underestimated.

Economic gouging and extraction of this kind had previously taken place, but the methods employed were usually indirect.[36] Few villagers identified the Kinshasa government, or the political system as a whole, as the cause of the daily exactions levied by the foreign merchants or, for that matter, the collectivity officials. The view from the villages was obscured by the intervening layers of government. There was not a direct appreciation of the role of the central authorities in the rural exploitation system. But this changed dramatically in the wake of the 30 November decisions. For perhaps the first time since independence, the villagers were able to perceive a direct link between their own life situations and the political activities of the highest levels of the politico-administrative leadership in the capital. As we have seen, most of the stores—even in the remotest corners of the region—were acquired by Kinshasa political figures. When they arrived to take over their new possessions, the first thing many did was to raise the prices of the merchandise already on the shelves. These arbitrary and illegal actions weighed heavily on the household budgets of most people. Before much time had elapsed, the word *acquirer* became an almost universal epithet.

In Lisala, for example, people appearing with a new shirt, or a new motorbike, would be asked by their companions if they had become acquirers. Remarks like "They wanted to create a bourgeois class"; or "Certain acquirers [raise prices] a bit more, in order to create another level apart from the rest of the population," were quite common.[37] One service chief bitterly noted that

> it is the fault of the government. They seized the merchandise; the goods of the Europeans, they carried them off and they shared them among themselves. You have to be a kid not to know that.[38]

Although the situation was vastly complex, most Lisala residents were quick to blame the difficult economic conjuncture on the activities of the acquirers.[39] Indeed, much hostility was created between the acquirers on one side and the rest of the population on the other. One of Lisala's acquirers lived in constant fear that his "jealous" (this is his adjective) fellow citizens would falsely accuse him of uncivic behavior, and the authorities would come and take away the store he had acquired.[40]

As mentioned above, perceptions of the social order may be reflected in everyday language. In this light it is possible to trace the evolution of words that, in different periods, have stood for the wealthiest and most politically powerful elements in Zairian society. We have already discussed the *évolué* group during the colonial period. In the popular perception, this term was based more on a distinct social status than on any economic criterion—although, of course, the two often go together. Shortly after independence the term *évolué* seemed to pass into disuse. As Nzongola suggests, the new term that generally designated those on top of the social and economic hierarchy was *intellectual.*[41] It is obvious that educational attainments may have been the determining factor in the minds of most people for inclusion in this category. This word, too, passed into relative disuse after a period of time. Common during the First Republic period, it has been heard less often under Mobutu. The term *Citizen* was introduced during the early part of the Second Republic. Although unintended, most people have attached an economic significance to it, and inclusion in this category in the popular mind seems to be based primarily on material wealth. Within the last few years the expression *acquirer* has gained much currency. In most instances it refers to those who benefited from the presidential decisions of 30 November 1973.[42]

The progression—from *évolué*, through intellectual and Citizen, to acquirer—bears some commentary. It should be noted that the first three words in this progression contain significant degress of ambiguity. The status of *évolué*, for example, was not usually clear-cut. Often any number of people were trying for inclusion in this category, but the criteria were not straight-forward. The same can be said, with even greater emphasis, for intellectual. A primary school teacher in Kinshasa might not make the grade, while in Lisala he probably would. This designation, then, depends upon the social context to a considerable degree. We have also seen that there are ambiguities inherent in the popular use of the expression Citizen. There are no precise delimita-tions of the amounts of wealth necessary for inclusion in this category. In the capital, or in any other large city, they are surely different from those in Lisala or any other small urban center. The connotations of these three terms, then, are likely to differ with the context in which they are used. But the word *acquirer* differs in this respect: Although it is occasionally used to single out those who are wealthy or display some newly purchased item, it generally has less contextual flexibility than any of the other three terms. It is, by and large, a distinctive social category, and there is little doubt or ambiguity about who is included or who is excluded. This expression almost always labels those who took over the economic enterprises of the expatriates.

Murray Edelman contends that we usually think of words as signals rather than as symbols and, consequently, the catalytic capacity of words is often ignored. He further argues that

> if a word is a symbol that condenses and rearranges feelings, memories, perceptions, beliefs, and expectations, then it evokes a particular structuring of beliefs and emotions, a structuring that varies with people's social situations. Language as symbol catalyzes a subjective world in which uncertainties are clarified and appropriate courses of action become clear.[43]

The point to be made here is that the widespread use of the word *acquirer* has engendered a similar symbolic process. Although previously present and manifest in the use of the other three expressions, the symbolic processes occurring when the term acquirer is used are less ambiguous, and therefore potentially more liberating. This term evokes a structuring of beliefs and perceptions that focuses on the role of the central authorities in the economic and commercial catastrophe following the economic reforms. In the perceptions of most Zairians it clearly identifies a numerically restricted category of people who profited from the presidential measures and whose standards of behavior have caused widespread hardship and suffering. Its use has channeled, catalyzed, and rearranged the perceptions of the villagers and other ordinary folk. They now discern more acutely the effects that the the political manipulations of the national authorities have on their own life situations and mobility chances. Above all, it focuses resentment, bitterness, and a sense of opposition to these same authorities. The symbolically charged epithet *acquirer*, may for the first time be creating the basis for a sense of identity among the village population that transcends ethnic lines. As such, it has introduced into the popular consciousness a relatively neat dichotomous distinction that had not previously existed. It may therefore be the first indication of an increasing rigidity in the subjective component of the class system.

Conclusions

In one of his later works, *Philosophical Investigations*, Ludwig Wittgenstein wrote that

> no *single* idea of exactness has been laid down; we do not know what we should be supposed to imagine under this head—unless you yourself lay down what it is to be so called. But you will find it difficult to hit upon such a convention; at least any that satisfies you.[44]

What are the exact criteria for determining the existence, or absence, of class consciousness? I have not answered this question. Instead, at this juncture we have to content ourselves with what must be considered a preliminary and somewhat tentative sketch of the features that compose class consciousness in contemporary Zaire. Other authors—Anthony Giddens and Ralph Miliband among them—have tried to elaborate levels, or stages, of class consciousness.[45] While these efforts are stimulating and take us well beyond

Marx's simple class-in-itself and class-for-itself distinction, they are not readily applicable to a contextual approach to the whole problem. At this stage the introduction of analytic levels of class consciousness would result in a confusing proliferation of theoretical parameters. We would then have to ask which level of consciousness is likely to be present during any particular context. This would restrict the flexibility inherent in a contextual approach and burden us with another unwieldy typology. Perhaps the best we can do is to set forth some simple conditions under which a contextual approach might prove useful.

In addition to the question of exactness, there is the related problem of the researcher's judgment. Given the nature of class consciousness, it is entirely possible for experienced observers to differ—not only about its appropriate level in any given circumstance, but also over its very existence. For example, we have the fine studies of Peter Lloyd on the Yoruba in Western Nigeria. Throughout his career Lloyd has consistently found that there is no class consciousness in this region or among these people. On the other hand, an equally perceptive observer, Peter Gutkind, disagrees. He argues that there is considerable evidence to suggest that "class consciousness is clearly revealed in the attitudes, and sometimes in the actions, of the urban poor in Ibadan."[46] Inevitably, then, one has to rely on one's own judgment and sense of the situation; this is what I have tried to do.

These reservations notwithstanding, it is possible to draw several conclusions from the evidence presented in this chapter. First, what are the conditions under which a contextual approach to class consciousness seems to be the most useful? In general, it can be argued that its most fruitful applications will be found in the middle layers of the social hierarchy. At these points, among the bureaucrats, teachers, and merchants, there is more room for contextual ambiguity. Although certain examples can be isolated at either the very highest or the very lowest levels of the social order, its utility there will be more limited. It is difficult to imagine very many situations in which the members of the National Executive Council or the MPR Political Bureau might believe themselves exploited. Similarly, there are probably few opportunities for village farmers to believe that they are exploiting someone else. The key, then, lies in the middle layers. Although these are numerically restricted when compared with the majority of the population, who still live and work on the land, they are a politically crucial grouping. For it is among them that many rapid shifts in the composition of Zairian social classes have occurred. Few villagers suceed in making it up the social ladder; while there is much rotation among the top officeholders, only a very small number slip all the way down the ladder. In addition, it is often people in these middle strata who manipulate—either consciously for personal profit or unknowingly from structural necessity—the society's closure mechanisms.

Among the middle layers themselves, the contextual approach is more likely to be of analytic utility when conditions of scarcity and insecurity obtain. When there are few economic resources to go around and when people do not know how long they will be able to retain those they have, the impulse will most probably be to accumulate wealth as rapidly as possible. In consequence, officials will try to convert small parcels of authority into wealth by using them to extract resources from those who can be coerced. It is thus that the school principal will require entry fees from the parents of would-be students; that the lower-level clerk will demand a *matabiche* from someone who needs an official document or signature; or the collectivity policeman will seize payment in kind from the villagers over whom he has some authority. In general we can say that the more economically secure the situation, the less probable these occurrences, and the less likely that people will regard those with higher positions in the hierarchy as exploiters.

Another conclusion to be drawn is that class consciousness may be more likely to emerge first in the higher levels of the social structure than in the lower. This is not to argue that it will be absent in the lower levels, but that it will be better defined and more explicitly articulated the higher one goes. This is by no means unusual. Miliband has noted the phenomenon in a French example and Wittfogel has detailed it for China.[47] In the broader African context, Balandier has observed the same process. He writes that

> class consciousness wakes slowly, except in the case of the social strata, very much in the minority, who have become the principal beneficiaries of independence. A solidarity of interests has been established among them which unites them or imposes on them, at least, a common strategy.[48]

Often this common strategy is not specifically voiced, but consists of simple cooperation and according each other certain privileges. When asked what professional problems he had, the director of Lisala's hospital replied that the

> problem is to organize the clinic. We are all human equals, but there are classes. We are not going to put the subregional commissioner or a member of his family in a common ward. The clinic was very dirty when I arrived. This year I would like to organize the clinic.[49]

Such expressions of class consciousness among the privileged strata are quite common.

Mutual courtesies and advantages are accorded to well-placed members of the community as far as *Salango* is concerned, too. One of Lisala's primary school principals affirmed that he, personally, had never cut a blade of grass or participated in any other way in *Salongo*. Indeed, no one had ever asked him to take part. He further maintained this was because of his elevated position in the social community. People in positions of authority in Zaire, like the cases cited above, have a well-defined and somewhat prickly sense of what is required to maintain the dignity of their positions. Certain tasks are thought to be demeaning, and high officials will not perform them unless coerced. When the regional director of the JMPR visited Lisala, he was accompanied by a member of the Disciplinary Brigade whose sole function was to carry the director's briefcase. In a like manner, one observer noted that when President Mobutu stood before the General Assembly to defend the world's poor, he had an aide place his speech on the podium for him and then remove it when he had concluded his address. Such exertions are apparently beneath his dignity.[50]

Although not so clearly pronounced or so well-defined, there is class consciousness on the lower levels of Zairian society. We have seen that the villagers have always felt themselves distinct from the bureaucratic officials in the countryside. Often the latter have been the targets of politically inspired violence. This is no less true under Mobutu than it was in either the colonial period or the First Republic, as the letters cited above requesting police protection for the territorial commissioners bear witness. The territorial officials are afraid of popular violence and are apprehensive about how people will react to their enviable life-styles. One MPR bureaucrat mentioned that if he had his choice, he would prefer to work in Kinshasa. "Here," he said, "if you wear a new shirt, they begin to make trouble for you. In Kinshasa they do not bother with you even if you have two or three cars. There are too many gossips here."[51] The gossips, of course, are Lisala's poor, and it is apparent that many bureaucrats and political officers are leery about agitating them through too open a display of wealth. Indeed, this is a common concern among all levels of the state apparatus; in July 1974 all territorial commissioners were instructed to curb the flagrantly conspicuous consumption of their wives.[52]

It might be objected that there really is no class consciousness in the lower levels of Zairian society because there is no political organization that represents the interests of this class. The villagers, in Marxian terms, have not yet banded together to organize their interests and to fight for them. In Zaire, however, such political organization is not now a possible or appealing alternative. The agents and informers of the state are everywhere and people are afraid to speak out openly against the regime. Under such conditions, political organization would seem to be out of the question, for suppression would be quick and violent were any foolhardy enough to try it. But the lack of an organizational arm must not be taken to mean that people in the villages are unaware, unconcerned, or unconscious of their own interests. Indeed, Scott has argued that Asian peasants "have a sharp appreciation of their relations with rural elites, [and] they have no difficulty in recognizing when more and more is required of them and less and less is given in return."[53] Zairians, too, know what their interests are. It has already been shown that there are instances when they will revolt against excessive taxation. More common, however, is flight to the forest. In the current context, revolts and migrations may well indicate that villagers are class-conscious. The government, however, possesses overwhelming military superiority as well as the will to use it freely.

Finally, we return to the question of context. Some analysts have tried to explain the lack of class-based mobilization in independent Africa by pointing to crosscutting identities. Often these were ethnic; occasionally they were religious or racial. The point, though, is that such treatments were looking primarily for the Marxian manifestations of social-class identity. Failure to appreciate contextual subtleties has led many scholars to deny the existence of class and class consciousness. The reason class has not usually appeared in its analytically identifiable Marxian trappings is that it is a contextual consciousness that often crosscuts itself. Africans, like others, can and do maintain more than one ethnic identity. Which one becomes salient in a given situation is very likely to depend upon the sociopolitical context of the moment.[54] So, too, for social class. As the context changes, the same individual may well display more than one class identity. I have shown how various categories of people in Lisala identify with one group in a given situation and with an entirely different group when the context changes. These shifts in consciousness depend upon the context and have little to do with any changes in the "objective" material conditions of the people involved. Most of us, no less than the bureaucrats in Lisala, maintain conflicting class identities. This is normal and we somehow manage to compartmentalize our ambivalences and ambiguities. To return to the citation that began this chapter, like Walt Whitman, we are all large and contain multitudes.

CHAPTER 9
Conclusion

> *"Cheshire-Puss,"* she began, rather timidly, as she did
> not at all know whether it would like the name: however,
> it only grinned a little wider. *"Come, it's pleased so
> far,"* thought Alice, and she went on. *"Would you tell
> me, please, which way I ought to go from here?"*
>   *"That depends a good deal on where you want to get
> to,"* said the Cat.
>   *"I don't much care where——"* said Alice.
>   *"Then it doesn't matter which way you go,"* said the
> Cat.
>   *"——so long as I get* somewhere," *Alice added as an
> explanation.*
>   *"Oh, you're sure to do that,"* said the Cat," *if you
> only walk long enough."*
>
> —Lewis Carroll[1]

Social research is a process of trying to comprehend an evanescent and highly fluid reality. Theory changes as it is exposed to data and, similarly, the meaning of data is transformed as newer and more refined theories are brought to bear in the interpretive enterprise. Confusion abounds in the dialectical interaction of theory and data. There is no straight, direct march to the understanding of social phenomena. It is, on the contrary, a slow, painful, and occasionally disorienting process. In a very real sense, like Alice, one must keep walking until one arrives somewhere.

I began this work by rejecting the linkage theory with which I had started my intellectual journey. In its place I have substituted a contextual approach to social-class formation. In this chapter I hope to weave a more cohesive picture of the political dynamics of class formation in Zaire. To this end I present an overall sketch of the current Zairian class system, discuss the pervasive feelings of insecurity characteristic of contemporary Zaire, and delineate some of the central contradictions of the Mobutu regime, so that attention is paid to both the objective and the subjective aspects of the dynamics of class formation.

Before turning to these subjects, though, one clarification is perhaps necessary. Although this study has largely been based on data gathered in Lisala, on numerous occasions national politics and policies have been discussed. My lack of reverence for the sanctity of neat levels of analysis has been both intentional and unavoidable. In a highly centralized polity such rigid analytic distinctions may well hinder our understanding. Lisala, like other small urban centers, is a microcosm of the larger society, and the processes of class formation occurring there are being repeated elsewhere in Zaire.[2] Nzongola's study of Kananga, data occasionally presented for other areas, and interactions with researchers working in different parts of the country all tend to support this contention.

The Zairian Class System

Much of the information presented in the preceding chapters describes the emergence, over many years, of a national politico-commercial bourgeoisie.[3] The seeds of this class were sown during the colonial period. Although the Belgians denied Zairians access to higher political and administrative office, clerks and typists were needed to make the administrative and commercial systems function efficiently. We have already seen that there was a tendency for those with high status in the early colonial years—chiefs and blacksmiths, for example—to bequeath their elevated positions to their children and grandchildren. This status transmission was usually contingent upon entry into the missionary school system. After finishing their education the sons of the chiefs and blacksmiths often became lower-level administrative and commercial clerks. While these positions were subordinate, the salaries attached to them still enabled these individuals to live much better than did the majority of their countrymen who remained village farmers. In turn, the members of this generation conveyed their status advantages to their own offspring. They, too, had access to the school system and could ensure their own children the educational opportunities necessary for social mobility under Belgian rule. Even today, the percentage of Lisala's elite who had fathers and grandfathers occupationally involved with the colonial agencies of Westernization is most impressive. But on the whole the colonial system provided few schools, and educational access was severely limited.

This fact was scarcely lost on the majority of the population. When independence was gained in 1960, the governments of the First Republic, at both the national and the provincial levels, embarked upon ambitious programs of educational expansion. The people demanded no less, and large portions of the budget were voted for the construction of schools throughout the country. For a time, access to these facilities was wide open. As the Belgians departed and the agencies of local government proliferated (the *provincettes*), Zairians increasingly took command of their own administration. But once these positions were filled, secondary education was no longer an almost automatic ticket to advancement. Still a necessary condition for mobility, it was no longer a sufficient one.

Access to politico-administrative office was crucial during the First Republic and has remained so during the Second. A steady salary, relative insulation from the vagaries of the agricultural pricing system, and frequent access to public funds has made government service a way station on the road to high economic standing. Once attained, such monies could be, and were, used to begin commercial establishments or plantations. As the commercially oriented bureaucrats became entrenched in their positions and amassed even more wealth, they took care to lay the foundations for the advancement of their own children. Education, of course, was a necessary first step. A regular salary facilitates the payment of school fees, and the difficult life in the rural areas means that relatively few village farmers can afford to send their children to school. Indeed, in Lisala's primary and secondary schools there is an important overrepresentation of the children of state employees. In addition, those in positions of influence often exert their power to ensure that their children will receive preference in the competition for places in the local educational institutions.

While already significant under the First Republic, the interpenetration of the commercial and political sectors has become even more prevalent since Mobutu's takeover. The new regime's politico-administrative authorities encourage commerce as a matter of policy. Lisala's subregional commissioner put it this way:

> We must favor and make contact with the businessmen. Their work is in their own interest first, but that also aids the population. Things must be facilitated for them where possible and they must be supported and assisted morally.[4]

This is especially convenient because the businessmen whom the territorial officials are duty-bound to aid are often themselves politicians or administrators. When asked how he had accumulated enough capital to begin a rice mill, one former minister ingenuously replied that

> the president-founder asked us to begin economic enterprises in the interior of the country. Credit for buying the rice mill came from the Banque du Peuple, the former Socobanque. No, there was not much a problem obtaining this credit because with the position I occupied these things were facilitated for me.[5]

This pattern of political-commercial interpenetration is by no means unique to Zaire. Referring to Uganda, John Saul has recently argued that "the creation of a stark and misleading dichotomy between entrepreneurial and bureaucratic 'fractions' of the petty bourgeoisie . . . obscures more than it illuminates."[6] Similarly, Miliband discusses the group of European managers and technocrats who work in parastatals, business, or government.

> These men belong exclusively neither to the world of government nor to the world of business. They belong [to] and are part of both, and move easily between them, the more easily in that the boundaries between these worlds are increasingly blurred and indistinct.[7]

The MPR, the regime's primary political instrument, can also be understood in light of the pervasive interpenetration of the political and commercial sectors. To reiterate, the party might best be seen as an avenue of upward mobility for a very small, but wealthy, segment of the population. The 1968 instructions on party staffing set the basic policy by restricting positions in the MPR to those who had independent means and could live decently. Inevitably, then, those who came to occupy posts in the party were merchants, bureaucrats, and others who were relatively wealthy and not dependent on the MPR for their livelihood. In consequence these wealthier elements were perceived as dedicated militants; as those who would work for the new order without payment; as the real apostles of *Mobutisme*. As a just reward for services rendered, benefits from certain political opportunities enabled them to increase their personal fortunes.

One such opportunity came during the 1970 legislative elections. We have already seen how the candidates were chosen and which criteria were applied. They were rated on their militancy, position in the party, and wealth. Substantial economic activities in the area were unquestionably an aid in receiving the party's approbation. Once in office, the Second Republic legislators had numerous chances to profit from their official positions. It was the explicit policy of the Mobutu government to aid them in setting up commercial and agricultural enterprises throughout the country. With this goal in mind, bank loans and credits were made available to the commissioners of the people. Naturally, similar outlets were found for the commercial enthusiasm of the rest of the regime's high officials. Members of the MPR Political Bureau, ambassadors, important territorial commissioners, and ministers all prospered at various times and in countless ways. The president and his entourage thus marched militantly into the business sector.

President Mobutu and his close collaborators also grabbed off most of the plantations and the commercial houses when these sections of the economy were taken over from the expatriates on 30 November 1973. With little regard for the smooth functioning of the economy, the new acquirers pilfered cash boxes, destroyed businesses, and let plantations go untended. The immediate rise in prices and the wave of conspicuous consumption, which followed these decisions, demonstrated to most Zairians that such actions were not designed for the public good. Since Zairianization has played a signal role both in the ongoing consolidation of the politico-commercial bourgeoisie and in the precipitation of a more rigidly dichotomous perception of the class structure, it might be worth placing the presidential decisions in historical perspective. A comparison of the political independence obtained on 30 June 1960 and the economic independence declared on 30 November 1973 would therefore appear useful. But since an impressive amount of ink has already been devoted to the "decolonization which went awry," there is little need to summarize what is now accepted as received wisdom.[8]

On a basic and superficial level there were numerous similarities between the two events. In both there was a social atmosphere of confusion and insecurity; whites were harassed and an exodus of expatriates resulted. Both decolonizations were ill-prepared, poorly thought out, and hastily executed. On deeper level, too, the two processes resemble each other. When political independence was obtained, there was an immediate and massive movement of clerks and *évolués* to fill the positions of the departing Belgian administrators. In the case of 30 November there was a similar action by the Zairian politico-administrative leadership. This time, however, the aim was to fill the economic void created by Zairianization. Whereas in 1960 political and administrative offices had been appropriated, in 1973 economic activities were taken over.

As has been amply demonstrated in the works cited above, one effect of the political decolonization was to throw the polity into confusion and disarray. As we have seen, the economic decolonization has also produced its share of disorder in the economy. Political decay in the first instance is paralleled by economic decay in the second.

The Mobutu regime and the extraordinary degree of centralization it has wrought can be interpreted, at least in part, as a response to the political chaos induced by decolonization. Although events in the economic sector have been temporally telescoped, 30 November and its concomitant disruptions have also produced a trend toward greater state control and economic centralization. This can most clearly be seen in the 30 December 1974 decisions, which attempted to "radicalize the revolution" by having the state take over many enterprises that had previously been Zairianized and distributed to individuals.

The course of Zairianization indicates that there may well be some justice to Marx's observation that all great events and characters of world history occur twice: first as tragedy, and then as farce. In Zaire, if the events surrounding the political decolonization gone awry were the tragedy (and there can be no doubt that they were), then those surrounding the economic decolonization can only be considered the farce.[9]

Since 30 November 1973 the Mobutu regime has continued to favor those who are wealthy at the expense of those who are not. The October 1975 legislative elections, for example, merely continued the party's staffing policy. Indeed, in March 1975 the state commissioner for political affairs informed the territorial authorities that the criteria and the procedures for selecting candidates would be substantially the same as they were in 1970. Specifically, those with economic enterprises, acquirers, and party militants were favored.[10] In Mongala Subregion there were only thirty-five candidates this time, and most of these came from the same categories of people who dominated the 1970 elections. Of the eight commissioners of the people chosen for the subregion, five were incumbents, one was the regime's foreign affairs commissioner, one was a lower-level bureaucrat, and one remains unidentified. Among the eight alternates, five were incumbent commissioners; I have been unable to identify the other three.[11] The MPR—indeed the whole state apparatus—has been used to promote the interests of a small and restricted segment of the population. The result to date has been the increasing solidification of an indigenous politico-commercial bourgeoisie.

As should by now be evident, the Zairian social system does not resemble a free market in which all have equal access and equal opportunity. Closure mechanisms bar the social, economic, and political mobility of most Zairians. In chapter 4 the exploitative character of collectivity administration was detailed. Accumulation of resources is all but impossible under such a system, as the villagers are served an almost daily fare of oppression, exaction, and violence. Their inability to amass resources all but precludes their children's eventual rise. Money is a prerequisite for entry into the educational system, and many villagers are increasingly unable to pay the necessary school fees. The disproportion of pupils whose parents are employed by the state eloquently demonstrates this point. Although the rural administration and educational establishments must be considered part of the institutional and structural settings, we have seen that they can be consciously manipulated by those in power for their own, often selfish, ends. The budgetary machinations of the collectivity officials as well as the pressures brought to bear on school principals to admit the children of those in power are also examples of this phenomenon. Class actions, therefore, can and do serve as closure mechanisms.

Many redistributive decisions taken by the Mobutu regime can also be interpreted as class actions. The economic decolonization is one example. Here decisions were made by the politico-commercial bourgeoisie, which increased its own access to significant economic resources. In a like fashion our investigation of the political economy of beer in Lisala showed the fate of the revenue gathered from the tax on consumption. Although theoretically slated for developmental expenses, most of the funds were used to provide amenities for territorial commissioners, chiefs, and collectivity employees. The result was a resource transfer from the consuming public to the already relatively advantaged administrators and clerks.

An examination of the redistributive patterns of both expatriate wealth and funds generated by beer consumption should perhaps induce us to rethink several key assumptions of those who have studied the development process in Africa. In most treatments of this subject it has been the norm to focus on the constraints that inhibit development. Often these obstacles are of a material nature. Indeed, we have seen that lack of passable roads and absence of an adequate communications system cause many problems in the implementation of policy in the Zairian hinterland. Furthermore, although it is well beyond the scope of this study, there is little doubt that the limitations posed by Zaire's dependence upon the price of copper in the international market is of great significance. In chapter 3 we saw that many Zairian bureaucrats enter government service with a sincere desire to serve their countrymen. But when asked what they themselves could do to help build their nation, they seemed profoundly demoralized. Most believe that little if anything can be done because they are not given the proper tools to accomplish their respective tasks. Lack of transportation, lack of seeds, lack of resources, are all motifs that recur in conversations with bureaucrats in the interior. Such impediments are real; it is not my intention to minimize them. It seems clear, though, that approaches focusing exclusively on these constraints are incapable of explaining the failure of Zaire and other postcolonial states to increase significantly the material well-being of their populations. The values, aims, and intentions of the postindependence leadership must be given equal weight.

Michael Cohen's study of urban policy in the Ivory Coast makes this point well. After examining the distribution of social services within the city of Abidjan, Cohen observes that Cocody—the residential neighborhood of the Ivoirian leadership—is blessed with excellent medical, cultural, and educational facilities while the more populous quarters have relatively few amenities. In short,

> this concentration of valued services is only explained by the fact that Cocody is the home of administrative personnel. This isolation of the facilities from the majority of the population raises the question of administrative priorities: is it the government's initial desire to provide services for all the population or just for certain groups—specifically its own members?[12]

But Cohen's work is an exception to the rule. Most previous studies of African politics have assumed that government leaders wish to achieve development, redistribute income, and enhance the life chances of their respective populations. In this, political scientists have tended to take political leaders at their word. Unfortunately, analytic errors have been made by specifically adopting the perspective of those at the summit of the political system. We have, for instance, the work of Warren Ilchman and Norman Uphoff on *The Political Economy of Change.* These authors note that government leaders have five key areas in which they can spend resources: (1) choices to cope with social and economic change; (2) choices to induce social and economic change; (3) choices to remain in authority at present; (4) choices to remain in authority in the future; and (5) choices to construct the political and economic infrastructure.[13] This list of alternative strategies is almost more interesting for what it fails to include. Nowhere do the authors consider that the aim of African leaders might be to suppress social change. Nowhere do they consider that the operative goals of government officials may be oriented more toward the personal accumulation of capital than any vaguely defined concept of development. Nowhere do they consider that those in power may be far more interested in extraction than construction. This examination of the political dynamics of class formation in Zaire has shown that these unpleasant and often unpalatable alternatives must at least be considered as empirical possibilities. The error, then, as been to *assume* the good faith of politically dominant elements when, in fact, it may or may not exist.

A second, and closely related, analytic error is of equal importance. In an essay on social and institutional change in independent Africa, Michael Lofchie has written:

> There is a strong tension between the two principal commitments of government, first to a process of representation and second to a goal of social transformation. As a norm for the determination of public policy, representation generally involves using available resources to respond to popular demands for improved conditions of life.[14]

Simply stated, it cannot be assumed that representation and social transformation are the "principal commitments" of government. They might well be, but this must be treated as an open empirical question to be determined on a case-by-case basis. The mistake here is to believe that African heads of state are guided by the norms of either American liberal pluralism or European social democracy. Imputing our ideas of development to African leaders and then arguing that failure to achieve these goals is due solely or primarily to certain obstacles ignores the central question of motives. It also confuses the statements of African leaders both with their intentions and with actual fact. Regrettably, this kind of confusion has occurred all too often. There was a time, for example, when we believed the assertions of African leaders that their societies were classless. Furthermore, their word was also accepted concerning the organizational efficacy of single parties.[15]

Put starkly, do the members of the Zairian politico-commercial bourgeoisie (or, for those who prefer, the Zairian political elite) genuinely wish to effect rural development and significant income redistribution in favor of the village farmers? With only rare exceptions, the answer is no. The weight of the evidence presented throughout this study forces this pessimistic conclusion. Oppressive and extractive bureaucrats abound; developmental administrators scarcely exist.

Attention to the redistributive aspects of the economic decolonization and the political economy of beer also directs our thoughts to the subject of ethnicity. In both cases we saw that ethnicity was vitally important. The ethnic dimension of political life seems to become particularly crucial when scarce resources are being allocated, appropriated, or competed for by members of the same class. Indeed, investigation of intraclass conflict can lend depth and nuance to our understanding of the political dynamics of class formation. The injection of ethnic criteria into intraclass squabbles indicates that an ethnic call to arms may well be a tactic in the accumulation of economic resources.[16] It is precisely at this point that ethnicity becomes analytically salient.

Many scholars have viewed Zairian politics primarily in ethnic terms. It is difficult to fault this interpretation for the 1960–65 period. There have been changes, however, under the Second Republic. The ever-increasing centralization and personalization of the regime since 24 November 1965 may be viewed as a reaction to the ethnic fragmentation of the early 1960s. The muting of ethnic strife has largely been accomplished by Mobutu's own brand of patrimonial pork barrel politics. Ironically, though, his very skill and great success at the game of ethnic balancing and representational redistribution may already have undermined the foundations of his regime. Two combined patterns have become evident to the villagers. On the one hand, they see their native sons acquire a share of the appropriated resources. On the other, this results in no appreciable amelioration of their own situations. Under these circumstances both their class consciousness and their bitterness toward the regime will increase. This was certainly true in the wake of the 30 November decisions, for example. This is one of the central contradictions in the Zairian polity today. The success of patrimonial politics coupled with the failure of resources to trickle down to the villages actually tend to increase class consciousness. Although ethnicity cannot and should not be removed from the analysis of Zairian politics, in the current context the explanatory power of social class is potentially greater.

Fluidity and change have always been central aspects of Zairian politics; the dynamics of social-class formation amply reflect this. The patrimonial politics of President Mobutu and the frequent rotation of those who hold high office has ensured a great turnover in the composition of the politico-commercial bourgeoisie. The middle levels of the class structure—merchants, clerks, teachers, and territorial administrators—have also been characterized by a continually changing composition. This is demonstrated by the modal biographies presented in chapter 3. Like their counterparts in the bourgeoisie, the careers of people in the middle levels have followed Zaire's political vicissitudes since independence. They have risen, and fallen, in the class system as the overall political and economic contexts have shifted. At any given moment within the space of a lifetime, the composition of the classes is not likely to be the same as it was a short time before. Great degrees of intragenerational mobility have resulted in an almost constant change in class composition. It would be incorrect to assume, however, that the level of fluidity is remaining constant. We have seen that closure mechanisms prevent upward mobility for most Zairian people. The financial and educational prerequisites for upward mobility are systematically denied to most village farmers. The outer boundaries of the politico-commercial bourgeoisie and the middle-level classes are thus becoming increasingly rigid. The inner boundaries (that is, those actually in power), however, have retained much of their permeability and are likely to do so as long as the constant rotation of officeholders is enforced from the president's office.

Insecurity and Scarcity

At many points in this study mention has been made of the widespread feelings of insecurity throughout the polity. A recurring theme in almost every chapter, it is one of the most striking features of contemporary Zairian life. To recapitulate, the frequent exactions of local officials and the difficult agricultural situation tend to make villagers insecure. Collectivity officials are also insecure; they have no job tenure guarantees and are rarely paid on time. Like the villagers, they do not know and cannot predict when they are likely to have money. Lower-level clerks who work in the territorial administration are also insecure. Although they are paid more regularly than their counterparts at the collectivity, they do not have the security of job tenure, and massive layoffs are commonplace. Territorial commissioners, chiefs, and party bureaucrats are primarily political officials. They are subject to five-year mandates that can be revoked at any time and for any reason. They, too, are insecure. On the highest levels of the apparatus, members of the MPR Political Bureau, the National Executive Council, and regional commissioners have become pawns on the chessboard of patrimonial politics. The Zairian political system has been characterized by frequent rotation of these top officials, and none of them has secure tenure in office.

Insecurity is manifest in other ways as well. We have noted the work of the CND, the state security agency, which, among other tasks, provides the president with an efficient network of informers. People in all walks of life are afraid to air openly their opinions about current happenings or political conditions. The fear of denunciation is real and contributes to what might be called an insecurity syndrome. This pervasive insecurity affects the policy process as well. Our examinations of the political economy of beer and economic decolonization have uncovered regular and dramatic reversals in announced policies—both in the disposition of beer tax revenues and in the general procedures to be followed in distributing the benefits of the 30 November decisions. Such frequent reversals make the bureaucrats who are responsible for the implementation of government decisions insecure because they do not know what the policy will be from one moment to the next. Finally, the initial and subsequent allocations of European wealth have made people insecure in their economic possessions.

Insecurity plays an important role in the political dynamics of class formation, as it dialectically interacts with the overwhelming condition of economic scarcity. Because people are insecure and know that economic resources are extremely limited, they come to believe that it would be best to accumulate whatever they can, as fast as they can. The almost inevitable tendency, therefore, is to extract whatever possible from those in contextually inferior positions in the hierarchy. This results in exploitation and oppression at every level of the class system and contributes directly to the contextual ambiguities of social self-placement in the class hierarchy. It is thus that the collectivity policeman will extract resources from the villagers under his jurisdiction, but believe that he himself is being oppressed by the chief who fails to pay his salary. As he sees it, since the chief does not ensure his payment, he has no choice but to take matters into his own hands. Assuredly, his family has to be fed, his children have to be educated, and his social obligations have to be discharged in local taverns. Though aspects of his behavior vis-à-vis the villagers are reprehensible, the context in which they occur must be understood. Like all of us, he is a being with imperative social needs, a being who is, after all, human.

A second central contradiction in the Zairian polity is that the measures designed to combat the First Republic's societal and political instability have produced a new form of personal insecurity under Mobutu. Greater centralization, frequent bureaucratic rotation, and all the trappings of patrimonial politics à la Mobutu Sese Soko have worked to increase regime stability at the expense of personal security. The personal insecurity explains how people driven by social necessity under conditions of economic scarcity begin to exploit their little parcels of authority. The result is a dialectic of oppression with insecurity and scarcity interacting in such a way as to create even more oppression and, perhaps, ultimately, new sources of regime instability.

Some Final Thoughts

We have argued that the Zairian polity may be conceived as a class system. At every level of the social hierarchy there are both a differential access to life and mobility chances and an unequal distribution of economic, social, and political resources. In addition, most people are socially conscious of these patterns and of how their own lives and opportunities are affected by them. Social class is thus a feature of life in Zaire. It must be stressed, however, that these social classes are perpetually appearing and disappearing, and this is why a contextual approach has been adopted. It should also be borne in mind that this does not necessarily mean that the future course of Zairian politics will be determined by a mechanistic dialectic in which only one outcome is possible.

What of the future? Unfortunately, the social scientist's crystal ball is never so clear as we should like it to be. We shall not, therefore, offer the reader a series of facile, and probably incorrect, predictions concerning the future evolution of politics in Zaire. But a few, brief, general observations are in order.

First, the picture of Zairian society presented here is not pleasant. Nonetheless, it is empirically accurate. At this time the system seems incapable of reforming itself. It is most unlikely that a change in leadership at the top will result in thoroughgoing change at the bottom. The social, political, and economic ills that sap the foundations of society are endemic. On an individual level, it is no longer possible to speak of a few rotten apples spoiling the barrel. Rather, we now have the reverse situation. The occasional unspoiled apple that remains is in danger of being corrupted by a completely rotten barrel. This point of view has been movingly expressed by Monseigneur Kabanga; his pastoral letter is worth citing once again.

> Happily, at all levels, from the high cadres to the most simple, there are still honest people who suffer from this situation and have not resigned themselves to it. We are proud of these brothers who struggle against the current in the middle of numerous ambushes. They are the living proof that the soul of our people has not died. But we must acknowledge that they are a minority and that the wound of dishonesty has attained all strata of society, to the point that public opinion sees these honest people as naive: 'they do not know how to get along.' And the others are quiet because they are afraid, afraid for their life, for their situation.[17]

Second, the dialectic of oppression—insecurity and scarcity—may provoke even greater degrees of centralization and repression. These factors, coupled with an ever-increasing level of economic inequality amid an unfavorable economic conjuncture could produce a condition of absolute insecurity. This condition would be characterized by the failure of the villagers to retain enough resources to subsist. If this should happen, they will probably continue to flee or, failing that, revolt. James Scott has argued that security of subsistence may be the key factor in explaining peasant revolts.[18] In the Zairian context, Monseigneur Kabanga has warned that even if the leadership does not fear God, they should at least fear a revolt of the poor.[19] But the outcome of such a revolt, were it to happen, is by no means predictable. The members of the politico-commercial bourgeoisie who control the state have both the capacity and the will to preserve their rule through violent repression. The success of any such rebellion is highly problematical. If, however, the disadvantaged succeed in overthrowing the system, the shape of the new order is not readily foreseeable.

Finally, it seems appropriate to ask: Where do we go from here? Although our application of a contextual approach to the political dynamics of class formation has borne some fruit, a richer harvest depends upon further investigation. As we have seen, this orientation is particularly well suited to Zairian events since independence. It seems likely that attention to the contextual aspects of social-class formation might also illuminate the experiences of other nations in Africa and Asia where governmental instability, political strife, and rapid social change remain watchwords. To this end, the economic, social, and political conditions under which con-textual shifts in class and class consciousness occur should be examined more completely. In addition, the impact of the international system on the formation of these social contexts and on the political dynamics of class formation ought to be studied. Its influence is not inconsiderable and deserves to be treated in a work more ambitious than this. One major advantage of this approach has been to highlight the ambiguities of social self-placement in the class hierarchy. If this varies with differing contexts—and there is good evidence that it does—it seems reasonable to assume that the relation of the political actor to the means of production may not be so important as many Marxists have thought. This topic merits far more sustained research and thought than I have been able to devote to it in this study. All these subjects can only be addressed in the crucible of further research in comparative politics, world history, and sociology. Our journey has just begun. Like Alice, we shall have to keep walking until we get somewhere.

Notes

Chapter 1

1. Agatha Christie, *The Mysterious Affair at Styles* (New York: Bantam, 1974), p. 71.
2. Colin Leys, *Politicians and Policies: An Essay on Politics in Acholi, Uganda 1962–1965* (Nairobi: East Africa Publishing House, 1967); Joel Samoff, *Tanzania: Local Politics and the Structure of Power* (Madison: University of Wisconsin Press, 1974); David Brokensha, *Social Change at Larteh, Ghana* (Oxford: Clarendon Press, 1966); Maxwell Owusu, *Uses and Abuses of Political Power: A Case Study of Continuity and Change in the Politics of Ghana* (Chicago: University of Chicago Press, 1970); and Nicholas S. Hopkins, *Popular Government in an African Town: Kita, Mali* (Chicago: University of Chicago Press, 1970).
3. James N. Rosenau, "Toward the Study of National-International Linkages," in *Linkage Politics: Essays on the Convergence of National and International Systems,* ed. James N. Rosenau (New York: Free Press, 1969), p. 45; Richard E. Stryker, "Political and Administrative Linkages in the Ivory Coast," in *Ghana and the Ivory Coast: Perspectives on Modernization,* ed. Philip Foster and Aristide R. Zolberg (Chicago: University of Chicago Press, 1971), p. 75.
4. Joseph LaPalombara, "Penetration: A Crisis of Government Capacity," in *Crises and Sequences in Political Development,* ed. Leonard Binder et al. (Princeton: Princeton University Press, 1971), p. 207.
5. Saul B. Cohen, ed., *Oxford World Atlas* (New York: Oxford University Press, 1973), p. 157.
6. Francis Dhanis, *Le District d'Upoto et la fondation du camp de l'Aruwimi,* Publications de l'Etat Indépendant du Congo, no. 3 (Brussels: Imprimerie Typo-Lithographique J. Vanderauwera, n.d.), pp. 10–11. A discussion of this expedition and the motives behind it may be found in Michael G. Schatzberg, "The Chiefs of Upoto: Political Encapsulation and the Transformation of Tradition in Northwestern Zaire," paper presented at the African Studies Association meeting, Houston, 2–5 November 1977, pp. 4–8.
7. Etat Indépendant du Congo, *Bulletin Officiel 1898* [hereafter *BO*] (Brussels: Etat Indépendant du Congo, 1898), pp. 242–243. On the early history of the Upoto mission, which was founded in 1890, see. E. M. Braekman, *Histoire du Protestantisme au Congo* (Brussels: Editions de la Librairie des Eclaireurs Unionistes, 1961), pp. 111–112. Ruth M. Slade, *English-Speaking Missions in the Congo Independent State (1878–1908)* (Brussels: Académie Royale des Sciences d'Outre Mer, Classe des Sciences Morales et Politiques, 16, fasc. 2, 1959), pp. 240, 290, 321, tangentially discusses the role of the Upoto mission in supplying testimony for E. D. Morel and others who were interested in ending the red rubber atrocities.
8. *BO 1902,* pp. 186–189; *BO 1905,* "Décret sur le personnel supérieur des districts et de la Force Publique," 17 January 1905, p. 5. On the early European populations of Lisala and Upoto, "Zaire Colonial Documents: De Ryck Collection of Material of General Administration, Equateur, Kivu, and Ruanda-Urundi" (University of Wisconsin—Madison Library) are also of interest. See especially reel III, no. 28.
9. Archives, Equateur Region, Political Affairs Department, Mbandaka. Bapoto Political Dossier, "Rapport préliminaire au rapport d'enquête," 11 September 1930, Territorial Administrator Denis. For the early history of Upoto under the Belgians, see Schatzberg, "The Chiefs of Upoto," pp. 8–14.
10. *Bulletin Officiel du Congo Belge 1911* 4 (30 December 1911): 940. Of some help in tracking down bits and pieces of this information was Léon de Saint Moulin, "Histoire des villes du Zaire: Notions et perspectives fondamentales," *Etudes d'histoire africaine* 6 (1974): 137–167.
11. Territories became administrative subdivisions of districts with the *Arrête Royal* of 28 March 1912. It is probable, however, that this measure was not implemented until several years

later. See J. L. Vellut, *Guide de l'étudiant en histoire du Zaire* (Kinshasa and Lubumbashi: Editions du Mont Noir, 1974), p. 117.

12. Archives, Equateur Region, Political Affairs Department, Mbandaka. Political Dossier, Center of Lisala, "Arrêté du 29 mars 1935 no. 35/SEC./AIMO créant le centre extra-coutumier de Lisala"; "Proposition en vue de la création du Centre Extra-Coutumier de Lisala," 4 October 1934, Territorial Administrator Denis; "Arrêté no. 143/SEC/ AIMO en date du 20 octobre 1935 créant des Quotités Additionnelles aux impôts dans les centres extra-coutumiers de Coquilhatville, Basankusu, Bumba, Lisala, et Libenge."

An extended discussion of the theory and practice of administration in the CECs is beyond the scope of this work. Interested readers may find general treatments of the theory in J. Magotte, *Les Centres extra-coutumiers: Commentaires des décrets des 23 novembre 1931, 6 et 22 juin 1934 coordonnés par l'arrêté royal du 6 juillet 1934* (Dison-Verviers: Imprimerie Disonaise, 1938); and Guy Baumer, *Les Centres indigènes extracoutumiers au Congo belge* (Paris: Dormat-Montchréstien, 1939). These works are largely legalistic and theoretical. More empirically oriented studies of a CEC in Equateur are provided by Franz M. De Thier, *Le Centre extra-coutumier de Coquilhatville* (Brussels: Université Libre, Institut de Sociologie Solvay, 1956); and Jacques Denis, "Coquilhatville: Éléments pour une étude de géographie sociale," *Aequatoria* 19 (1956): 137–144.

13. The literature on postindependence politics in general, and on the *provincettes* in particular, is voluminous. Of special interest are Crawford Young, *Politics in the Congo: Decolonization and Independence* (Princeton: Princeton University Press, 1965), pp. 533–571; Jean-Claude Willame, *Patrimonialism and Political Change in the Congo* (Stanford: Stanford University Press, 1972), pp. 34–56; Benoît Verhaegen, "Présentation morphologique des nouvelles provinces," *Etudes congolaises* 4 (April 1963): 1–25; and J. C. Willame, "La Réunification des provinces du Congo," *Etudes congolaises* 9 (July–August 1966): 68–86.

Specific treatments of Equateur may be found in Edouard Mokolo wa Mpombo, "Structure et évolution des institutions politiques et administratives de la Province de l'Equateur," (Mémoire de licence, Université Lovanium, Kinshasa, July 1968). This author is also responsible for two extremely valuable monographs on postindependence politics in Equateur. See "La Province de l'Equateur: Présentation morphologique des institutions politiques 1960–1967," *Courrier africain*, no. 82–83 (30 October 1968); and "Poids socio-politique des ressortissants de l'Equateur à Kinshasa," *Courrier africain*, no. 84 (8 November 1968).

With the exception of Laurent Monnier's *Ethnie et intégration régionale au Congo: Le Kongo central 1962–1965* (Paris: Edicef, 1971), the most probing studies of the individual *provincettes* are in J. C. Willame, *Les Provinces du Congo: Structure et fonctionnement*, 5 vols., Cahiers Economiques et Sociaux, Collection d'Etudes Politiques (Kinshasa: Université Lovanium, 1964–65). Volume 5 contains the most detailed treatment of Moyen-Congo and is an invaluable source of information on that period of Lisala's history.

In addition, more detailed information on Moyen-Congo may be found in the series published jointly by the Centre de Recherches et d'Information Socio-politique (CRISP) and the Institut National des Etudes Politiques (INEP). See Jules Gérard-Libois and Benoît Verhaegen, eds., *Congo 1962* (Brussels and Léopoldville: CRISP and INEP, 1963), pp. 264–267; Benoît Verhaegen, Jorge Beys, Paul Henry Gendebien, eds., *Congo 1963* (Brussels and Léopoldville: CRISP and INEP, 1964), pp. 305, 330–332; as well as the other volumes in the series for occasional references.

14. This inability is understandable. Ethnicity is a sensitive subject in Zaire because of the country's tumultuous postindependence history.

15. For a general treatment of this area and these migrations, see Jan Vansina, *Introduction à l'ethnographie du Congo* (Kinshasa: Editions Universitaires du Congo, 1966), pp. 62–72. B. M. Heijboer, "Esquisse d'histoire des migrations ngombe depuis le début du XVIIIè siècle," *Aequatoria* 10 (1947): 63–66, deals with this subject in detail. Curiously, the one major study of the Ngombe, by Alvin W. Wolfe, scarcely considers this question. See Alvin W. Wolfe, *In the Ngombe Tradition: Continuity and Change in the Congo* (Evanston: Northwestern University Press, 1961), pp. 3–5.

The hypothesis that the migrations would have continued had the Europeans not occupied the territory is suggested by Territorial Administrator Lardinois, "Rapport d'enquête préalable à la création du Secteur de Lisala du Territoire de Lisala," 7 July 1936 (Archives, Equateur Region, Political Affairs Department, Mbandaka), Political Dossier, Gombe-Doko Collectivity. Van Der Kerken places the Ngombe migration across the Zaire River between 1870 and 1907. See Georges Van Der Kerken, *L'Ethnie Mongo*, 2 vols. (Brussels: Institut Royal Colonial Belge, Section des Sciences Morales et Politiques, 13, fasc. 1 and 2, 1944), p. 471. This work has recently been criticized by Gustave Hulstaert, "Une Lecture critique de *l'Ethnie Mongo* de G. Van Der Kerken, " *Etudes d'histoire africaine* 3 (1972): 27–60.

16. A possible exception would be the *provincette* period, when ethnic polarization was the order of the day. From 1963 to 1966 Lisala was a Ngombe city. Mongo returned to Mbandaka; Budja left for Bumba; and Ngwaka-Mongwandi traveled to Gemena. At present, though, the ethnic composition once again resembles its preindependence profile.

Parenthetically, the reason the Bapoto are listed in neither the 1934 nor the 1958 census is fairly simple. In 1931, a few years before Lisala's incorporation as a CEC, the colonizers decided to merge the four Bapoto chieftaincies. A new chief was imposed in 1931 and Bapoto became a *groupement*. The boundaries of Lisala had changed somewhat by this time, and the new Bapoto *groupement* found itself outside the town limits.

On the Ngombe, in addition to the works cited above, see Alvin W. Wolfe, "The Dynamics of the Ngombe Segmentary System," in *Continuity and Change in African Cultures*, ed. William R. Bascom and Melville J. Herskovits (Chicago and London: University of Chicago Press, 1959), pp. 168–186; Wolfe, "The Institution of Demba among the Ngonje Ngombe," *Zaire* 8 (October 1954): 843–851 et passim. Early and often inaccurate descriptions of the Ngombe may be found in Camille Coquilhat, *Sur le haut Congo* (Paris: J. Lebègue, 1888), pp. 207–208; Charles Le Maire, *La Région de l'Equateur* (Brussels: Imprimerie et Lithographie A. Lesigne, 1895), p. 19.

In early works the Ngombe were often treated as part of the mythical Bangala group. For example, see Cyrille Van Overbergh, *Les Bangala* (Brussels: Institut International de Bibliographie, 1907), pp. 56–65, 68–69. The myth of the Bangala has been treated in detail by Young in *Politics in the Congo*, pp. 242–246, and more recently in his *The Politics of Cultural Pluralism* (Madison: University of Wisconsin Press, 1976), pp. 171–173. The debate on the Bangala has not yet been laid to rest. See Mumbanza mwa Bawele, "Y a-t-il des Bangala?: Origine et extension du terme," *Zaire-Afrique*, no. 78 (October 1973), pp. 471–483; a critique by Gustave Hulstaert, "A propos des Bangala," *Zaire-Afrique*, no. 83 (March 1974), pp. 173–185; and a rejoinder by Mumbanza, "Les Bangala du fleuve sont-ils apparentés aux Mongo?" *Zaire-Afrique*, no. 90 (December 1974), pp. 625–632.

Although I have not paid detailed attention to the other ethnic groups in question, an extensive literature exists on the Mongo. In addition to the works by Van Der Kerken and Hustaert already cited, Hustaert, *Les Mongo: Aperçu général*, Archives d'éthnographie 5 (Tervuren: Musée Royal de l'Afrique Centrale, 1961) is useful. See, too, his "La Société politique nkundo," *Etudes zairoises* 2 (June–July 1974): 85–107. On the Mongwandi and Ngwaka, see H. Burssens, *Les Peuplades de l'entre Congo-Ubangi* (Tervuren: Annales du Musée Royal du Congo Belge, 1958). Unfortunately this work is not based on field research, but it remains—however limited—a useful introduction. On the Lokele, see Lokomba Baruti, "Structure et fonctionnement des institutions politiques traditionnelles chez les Lokele (Haut Zaire)," *Cahiers du CEDAF*, no. 8 (1972).

17. Région de l'Equateur, Division Régionale de l'Agriculture, *Rapport annuel 1974*, pp. 84–89, 91, 93. Such agricultural statistics are often inaccurate and must be treated as approximations.

18. Province de l'Equateur, *Rapport annuel économique 1957*, p. 10, cited in Paule Bouvier, *L'Accession du Congo belge à l'indépendance: Essai d'analyse sociologique* (Brussels: Editions de l'Institut de Sociologie, Université Libre de Bruxelles, 1965), p. 187.

19. Province de l'Equateur, *Conseil de Province 1954*, Première Partie, p. 23. This and all subsequent translations are mine unless otherwise noted.

20.   Young, *Politics in the Congo*, pp. 242–246 on the Bangala; Willame, *Les Provinces du Congo*, vol. 5, p. 17. In this context Mokolo's monograph "Poids socio-politique des ressortissants de l'Equateur à Kinshasa" is noteworthy, as is B. Verhaegen's "Les Associations congolaises à Léopoldville et dans le Bas-Congo de 1944 à 1958," *Etudes africaines du CRISP*, no. 112–113 (1970), pp. 11–17.

21.   This is not an unusually high percentage of students for a town the size of Lisala. In other small towns in Africa the percentage of students may vary from 20 to 45. See Michael G. Schatzberg, "Islands of Privilege: Small Cities in Africa and the Dynamics of Class Formation," paper presented at the Conference on the Small City and Regional Community, Stevens Point, Wisconsin, 30–31 March 1978, pp. 4–6.

22.   Samoff, *Tanzania: Local Politics and the Structure of Power*, pp. 7–8. Like Samoff, I am eclectic.

23.   Benoît Verhaegen, *Introduction à l'histoire immédiate: Essai de méthodologie qualitative* (Gembloux: Duculot, 1974).

CHAPTER 2

1.   Richard L. Sklar, *Nigerian Political Parties: Power in an Emergent African Nation* (Princeton: Princeton University Press, 1963), p. 230.

2.   Young, *Politics in the Congo*, p. 602.

3.   See Charles W. Anderson, Fred R. von der Mehden, and Crawford Young, *Issues of Political Development* (Englewood Cliffs, N.J.: Prentice-Hall, 1967); and Young, *The Politics of Cultural Pluralism*, for the evolution of his theoretical views on the important questions of ethnicity and cultural pluralism. In an earlier article Young tried—unsuccessfully, in my opinion—to compare Zaire and Uganda, using the crisis framework of the Social Science Research Council as a theoretical fulcrum. See his "Congo and Uganda: A Comparative Assessment," *Cahiers économiques et sociaux* 5 (October 1967): 379–400.

4.   Young, *Politics in the Congo*, p. 607.

5.   In addition to the general studies of Zairian politics cited in the first chapter, the following works are also important for the events listed. See René Lemarchand, *Political Awakening in the Belgian Congo: The Politics of Fragmentation* (Berkeley and Los Angeles: University of California Press, 1964); Herbert F. Weiss, *Political Protest in the Congo: The Parti Solidaire Africain during the Independence Struggle* (Princeton: Princeton University Press, 1967); Catherine Hoskyns, *The Congo since Independence: January 1960–December 1961* (London: Oxford University Press for the Royal Institute of International Affairs, 1965); Jules Gérard-Libois, *Katanga Secession*, trans. Rebecca Young (Madison: University of Wisconsin Press, 1966); Benoît Verhaegen, *Rébellions au Congo*, 2 vols. (Brussels: CRISP, 1966 and 1969); Edouard Bustin, *Lunda under Belgian Rule: The Politics of Ethnicity* (Cambridge, Mass., and London: Harvard University Press, 1975); and [Maurice Lovens], "Le Régime présidentiel au Zaire," *Etudes africaines du CRISP*, no. 144 (20 December 1972).

6.   Verhaegen, *Introduction à l'histoire immédiate*, p. 68.

7.   Ibid., pp. 68, 131, 170. Verhaegen's methodology has been greatly influenced by current discussions among European Marxist scholars—for instance, the emphasis on praxis, the commitment to societal transformation, and the importance of the dialectic.

8.   Immediate history can nevertheless be criticized on a number of grounds. The notion of crisis is ambiguous; the methodology may be limited to only those societies characterized by frequent upheavals; and the role of nonnational researchers in transforming a society that is not their own needs elaboration. Moreover, Verhaegen seems to have erected some sophisticated but unnecessary ideological paraphernalia around long-used social scientific methods. For a treatment of these ideas see Michael G. Schatzberg, "Bureaucracy, Business, Beer: The

Political Dynamics of Class Formation in Lisala, Zaire" (Ph.D. dissertation, University of Wisconsin—Madison, 1977), pp. 35–38.

9.   Willame, *Patrimonialism and Political Change in the Congo*, p. 2. This is an apt assessment.

10.   Ibid., p. 2.

11.   Ibid., p. 129.

12.   Ibid., pp. 77–101. This duality in Willame's work is most puzzling. In other contexts he has adopted a Marxist perspective. See, for example, his "Patriarchal Structures and Factional Politics: Toward an Understanding of the Dualist Society," *Cahiers d'études africaines* 12 (1973): 326–355. A skeptic might even suggest that the Weberian framework was a genuflection to the political exigencies of obtaining a Ph.D. in an American university.

13.   Mukenge Tshilemalema, "Businessmen of Zaire: Limited Possibilities for Capital Accumulation under Dependence" (Ph.D. dissertation, McGill University, 1974), p. 106. For early examples of this literature see L. Henrard, "Note sur la situation du commerce et de l'artisanat pratiqués par les indigènes au Centre Extra-Coutumier d'Elisabethville," *Problèmes sociaux congolais*, no. 7 (1948), pp. 100–118; and A. Van Cauwenbergh, "Le Développement du commerce et de l'artisanat indigènes à Léopoldville," *Zaire* 10 (June 1956): 637–654.

One such study, performed in Lubumbashi shortly after independence, reflected many of these concerns. Anselin noted that while there was a middle class in the city, it had unusual characteristics. He observed that it "was composed in large part of people whose independent activity is the last means of subsistence. The conscious choice of the situation is rarely frequent; one can therefore predict in this middle class an important diminution and a strong rotation in the number of African enterprises which compose it." M. Anselin, "La Classe moyenne indigène à Elisabethville," *Problèmes sociaux congolais*, no. 53 (June 1961), p. 109. For more on the composition of this class, see below.

14.   Bouvier, *L'Accession du Congo belge à l'indépendance*, p. 73.

15.   Young, *Politics in the Congo*, p. 74.

16.   B. Jewsiewicki, "La Contestation sociale et la naissance du prolétariat au Zaire au cours de la première moitié du XXe siècle," *Canadian Journal of African Studies* 10 (1976):69.

17.   Roger Anstey, "Belgian Rule in the Congo and the Aspirations of the 'Evolué' Class," in *Colonialism in Africa 1870–1960*, 5 vols. (Cambridge: Cambridge University Press, 1970), vol. 2: *The History and Politics of Colonialism 1914–1960*, ed. L. H. Gann and Peter Duignan, pp. 196–201, especially p. 200. See, too, L. Baeck, "An Expenditure Study of the Congolese Evolués of Leopoldville, Belgian Congo," in *Social Change in Modern Africa*, ed. Aidan Southall (London: Oxford University Press for the International African Institute, 1961), pp. 159–181. Also of interest in this regard is Patrice Lumumba, *Congo, My Country* (New York: Praeger, 1962), pp. 59, 68.

18.   Christian Comeliau, *Fonctions économiques et pouvoir politique: La Province de l'Uélé en 1963–1964* (Léopoldville: Institut de Recherches Economiques et Sociales, n.d. [1965]), pp. 24, 81, 82, 98.

19.   Ibid., pp. 87–98.

20.   Ibid., pp. 98–99.

21.   Jean-Louis Lacroix, *Industrialisation au Congo: La Transformation des structures économiques* (Paris and The Hague: Mouton, 1967), p. 352, n. 10.

22.   Ibid., pp. 199–200.

23.   Ibid., pp. 200, 211.

24.   Georges N. Nzongola, "The Bourgeoisie and Revolution in the Congo," *Journal of Modern African Studies* 8 (December 1970): 511–530.

25.   Ibid., pp. 517–520.

26.   Ibid. Nzongola's article has been criticized from a Marxist perspective by Paul Demunter, "Structure de classes et lutte des classes dans le Congo colonial," *Contradictions*, no. 1 (January–June 1972), pp. 67–109.

27.   Nzongola-Ntalaja, "Urban Administration in Zaire: A Study of Kananga, 1971–1973" (Ph.D. dissertation, University of Wisconsin—Madison, 1975), p. 98.

28.   Ibid., pp. 98–101. The entire description of five social classes is contained in these four pages, and it is almost as though the author included them as an afterthought. It will be noted that there are differences between the class structure and the categories described here and those presented in his earlier article. They are not crucial to my argument and probably represent the normal evolution of Nzongola's thought on the subject over a five-year period.

29.   Fred W. Riggs, *Administration in Developing Countries: The Theory of Prismatic Society* (Boston: Houghton Mifflin, 1964).

30.   Paul Demunter, *Luttes politiques au Zaire: Le Processus de politisation des masses rurales du Bas-Zaire* (Paris: Editions Anthropos, 1975), p. 105.

31.   Ibid., p. 106.

32.   Ibid. pp. 304–315, especially p. 304.

33.   Immanuel Wallerstein, "Class and Class Conflict in Contemporary Africa," *Canadian Journal of African Studies* 7 (1973): 375–376. On the myth of classlessness as a justification for the policies of the ruling elements, see Kenneth W. Grundy, "The 'Class Struggle' in Africa: An Examination of Conflicting Theories," *Journal of Modern African Studies* 2 (November 1964): 379–393.

34.   Georges Balandier, *Sens et puissance: Les Dynamiques sociales* (Paris: Presses Universitaires de France, 1971), p. 267.

35.   Colin Leys, *Underdevelopment In Kenya: The Political Econoy of Neo-Colonialism 1964–1972* (Berkeley and Los Angeles: University of California Press, 1974), p. xii.

36.   Leys, "Politics in Kenya: The Development of Peasant Society," *British Journal of Political Science* 1 (July 1971): 307.

37.   R. H. Jackson, "Political Stratification in Tropical Africa," *Canadian Journal of African Studies* 7 (1973): 381, 382.

38.   Sklar has cogently argued that "tribal movements may be created and instigated to action by the new men of power in furtherance of their own special interests which are, time and again, the constitutive interests of emerging social classes. Tribalism then becomes a mask for class privilege." Richard L. Sklar, "Political Science and National Integration—A Radical Approach," *Journal of Modern African Studies* 5 (May 1967): 6.

Sklar's point is valid, but there are often cases in which ethnicity has some independence as a variable and situations in which it may exist apart from the motives of the emerging social classes. It would be difficult, for example, to explain the Biafran secession on the basis of social class. My position, rather, is closer to that of Robin Cohen, who assigns to ethnicity a certain independence. See his "Class in Africa: Analytical Problems and Perspectives," in *The Socialist Register 1972*, ed. Ralph Miliband and John Savile (London: Merlin Press, 1972), p. 244.

39.   Georges Gurvitch, *Etudes sur les classes sociales* (Paris: Editions Gonthier, 1966), p. 234. This is also implicit in the work of Michel Merlier, who notes that a true industrial proletariat does not exist in Zaire. See his *Le Congo de la colonisation belge à l'indépendance* (Paris: François Maspero, 1962), p. 171.

40.   Anthony Giddens, *The Class Structure of the Advanced Societies* (London: Hutchinson University Library, 1973), p. 132. The footnotes in the remainder of this chapter reflect only partially my intellectual debt to this stimulating work.

41.   An example of this lack of flexibility is Majhemout Diop, *Histoire des classes sociales dan l'Afrique de l'ouest*, vol. 2: *Le Sénégal* (Paris: François Maspero, 1972), which is a standard and totally inappropriate Marxian analysis. In addition, see Kwame Nkrumah, *Class Struggle in Africa* (New York: International Publishers, 1970), and the earlier work of Raymond Barbé, who maintains, in relation to the African peasantry, that "by basing themselves on the spontaneous ideology of the peasants, on their more or less natural consciousness, these doctrines—which return to the populist theories refuted in his time by Lenin—can only mislead the movement, by refusing the authentic conditions of socialist transformations." Barbé, *Les Classes Sociales en Afrique noire* (Paris: Economie et Politique, 1964), p. 52.

Equally rigid is the attempt by V. L. Allen to group the wage earners and peasants under a single definitional heading. V. L. Allen, "The Meaning of the Working Class in Africa," *Journal of Modern African Studies* 10 (July 1972): 184. Mahmood Mamdani, *Politics and Class Formation in Uganda* (New York and London: Monthly Review Press, 1976); and Issa G. Shivji, *Class Struggles in Tanzania* (New York and London: Monthly Review Press, 1976), are other examples. In addition to Sklar's work, useful and intellectually supple studies include John Markakis, *Ethiopia: Anatomy of a Traditional Polity* (Oxford: Clarendon Press, 1974); and Hugues Bertrand, *Le Congo: Formation sociale et mòde de développement économique* (Paris: François Maspero, 1975).

42. Nzongola, "The Bourgeoisie and Revolution in the Congo," p. 519.

43. V. Y. Mudimbe, "Les Intellectuels zairois," *Zaire-Afrique*, no. 88 (October 1974), pp. 451–463, especially p. 451.

44. Ali A. Mazrui, "The English Language and Political Consciousness in British Colonial Africa," *Journal of Modern African Studies* 4 (November 1966): 298.

45. Ralf Dahrendorf, *Class and Class Conflict in Industrial Society* (Stanford: Stanford University Press, 1959), p. 126. The basic dichotomous notion did not, of course, originate with Marx. Ossowski traces the idea back as far as the Bible and observes that in the Christian world view "the dichotomic image of the social structure was transposed into the next world, the spatial metaphor finding a literal application in the topography of heaven and hell." See Stanislaw Ossowski, *Class Structure in the Social Consciousness*, trans. Sheila Patterson (New York: Free Press, 1963), p. 22. Ossowski further notes that throughout time the basic dichotomy has had three major manifestations, corresponding roughly to three categories of privileges enjoyed by some and denied to others: (1) the rulers versus the ruled; (2) the rich versus the poor; and (3) employers versus employees. Ibid., p. 23.

46. Frank Parkin, *Class Inequality and Political Order: Social Stratification in Capitalist and Communist Societies* (London: MacGibbon & Kee, 1971), p. 9. Parkin's views on the utility of the basic dichotomy may have changed since 1971. See Frank Parkin, ed., *The Social Analysis of Class Structure* (London: Tavistock Publications, 1974), p. 12. The passage in mind is cited in note 67.

47. Aidan W. Southall, "Stratification in Africa," in *Essays in Comparative Social Stratification*, ed. Leonard Plotnicov and Arthur Tuden (Pittsburgh: University of Pittsburgh Press, 1970), p. 234.

48. Giddens, *The Class Structure of the Advanced Societies*, p. 101.

49. On the question of false consciousness, see James C. Scott, *The Moral Economy of the Peasant: Rebellion and Subsistence in Southeast Asia* (New Haven and London: Yale University Press, 1976). Scott argues that "the concept of false consciousness overlooks the very real possibility that the actor's 'problem' is simply not one of misperception. It overlooks the possibility that he may, in fact, have his own durable standards of equity and exploitation—standards that lead him to judgments that are quite different from those of an outside observer equipped with a deductive theory." Ibid., p. 160.

50. Claude Rivière, "Classes et stratifications sociales en Afrique noire," *Cahiers internationaux de sociologie* 59 (1975): 287.

51. Robin Cohen, "Class in Africa: Analytical Problems and Perspectives," p. 241. Emphasis in original.

52. Karl Marx and Frederick Engels, *The German Ideology*, edited and with an introduction by C. J. Arthur (New York: International Publishers, 1970), p. 80.

53. This pattern is partially confirmed by a recent examination of urban policy in the Ivory Coast. Michael Cohen argues persuasively that "public authority precedes the acquisition of property" and that "government officials [have] used their positions to create both property and the rules for its use." Michael A. Cohen, *Urban Policy and Political Conflict in Africa: A Study of the Ivory Coast* (Chicago and London: University of Chicago Press, 1974), pp. 6, 62. In more general terms Parkin believes that "the ability of the dominant class to maintain a privileged position for themselves and their progeny rests largely on the fact that representatives of this class have greater access to or control over the various agencies which govern the allocation of rewards than have members or representatives of the subordinate class." Parkin, *Class Inequality and Political Order*, p. 27. See also Norman Birnbaum, "La Crise de la

sociologie marxiste," *l'homme et la société*, no. 23 (January, February, March 1972), pp. 23–29.

54.   Balandier, *Sens et puissance*, p. 270; Rivière, "Classes et stratifications sociales en Afrique noire," p. 289. Of note in this context is Richard Sklar's most recent work on Zambia, *Corporate Power in an African State: The Political Impact of Multinational Mining Companies in Zambia* (Berkeley, Los Angeles, London: University of California Press, 1975). Sklar argues against the use of the term *bureaucratic bourgeoisie*, popularized by Franz Fanon and René Dumont. He believes that it tends to underestimate the importance of the private business elite and proposes a new term, *managerial bourgeoisie*, which encompasses both the state managers and those in the private sector. While perhaps true in the Zambian context, in Zaire this group of private sector managers might more fruitfully be viewed as an appendage of the state. The state, of course, has come to exert more and more control over the economy. One of my major arguments will be that the almost complete interpenetration of these two groups makes such a distinction unnecessary. For Sklar's argument, ibid., pp. 198–199.

55.   In the case of Guinea, Claude Rivière has remarked that the state is more oppressive than capital thanks to its control of organized violence. Rivière, "Classes et stratifications sociales en Afrique noire," p. 290.

56.   Paul Mercier, "Remarques sur la signification du 'tribalisme' en Afrique noire," *Cahiers internationaux de sociologie* 31 (1961): 64, 65, 67.

57.   Jan Vansina, *Kingdoms of the Savanna* (Madison: University of Wisconsin Press, 1966), pp. 14–15.

58.   Young, *The Politics of Cultural Pluralism*, p. 11.

59.   Ibid., pp. 12–13.

60.   Dahrendorf, *Class and Class Conflict in Industrial Society*, p. 201.

61.   Marx wrote, "Insofar as millions of families live under economic conditions of existence that separate their mode of life, their interests and their cultural formation from those of the other classes and bring them into conflict with those classes, they form a class. Insofar as these small peasant proprietors are merely connected on a local basis, and the identity of their interests fails to produce a feeling of community, national links, or a political organization, they do not form a class." See Karl Marx, *The Eighteenth Brumaire of Louis Bonaparte*, in *Surveys from Exile*, ed. David Fernbach, trans. Ben Fowkes (New York: Vintage Books, 1974), p. 239.

62.   Nicos Poulantzas, "Les Classes sociales," *l'homme et la société*, no. 24–25 (April–September 1972), p. 23; Theontonio dos Santos, "The Concept of Social Classes," *Science and Society* 24 (Spring 1970): 188; Giddens, *The Class Structure of the Advanced Societies*, p. 192; and Max Weber, *From Max Weber: Essays in Sociology*, translated, edited, and with an introduction by H. H. Gerth and C. Wright Mills (New York: Oxford University Press, 1946), p. 405.

63.   Richard Centers, *The Psychology of Social Classes: A Study of Class Consciousness* (Princeton: Princeton University Press, 1949), pp. 27, 78; Georges Gurvitch, *The Spectrum of Social Time*, trans. Myrtle Korenbaum (Dordrecht, Holland: D. Reidel, 1964), p. 86.

64.   T. H. Marshall, *Citizenship and Social Class and Other Essays* (Cambridge: Cambridge University Press, 1950), pp. 90–91; Parkin, *Class Inequality and Political Order*, p. 13.

65.   Martin L. Kilson, Jr., "Nationalism and Social Classes in British West Africa," *Journal of Politics* 20 (May 1958): 374–375.

66.   Frank Parkin, "Strategies of Social Closure in Class Formation," p. 3. On the way in which Weber applied the notion of closure—in this case closure by marriage—see Weber, *From Max Weber*, p. 188.

67.   Parkin, "Strategies of Social Closure in Class Formation," p. 12. Emphasis in original.

68.   Ossowski, *Class Structure in the Social Consciousness*, p. 141.

69.   Jean-Paul Sartre, *Questions de méthode* (Paris: Gallimard, 1960), p. 177. Emphasis in original.

70.   Cohen, "Class in Africa: Analytical Problems and Perspectives," p. 248.

71.   There are two major areas of difference. The first concerns the so-called radical incompatibility of classes. Gurvitch maintains, wrongly, that it is impossible for one to be a

member of more than one class at a time. A second area of difference flows from the first. If an actor may identify with different classes in different contexts, it then follows that it is no longer possible to place him or her in a consistent location in the class structure. Compare Marshall, *Citizenship and Social Class*, p. 94.

Gerhard Lenski more realistically defines a power class as an "aggregation of persons in a society who stand in a similar position with respect to force or some specific form of institutionalized power." In light of this definition, "an individual may well be a member of half a dozen power classes. This is inevitable whenever the various forms of power are less than perfectly correlated with one another. To illustrate, in contemporary American society a single individual may be a member of the middle class with respect to property holdings, a member of the working class by virtue of his job in a factory, and a member of the Negro 'caste.' Each of the major roles he occupies, as well as his status in the property hierarchy, influences his chances of obtaining the things he seeks in life, and thus each places him in a specific class. Since these resources are so imperfectly correlated, he cannot be located in any single class." Gerhard E. Lenski, *Power and Privilege: A Theory of Social Stratification* (New York: McGraw-Hill, 1966), p. 75. Lenski is, however, primarily concerned with different dimensions of class as well as the influence of different roles. In the case of the collectivity policeman, for example, the actor may belong to different classes in different contexts while *retaining* the same role (that is, he is still a policeman).

72.   Giddens, *The Class Structure of the Advanced Societies*, p. 105. Emphasis in original.

73.   Lucien Goldmann, *Marxisme et sciences humaines* (Paris: Gallimard, 1970), p. 85.

74.   In partial support of this idea see Cohen, "Class in Africa: Analytical Problems and Perspectives," p. 238; and Rivière, "Classes et stratifications sociales en Afrique noire," p. 313.

75.   Giddens, *The Class Structure of the Advanced Societies*, pp. 106, 273.

76.   Sartre, *Questions de méthode*, p. 176.

77.   Balandier, *Sens et puissance*, p. 273.

78.   Parkin, *Class Inequality and Political Order*, p. 14.

CHAPTER 3

1.   Marc Bloch, *The Historian's Craft*, trans. Peter Putnam (Manchester: Manchester University Press, 1954), p. 26.

2.   Three interviews have been eliminated from this exercise. One was with a territorial commissioner present in Lisala before my research; two were with local clergymen. In the first case, I wished to deal only with those actually present in Lisala at the time of my work. In the second case, an N of two would not have permitted me to preserve the anonymity of the respondents.

3.   The "merging" of officially distinct levels of government has been noted elsewhere in Zaire. See Nzongola, "Urban Administration in Zaire," pp. 115, 142, 166–167.

4.   A further word about the methodology employed here is perhaps necessary. Modal career pattern A was compiled in the following manner. The birth date, 1930, was derived by figuring the average birth date of the eleven bureaucrats in this pattern. The number of years in school, the year studies were completed, the year service was begun, the year of arrival in Lisala, and the salary were calculated on the basis of averages of the eleven respondents. For nonnumerical variables such as religion, ethnic affiliation, and reason for entering the bureaucracy, I was guided by simple frequency counts. Thus, in pattern A, the Mongo ethnic group was chosen because six of the eleven bureaucrats were members of this group. Where there was no clear numerical preponderance, I was guided by an intuitive appreciation of the people involved and tried to present an overall picture that is faithful to reality. The method closely resembles what historians call prosopography. For a discussion of the role of prosopography in historical research, see Lawrence Stone, "Prosopography," *Daedalus* 100 (Winter 1971): 46–79. For an application

of this method to the African scene, see Helen Codère, *The Biography of an African Society, Rwanda 1900–1960: Based on Forty-eight Rwandan Autobiographies* (Tervuren: Musée Royal de l'Afrique Centrale, 1973).

5. At the time of my stay the official exchange rate between U.S. dollars and Zairian currency, the zaire (Z), was Z1.00 = $2.00. There was a subsequent devaluation, but for convenience I use the old exchange rate throughout. The dollar equivalent of any sum is therefore twice the total in zaires. Parenthetically, Z1.00 is divided into 100 makuta (k).

6. Chiefs appointed by the Belgians were usually given medals to symbolize their authority.

7. Interview, Lisala, 13 November 1974, no. 1, p. 2.

8. Interview, Lisala, 6 February 1975, no. 9, p. 2.

9. One service chief noted that "it sometimes happens that orders given are not executed because the agents of execution do not understand them." Interview, Lisala, 4 April 1975, no. 22, p. 3.

10. This pattern may have been especially characteristic of the early 1950s. Similarly, in Lisala today the state usually pays better than the private sector, but there is evidence that this is not true everywhere in Zaire. Seniors at the National University at Kinsangani would much prefer to seek employment in the private sector because they perceive greater financial rewards there. See Kasongo Ngoyi Makita Makita et al., "Les Etudiants et les élèves de Kisangani (1974–1975): Aspirations, opinions et conditions de vie," *Cahiers du CEDAF*, nos. 7–8 (1977), p. 100.

11. Interview, Lisala, 21 November 1974, no. 24, p. 1.

12. *Débrouillez-vous* and Article 15 are common expressions in Zaire that refer to the general phenomenon of fending for oneself by whatever means necessary. The latter term stems from Albert Kalonji's Kasai secessionist state of 1960. His constitution had fourteen articles, but no formal budget. When asked how Kasaian bureaucrats would get on without salaries, they were told *"débrouillez-vous."* This watchword became "Article 15" of the constitution. David J. Gould, "Local Administration in Zaire and Underdevelopment," *Journal of Modern African Studies* 15 (September 1977): 359.

13. The existence of blacksmiths in the antecedent generations of other groups needs some comment. Three of the seventy respondents had either fathers or grandfathers indentifiable as blacksmiths. (In one case, both the father and grandfather had this status.) The important point here, as Vansina reminds us, is that blacksmithing "was therefore a status as much as an occupation. People did not just become smiths. The craft was hereditary, often learned from one's father, and the tools were inherited from the father. . . . The craft was thus limited to ascribed status groups, but smiths were not a caste . . . because they were free to marry whom they chose." Jan Vansina, *The Tio Kingdom of the Middle Congo 1880–1892* (London, New York, Toronto: Oxford University Press for the International African Institute, 1973), p. 142. That even three of the seventy respondents would have ancestors with this status seems to argue for the proposition that high traditional status has tended to reproduce itself over time by adapting to the new avenues of upward mobility.

14. Jacques S. Kazadi wa Dile, *Politiques salariales et développement en République démocratique du Congo* (Paris: Editions Universitaires, 1970), pp. 47–48.

15. The Z12–25 figure comes from Guy Gran, "Policy Making and Historic Process: Zaire's Permanent Development Crisis," paper presented at the African Studies Association meeting, Boston, 3–6 November 1976, p. 2. Jean-Philippe Peemans puts the average peasant money income at $2–6 per month. See his "The Social and Economic Development of Zaire since Independence: An Historical Outline," *African Affairs* 74 (April 1975): 169.

16. *Matabiche* is a bribe. Such "presents" and "considerations" are required before many simple administrative tasks will be performed.

17. Field Log, 19 August 1975, p. 112.

18. An analysis of the wealth controlled by the Catholic church is beyond the scope of this work. Suffice it to say that in the Diocese of Lisala there are ranches, plantations, farms, garages, and stores owned and operated by the church.

19. Young, *Politics in the Congo*, pp. 10–19. Young's presentation of the colonial behemoth as a "virtually seamless web" has been criticized by Jan Vansina. See Vansina, "Les Kuba et

l'administration territoriale de 1919 à 1960," *Cultures et développement* 2 (1972): 283. Perhaps the differences between these two interpretations are more a result of the difference in their respective levels of analysis than anything else.

20. Kasongo's study confirms that this desire is fully shared by many students. See his "Les Etudiants et les èléves de Kisangani," p. 42.

21. "The Queen had only one way of settling all difficulties, great or small. 'Off with his head!' " Lewis Carroll, *Alice's Adventures in Wonderland* and *Through the Looking-Glass: And What Alice Found There*, chap. 8.

22. Field Log, 18 March 1975, p. 60.

23. On the question of solidarity, see Mpase Nselenge Mpeti, *L'Evolution de la solidaritè traditionnelle en milieu rural et urbain au Zaire: Le Cas des Ntomba et des Basengele du Lac Mai-Ndombe* (Kinshasa: Presses Universitaires du Zaire, 1974).

24. Mukenge has discussed the ways in which family obligations can act as a brake on Zairian businesses. See his "Businessmen of Zaire," p. 397.

25. Interview, Lisala, 18 February 1975, no. 10, p. 2.

26. Figures for the educational expansion since independence may be found in Thérèse Verheust, "L'Enseignement en République du Zaire," *Cahiers du CEDAF*, no. 1 (1974), p. 45.

27. *Mambenga* (Mbandaka), 13 April 1974, p. 7.

28. Interview, Lisala, 29 April 1975, no. 48, p. 3.

29. In the Zone of Bongandanga, for example, which has no real administrative or educational center, there are thirty-one primary schools and six secondary schools. On the primary level 9.53 percent (N = 956) of the children's parents work for the state; 73.38 percent (N = 7,355) are village farmers; and 17.07 percent (N = 1,711) work in the private sector. On the secondary level 17.91 percent (N = 86) work for the state; 62.08 percent (N = 298) are village farmers; and 20 percent (N = 96) work in the private sector. Like the data on Lisala, these figures come from the JMPR census of schools.

30. A similar pattern of overrepresentation of children whose parents work for the state is evident in the data presented by Kasongo. Thirty-eight percent of their sample of Kisangani high school seniors had fathers working for the state, while only 20 percent had fathers who were farmers or fishermen. See Kasongo et al., "Les Etudiants et les élèves de Kisangani," pp. 34–35. Studies of schools in Cameroon and Algeria make similar points. See Jacques Champaud, "L'Utilisation des équipements tertiaires dans l'ouest du Cameroun," in *La Croissance urbaine en Afrique noire et à Madagascar*, vol. 1 (Paris: Centre National de la Recherche Scientifique, 1972), p. 413; and C. Nesson, "Ecole et promotion sociale au Sahara algérien: Les Élèves de première du lycée de Touggourt (1964–1970)," in *Maghreb & Sahara: Études géographiques offertes à Jean Despois* (Paris: Société de Géographie, 1973), pp. 289–306.

31. Interview, Lisala, 17 June 1975, no. 49, p. 5; and Field Log, 4 July 1975, pp. 92–93. There is also much administrative correspondence on this subject. Administrative correspondence, 13 August 1974, 14 August 1974, and November 1970. Unless otherwise noted, all administrative correspondence and other documents were consulted in the Archives, Mongala Subregion, Political Affairs Department, Lisala. I have chosen to cite all letters, telegrams, and similar documents as "administrative correspondence" for simplicity and also to guard the anonymity of certain respondents. Complete information on any document is available on request.

CHAPTER 4

1. Interview, Lisala, 4 February 1975, no. 28, p. 4.
2. Interview, Lisala, 25 June 1975, no. 56, p. 3.
3. Ibid., p. 1.

4. Administrative correspondence, 27 December 1973.

5. Région de l'Equateur, Division Régionale de l'Agriculture, *Rapport annuel 1974*, p. 86. Emphasis in original.

6. Giddens, *The Class Structure of the Advanced Societies*, p. 130. This notion of exploitation is essentially Weberian and departs from the Marxian idea of surplus value. On the general question of exploitation one might also consult James C. Scott, "Exploitation in Rural Class Relations: A Victim's Perspective," *Comparative Politics* 7 (July 1975):489–532; and George Dalton, "How Exactly Are Peasants 'Exploited'?" *American Anthropologist* 76 (September 1974):553–561. Dalton puts forth two definitions. The first is a commonsense meaning, which amounts to "self-gain at another's expense." The second, or technical, meaning is the coerced payment of surplus to nonpeasants.

7. I have deliberately avoided the term *peasant* for two reasons. First, there is much debate among anthropologists as to the word's precise meaning. Second, since Faller's classic article there has also been confusion about the concept's applicability in Africa. For those interested in the question, the following works might be consulted: Eric Wolf, *Sons of the Shaking Earth* (Chicago and London: University of Chicago Press, 1959), p. 67; Wolf, *Peasants* (Englewood Cliffs, N.J.: Prentice-Hall, 1966), pp. 3–4, 50–51; Walter Goldschmidt and Evalyn Jacobson-Kunkel, "The Structure of the Peasant Family," *American Anthropologist* 73 (October 1971): 1058–1076; and John S. Saul and Roger Woods, "African Peasantries," in *Essays on the Political Economy of Africa*, ed. Giovanni Arrighi and John S. Saul (New York and London: Monthly Review Press, 1973), p. 407. All these sources deal with definitional questions.

The relevance of this concept to the African experience is questioned in Lloyd A. Fallers, "Are African Cultivators to Be Called 'Peasants'?" *Current Anthropology* 2 (1961): 108–110. Sharp dissents to the exclusion of peasantries from Africa may be found in William Derman, *Serfs, Peasants, and Socialists: A Former Serf Village in the Republic of Guinea* (Berkeley and Los Angeles: University of California Press, 1973), p. 63 et passim; and Derman, "Peasants: The African Exception? Reply to Goldschmidt and Kunkel," *American Anthropologist* 74 (June 1972): 779–782.

8. A full examination of these reforms would take us well beyond the intended scope of this chapter. The law of 5 January 1973 is extremely important, however, and I hope to examine its effects at a later date.

9. For the colonial rules and regulations concerning the head tax, see Royaume de Belgique, Ministère des Colonies, *Receuil à l'usage des fonctionnaires et des agents du service territorrial du Congo belge*, 4th ed., (Brussels: Société Anonyme M. Weissenbruch, 1925), pp. 254–259. On the transition between the head tax and the CPM in 1960, see Hugues Leclercq, "L'inflation, sa cause: Le Désordre des finances publiques," in *Independance, inflation, développement: L'economie congolaise de 1960 à 1965*, ed. Institut de Recherches Economiques et Souales [IRES] (Paris and The Hague: IRES and Editions Mouton, 1968), pp. 109–110. Current CPM rates were set by decree of the Political Affairs Department on 7 June 1975. See "Arrêté Départemental No. 0154 du 7 juin 1975 fixant pour l'exercice 1975 les taux de la Contribution Personnelle Minimum et determinant les teintes de fond des acquits de payment et d'exemption."

10. Administrative correspondence, 27 June 1962, 16 September 1967; "Ordonnance-Loi No. 69–012 du 12 mars 1969 portant organisation des collectivités locales," articles 70; and administrative correspondence, 13 May 1970.

11. Merlier, *Le Congo de la colonisation belge à l'indépendance*, p. 82. Peemans notes that before 1940 yearly poll taxes absorbed 20 to 60 percent of the Zairians' annual cash income. See Jean-Philippe Peemans, "Capital Accumulation in the Congo under Colonialism: The Role of the State," in *Colonialism in Africa 1870–1960*, 5 vols. (Cambridge: Cambridge University Press, 1975), vol. 4: *The Economics of Colonialism*, ed. Peter Duignan and L. H. Gann, p. 175.

12. Scott, *The Moral Economy of the Peasant*, pp. 52, 93. Emphasis in original.

13. "Compte rendu de la réunion mensuelle du parti présidée le 19 juillet 1972, pour le mois de juillet"; and Zone de Bumba, *Rapport annuel des affaires politiques, 1974*, p. 20.

14. Charles E. Lindblom, "The Science of 'Muddling Through,' " *Public Administration Review* 19 (1959): 79–88; and Aaron Wildavsky, *The Politics of the Budgetary Process* (Boston:

Little, Brown, 1964). In Wildavsky's more recent work he argues that finance ministries in poor countries tend to deflate rather than inflate budget estimates in order to reduce uncertainty. In general his arguments are not relevant to budgeting at this level in Zaire because he deals only with the central government, assumes more political give and take than may actually occur in a highly centralized system, and assumes that financial officials operate in good faith with the well-being of their governmental unit—be it national, local, or departmental—uppermost in their minds. See, though, Aaron Wildavsky, *Budgeting: A Comparative Theory of the Budgetary Process* (Boston, Toronto: Little, Brown, 1975), pp. 136–165, especially p. 162.

15. F. G. Bailey, *Stratagems and Spoils: A Social Anthropology of Politics* (New York: Schocken Books, 1969).

16. Collectivité de Ngombe-Mombangi, *Comptes des recettes et des dépenses, 1974*. Of the Z6,429.00, the chief in question actually collected Z4,312.34 under this rubric. The difference was carried over and incorporated into the next year's estimates so the chief would not lose his indemnities.

17. Administrative correspondence, 9 May 1973.

18. Field Log, 3 August 1975, p. 106.

19. Ibid., 10 August 1975, pp. 112–113. *Salongo* is discussed below.

20. Figures on the average educational level of the collectivity employees are derived from collectivity personnel documents, 1974.

21. Bureaucratic efficiency reports, 1973.

22. Field Log, 11 July 1975, p. 97.

23. Administrative correspondence, 5 June 1974, 14 May 1974, and 23 June 1975.

24. This figure is arrived at by dividing Z1,118.12 by 12 and again by the number of policemen.

25. We get the sum of Z2.30 by dividing the yearly average shortfall (Z1,152.22) by 12 and again by the number of administrative personnel.

26. Interviews, Lisala, 21 March 1975, no. 30, p. 3; and 7 March 1975, no. 36, p. 4.

27. Interview, Lisala, 3 May 1975, no. 37, p. 6.

28. Collectivité de Mongala-Motima, *Prévisions budgétaires, 1975.*

29. Collectivité de Boso-Simba, *Comptes des recettes et des dépenses, 1974*; and administrative correspondence, 25 October 1972. These expenses were roughly 28 percent of the budget.

30. Administrative correspondence, 11 October 1974; Field Log, 13 September 1975, p. 119.

31. Administrative correspondence, 23 July 1975, 25 July 1975, 21 January 1973.

32. Administrative correspondence, 19 April 1973, 23 September 1969, 3 July 1972, 19 November 1974.

33. Administrative correspondence, 22 May 1975.

34. Administrative correspondence, 15 August 1972.

35. Interview, Lisala, 12 August 1975, no. 44, p. 3.

36. Administrative memorandum, 18 October 1974, p. 3. The citation is from administrative correspondence, 16 June 1975.

37. "P. V. de la réunion de service tenue lundi 10 avril 1972." Archives, Mongala Subregion, Political Affairs Department, Lisala.

38. Field Log, 28 March 1975, p. 63; and interview, Lisala, 18 July 1975, no. 43, pp. 5, 6.

39. Administrative correspondence, 26 May 1972; "Rapport administratif relatif au licenciement massif du personnel administratif de la collectivité de la Loeka," 22 June 1972; and "Procès verbal de la réunion de service tenue le 16 juin 1972." Archives, Mongala Subregion, Political Affairs Department, Lisala.

40. Roger Anstey, *King Leopold's Legacy: The Congo under Belgian Rule 1908–1960* (London: Oxford University Press, 1966), p. 152; Mulambu Mvuluya, "Cultures obligatoires et colonisation dans l'ex-Congo belge," *Cahiers du CEDAF*, no. 6–7 (1974), p. 94; "Ordonnance-Loi No. 69–012 du 12 mars 1969 portant organisation des collectivités locales," article 59; administrative correspondence, 12 June 1974, 22 April 1971.

41. Région de l'Equateur, Division Régionale de l'Agriculture, *Rapport annuel 1974*, p. 1;

administrative correspondence, 25 December 1974; interview, Lisala, 1 July 1975, no. 41, p. 3; Field Log, 4 July 1975, p. 93; administrative correspondence, 6 August 1974; and Field Log, 18 June 1975, p. 87.

42. The responsibility for attributing buying zones is now handled by the Office National des Céréales (ONACER). Interview, Lisala, 1 July 1975, no. 41, p. 3; administrative correspondence, 5 March 1974, 21 February 1975, and 19 March 1975.

43. Administrative correspondence, 22 February 1974.

44. "Rapport produits agricoles invendus," Businga, 21 April 1975; "Compte rendu de la réunion annuelle des inspecteurs sous-régionaux des affaires économiques tenue à Mbandaka de 29 mai au 3 juin 1975"; Région du Shaba, Division Régionale de l'Agriculture, *Rapport annuel 1974*, p. 6; and Région du Haut-Zaire, Division Régionale de l'Agriculture, *Rapport annuel 1974*, p. 52.

45. "Prise de contact du Commissaire de District," 21 January 1969; "Premier rapport du Commissaire de District," 10 February 1969; "Rapport effectué du 10 au 19 mai 1972 dans les territoires de Businga-Mobayi-Mbongo-Bumba et Bongandanga," 25 May 1972; "Rapport d'activitiés mois de février 1972," 8 March 1972; and interview, Lisala, 18 July 1975, no. 43, p. 3.

46. Zone de Lisala, *Rapport annuel des affaires politiques, 1972*, administrative section, p. 4.

47. "Memorandum à l'intention du président régional et gouverneur de la province de l'Equateur," 13 November 1969; and administrative correspondence, 9 June 1971.

48. Interview, Lisala, 16 June 1975, no. 23, p. 4; Zone de Mobayi-Mbongo, *Rapport annuel des affaires politiques, 1974*, p. 7.

49. Administrative correspondence, 25 October 1971, 12 August 1974, 2 January 1974, 19 February 1971; "Rapport d'activités mensuelles du Comité de Zone du MPR pour le [sic] mois d'août, septembre, et octobre 1974," 8 November 1974; administrative correspondence, 7 December 1972, 26 September 1973, 26 March 1975.

50. Administrative correspondence, 18 January 1971; and interview, Lisala, 4 February 1975, no. 28, p. 4.

51. The Kitawalists, who live in the forest, are the most notable example. It is impossible to say with certainty how many people live in these communities, but conservative estimates put their number at about ten thousand in Equateur alone.

52. Administrative correspondence, 3 April 1975, 29 March 1973, 2 August 1974.

53. Scott, *The Moral Economy of the Peasant*, p. 226.

54. The first of these points is underscored by the Zairian army's minimal performance against rebels who invaded Shaba both in 1977 and in 1978. These routs notwithstanding, the Zairian military was still able to deal quickly and brutally with antigovernment demonstrations in Idiofa in January 1978. Reports indicate that as many as 2,000 people were killed. See *West Africa* (London), 6 March 1978, p. 483; ibid., 13 March 1978, p. 537; and *Afrique-Asie* (Paris), 20 March–2 April 1978, p. 24.

55. Administrative correspondence, 3 April 1975, 24 October 1968, 14 June 1972, 25 September 1972, 2 January 1973; and interview, Lisala, 16 June 1975, no. 23, p. 5. In this account I have not mentioned the Disciplinary Brigade of the party youth wing. They, too, are often guilty of the same sorts of abuse. The annual JMPR report for 1974 noted that "our elements of the Mongala Disciplinary Brigade do not behave as they should. Most of them are undisciplined and incorrigible. . . . The program which we have outlined for them is not always followed and respected." "Rapport annuel d'activités de la JMPR Mongala exercise 1974."

56. Engulu Baanga Mpongo Bakokele Lokanga, "La Territoriale et la radicalisation du M.P.R.," exposé aux auditeurs de la Session Mobutu Sese Soko de l'Institut Makanda Kabobi, Kinshasa-N'Sélé, 5 September 1974, cited in Thomas M. Callaghy, "State Formation and Centralization of Power in Zaire: Mobutu's Pre-eminent Public Policy," paper presented at the African Studies Association meeting, Boston, 3–6 November 1976, p. 20.

57. Such instances are not rare. See administrative correspondence, 2 October 1970.

58. Nzongola, "Urban Administration in Zaire," p. 316.

59. Karl A. Wittfogel, *Oriental Despotism: A Comparative Study of Total Power* (New Haven and London: Yale University Press, 1957), pp. 255–256.

CHAPTER 5

1. The original idea for a study of beer stems from a series of conversations with my colleague Okello Oculi. A previous and slightly different version of this chapter was delivered at the annual meeting of the African Studies Association, Boston, 3–6 November 1976.

2. Interview, Lisala, 21 April 1975, no. 59, p. 2.

3. One interesting but partial exception is G. Bernier and A. Lambrechts, "Etude sur les boissons fermentées du Katanga," *Problèmes sociaux congolais*, no. 48 (March 1960), pp. 5–41. 41. The authors made a sustained effort to measure the economic importance of indigenous alcoholic beverages in one Katanga village. It should be made clear from the outset that this chapter deals *only* with beer that is produced in breweries. A study of the sort carried out by Bernier and Lambrechts would not have been feasible in a town the size of Lisala, as the measurement difficulties they experienced would have been compounded a hundredfold. A second, more partial exception is Samoff, who discusses the politics of liquor licensing in Moshi, Tanzania. See his *Tanzania: Local Politics and the Structure of Power*, pp. 59–73.

4. République de Zaire, Département de l'Economie Nationale, *Conjoncture économique: année 1973 et 1ᵉ trimestre 1974* 14 (December 1974):229–233. In 1974 Zaire produced 5,723,000 hectoliters (hl) of beer. The second leading producer, South Africa, accounted for 4,948,000 hl. Zaire was third to Zambia and Gabon in per capita consumption (Zaire, 23.62 liters; Zambia, 57.54 liters; and Gabon, 42.88 liters).

5. Jean-Louis Lacroix, *Industrialisation au Congo*, pp. 259–260, 316. Lacroix also discusses the importance and effects of the industry on pp. 261–263. Jean-Philippe Peemans, *Diffusion du progrès économique et convergence des prix; le cas Congo-Belgique, 1900–1960: La Formation du système des prix et salaires dans une économie dualiste* (Louvain: Editions Nauwelaerts, 1968), p. 142.

6. For example, in 1974 the United States produced 179,604,000 hl; Belgium, 14,604,000 hl.

7. One 0.72-liter bottle is roughly equivalent to two 12-ounce bottles. In many respects the figure of Z6.60 per year masks as much as it shows. In the first place, most women and children do not drink much. Second, I have used the official government price for these calculations. But the prescribed price almost always varies from region to region. Furthermore, it is rarely, if ever, enforced. The net result is that the amount spent on beer is much greater than the government price would indicate. In addition, the per capita income figure of Z50 is almost surely an overestimate. It is thus probable that expenditures for beer represent a much higher percentage of the per capita income than the conservative figures presented here would lead one to believe.

9. See table 5 in chapter 1 for these calculations.

10. In general, Houyoux found that the monthly expenditures for beer were higher in Kinshasa. In 1969 he calculated that each household in the capital spent about Z4.01 for beer per month. It should be pointed out that there are two major breweries in Kinshasa and none in Lisala. Consumption there is thus less dependent upon the whims of the distributive system. See Joseph Houyoux, *Budgets ménagers, nutrition et mode de vie à Kinshasa* (Kinshasa: Presses Universitaires du Zaire, 1973), p. 141.

11. Interview, Lisala, 30 May 1975, no. 63, p. 2.

12. Lacroix, *Industrialisation au Congo*, p. 263. Another crucial economic dimension will not be discussed here for it would take us well beyond our chosen focus: namely, that Zaire is dependent upon Europe and North America for the hops and malt necessary for the beer industry.

13. Field Log, 22 May 1975, p. 79.

14. Administrative correspondence, 26 July 1975.

15. Field Log, 6 October 1975, p. 121.

16. Interview, Lisala, 26 May 1975, no. 61, p. 4.

17. Field Log, 13 September 1975, pp. 115–116.

18. Interview, Lisala, 11 June 1975, no. 65, p. 4.

19. Field Log, 6 October 1975, p. 121.

20. Field Log, 22 September 1975, p. 118.
21. Field Log, 10 April 1975, p. 68.
22. Field Log, 2 July 1975, pp. 91–92.
23. Regional Archives, Economic Affairs Department, Mbandaka. "Compte rendu de la réunion annuelle des inspecteurs sous régionaux des affaires économiques tenue à Mbandaka du 29 mai au 3 juin 1975."
24. Interview, Lisala, 22 June 1975, no. 66, p. 5.
25. *Mambenga*, 4 January 1975, p. 10; ibid., 8 February 1975, p. 9.
26. Archives, Mongala Subregion, Political Affairs Department, Lisala. "Calcul des prix de vente de la bière locale en provenance de la brasserie de Mbandaka."
27. Interview, Lisala, 1 July 1975, no. 41, p. 4.
28. Administrative correspondence, 9 March 1971.
29. Administrative correspondence, 9 September 1973, 28 July 1975.
30. Interview, Lisala, 3 May 1975, no. 37, p. 9.
31. Cité de Lisala, *Comptes des recettes et des dépenses, 1973.*
32. Nzongola, "Urban Administration in Zaire," p. 140.
33. Administrative correspondence, 26 June 1970.
34. Ibid., 6 October 1973, 14 October 1972.
35. Ibid., 18 December 1972, 18 September 1973; administrative decision, 30 December 1972. At that time each likuta (1k, $0.02) was further divided into 100 sengi.
36. Administrative correspondence, 26 February 1974, 20 March 1974.
37. Ibid.
38. Ibid., 11 October 1974.
39. Ibid., 12 November 1974.
40. Beer is also of social significance and has been incorporated into the daily social life of Lisala's residents. For a discussion of this see Schatzberg, "Bureaucracy, Business, Beer," pp. 235–237, 374.
41. Administrative correspondence, 26 June 1970.

CHAPTER 6

1. Engulu Baangampongo Bakokele Lokunga, Vigilance et engagement révolutionnaire," exposé aux cadres de la JMPR en session spéciale de l'Institut Makanda Kabobi, N'Sélé, 1 March 1975, p. 5.
2. By way of a caveat I deal neither with the general subject of party ideology nor the question of the MPR's efficacy in inducing change. Those interested in ideology are referred to N. Tutashinda, "Les Mystifications de l' 'authenticité,' " *La Pensée*, no. 175 (June 1974), pp. 68–81; and Nzongola-Ntalaja, "The Authenticity of Neocolonialism: Ideology and Class Struggles in Zaire," paper presented at the African Studies Association meeting, Boston, 3–6 November 1976. For skeptical views of the party's prowess and the intentions of its leaders, see Cléophas Kamitatu, *La Grande mystification du Congo-Kinshasa: Les Crimes de Mobutu* (Paris: François Maspero, 1971), pp. 212–214; Wyatt MacGaffey, "Revolution or Repression?: The View From Matadi," *Africa Report* 16 (January 1971): 18, 20; Nzongola, "Urban Administration in Zaire," pp. 1–2, 316 et passim. Compare, though, Alan P. Merriam, "Politics and Change in a Zairian Village," *Africa-Tervuren* 26 (1975): 18–22. Finally, questions of party structure will be treated in a cursory fashion, only to provide the reader with the background necessary to understand the analyses that follow.
3. Much of this section is based on the following sources: Jules Gérard-Libois, ed., *Congo 1967* (Brussels and Kinshasa: CRISP and INEP, 1969), pp. 91–128; Office National de la Recherche et du Développement (ONRD), *Année politique au Congo 1968* (Kinshasa: ONRD,

1970), pp. 19–28; [Maurice Lovens], "Le Régime présidentiel au Zaire"; Maurice Lovens, "La R.D.C., du Congrès de la N'Sélé au nouveau mandat présidentiel (mai–décembre 1970) I," *Etudes africaines du CRISP*, no. 124 (30 January 1971); Callaghy, "State Formation and Centralization of Power in Zaire: Mobutu's Pre-eminent Public Policy," pp. 22–25; and Gatarayiha Majinya, Kangafu Gudumbagana, and Didier De Lannoy, "Aspects de la réforme administrative au Zaire: l'Administration publique et la politique de 1965 à 1975," *Cahiers du CEDAF*, nos. 4–5 (1976).

    4.   To avoid later confusion let me inject a word on party terminology. Between 1968 and 1972 the party and the state used different terms for each of their respective levels. The party's region corresponded to the state's province; the subregion to the district; the section to the territory; the subsection to the sector, chieftaincy, or *cité*; the cell to the *groupement*; and the subcell to the village. In 1972 the state adopted most of the party's terminology. Since then the names used by the state-party are region, subregion, zone (former territory and section), collectivity (former sector and subsection), locality (former *groupement* or cell), and sublocality (former village or subcell). For clarity I have used the post-1972 state-party terms throughout.

    5.   Gérard-Libois, *Congo 1967*, p. 104.

    6.   This change may actually have occurred in 1971. The Administrative circular of 11 January 1972 outlined the modifications.

    7.   *Salongo* (Kinshasa), 7 November 1974, p. 5. The Constitution of 15 August 1974, which declares that the MPR is the only institution in Zaire, may be found in "Documents," *Etudes zairoises*, no. 2 (June–July 1974), pp. 209–230.

    8.   Callaghy, "State Formation and Centralization of Power in Zaire," p. 23.

    9.   Frantz Fanon, *Les Damnés de la terre* (Paris: François Maspero, 1968), p. 112.

    10.   Interview, Lisala, 17 April 1975, no. 37, p. 2; and interview, Mbankada, 29 August 1975, no. 46, pp. 2–3. Note the discrepancy between the interview data and the written documentation. In general my respondents tended to view popular reaction *en gros* rather than day-to-day operations as paramount. Undeniably, people in Mongala did have enthusiastic initial reactions to the MPR. Although the citizenry was in favor, the implantation of the party machinery was fraught with difficulties.

    11.   Administrative correspondence, 30 September 1968, 17 March 1970.

    12.   Administrative and MPR reports for the zones of Mobayi-Mbongo, Bongandanga, and Bumba, 1969–70.

    13.   Ibid.

    14.   Administrative correspondence, 27 July 1970.

    15.   Field Log, 22 December 1974, p. 19; Field Log, 20 July 1975, p. 102; administrative correspondence, 28 April 1973; and bureaucratic efficiency reports, 1973.

    16.   Such cells were tried for a time, but were eliminated in 1971 because of the problem in reconciling conflicts between residential and professional *encadrement*. See Gatarayiha et al., "Aspects de la réforme administrative au Zaire," p. 55.

    17.   Administrative correspondence, 11 July 1972.

    18.   Ibid., 18 August 1972, 9 October 1973, 9 December 1974.

    19.   Interview, Lisala, 27 November 1974, no. 26, p. 3.

    20.   Field Log, 3 January 1975, p. 21; Field Log, 20 July 1975, p. 102.

    21.   Administrative decision, 25 October 1974.

    22.   Interview, Lisala, 4 February 1975, no. 31, p. 4.

    23.   Interview, Kinshasa, 8 October 1975, no. 71, p. 3.

    24.   While especially true at the subregional and zonal levels, this may not have been so at the regional level.

    25.   The sketches of these two officials are drawn from their résumés, which form part of the 1970 Election File.

    26.   Police report for November 1968, 13 December 1968. See, too, administrative correspondence, 27 October 1969, 22 November 1969, ? September 1971.

    27.   "Ordonnance No. 73-250 du 3 septembre 1973 portant le statut des authorités chargés de l'administration des circonsciptions territoriales."

28.   The cited document is not dated, but on the basis of internal evidence it can be placed between 16 March and 9 July 1968. It is a letter from the first secretary of the MPR to all provincial presidents of the party.

29.   In most cases the money was never refunded. As late as 1975 there were still active exchanges of letters from former candidates to party authorities claiming these refunds.

30.   Administrative correspondence, 5 July 1971.

31.   Ibid., 15 October 1973, 21 May 1974.

32.   Field Log, 10 April 1975, pp. 68–69.

33.   1970 Election File, no. 3.

34.   In addition, all the candidacies at the national, regional, and subregional levels were rated "elite" by the subregional committee.

35.   This case probably constitutes an exception to the general rule. The candidate was a long-term employee of the immense plantation at Binga. The authorities in Kinshasa may have wanted to ensure that this important agro-industrial enterprise was represented in the new legislature.

36.   Maurice Lovens, "La R.D.C., du Congrèe de la N'Sélé au nouveau mandat présidentiel (mai–décembre 1970) II," *Etudes africaines du CRISP*, no. 125 (20 March 1971), p. 10.

37.   République Démocratique du Congo, Assemblée Nationale, *Compte rendu analytique*, no. 14/71 (4 October 1971), p. 4.

38.   Ibid., no. 34/72 (5 May 1972), p. 4. Emphasis in original.

39.   Interview, Lisala, 9 August 1975, no. 44, p. 4.

CHAPTER 7

1.   Chinua Achebe, *A Man of the People* (London, Ibadan, Nairobi: Heinemann Educational Books, 1966), p. 97.

2.   Interview, Kinshasa, 8 October 1975, no. 71, p. 5. The term *acquirer* (*acquéreur* in French) became a widely used expression denoting Zairians who took over European enterprises after 30 November 1973. For an analysis of the connotation of the word *acquirer*, see chapter 8, especially the section entitled "30 November and Consciousness."

3.   "Discours présidentiel de politique générale prononcé le 30 novembre 1973 devant le Conseil Législatif National," *Jiwe*, no. 3 (June 1974), pp. 107–139. See especially pp. 127–139.

4.   For an overview of nationalization in the Third World, see M. L. Williams, "The Extent and Significance of the Nationalization of Foreign-Owned Assets in Developing Countries, 1956–1972," *Oxford Economic Papers, N.S.* 27 (July 1975): 260–273. For the Nigerian case, see Paul Collins, "The Political Economy of Indigenization: The Case of the Nigerian Enterprises Promotion Decree," *African Review* 4 (1975): 491–508.

5.   There was, for example, the Bakajika Law and the rest of the campaign against the Union Minière du Haut Katanga as early as 1966. In May 1972 the First Regular Congress of the MPR called for the return of import houses and local commerce to Zairian control. In addition, in October 1972 a long article in one of the Kinshasa daily newspapers detailed some of the problems to be encountered if citizens were to take over the commercial sector. See *Salongo* (Kinshasa), 18 October 1974, p. 20. Throughout the year immediately preceding the 30 November decisions, many of Mobutu's speeches strongly hinted at his discontent with foreign control in the commercial sphere. See *Salongo*, 27 November 1972, p. 4; and *Salongo*, 25 June 1973, p. 10.

6.   Administrative correspondence, 30 November 1973.

7.   Ibid., 6 December 1973, citing telegram of 2 December 1973.

8.   Ibid., 6 December 1973, citing telegram of 2 December 1973.

9.   Ibid., 6 December 1973, citing telegram of 4 December 1973.

10.   Administrative circular, 5 December 1973.

11.   Administrative correspondence, 9 February 1974, citing telegram of 14 December 1973.

The fact that this message, though sent on 14 December 1973, did not reach the zones until 9 February 1974 may be of some interest in itself. Because this is far longer than the usual transmission time, a cynic might wonder if the delay was deliberate to lengthen the time during which certain commissioners had access to business receipts.

12. Administrative correspondence, 11 December 1973, citing radio message of 8 December 1973; ibid., 21 December 1973.

13. Ibid., 10 December 1973.

14. Ibid., 31 December 1973.

15. Ibid., 14 January 1974.

16. *Salongo*, 4 December 1973, p. 2.

17. Administrative circular, 5 December 1973.

18. Administrative correspondence, 14 December 1973.

19. *Salongo*, 27 December 1973, p. 2.

20. Ibid., 31 December 1973, p. 2.

21. Ibid., 2 January 1974, p. 3.

22. Ibid., pp. 1–2.

23. Ibid., 14 March 1974, p. 2.

24. Ibid., 23 March 1974, p. 2.

25. Ibid., 23 March 1974, p. 2.

26. "Compte rendu de la séance du travail qui a réuni les commissaires de région sous la présidence du citoyen commissaire d'état aux affaires politiques en date du 23 mars 1974 à Kinshasa," 17 April 1974.

27. Ibid., "Réunion du 26 Mars 1974."

28. *Salongo*, 28 March 1974, p. 2; and "Chronologie (février à mai 1974)," *Etudes zairoises* 2 (June–July 1974): 143.

29. Administrative correspondence, 23 April 1974.

30. "Le Discours du Président-Fondateur du Mouvement Populaire de la Révolution à l'occasion de l'ouverture de l'Institut *Makanda Kabobi* à la Cité du Parti le 15 août 1974," *Etudes zairoises* 2 (June–July 1974): 205.

31. *Salongo*, 26 November 1974, p. 12.

32. The ten scourges may be found in Yabili Yalada Asani, *Code de la zairianization: Receuil de textes et règlements des décisions du 30 novembre 1973 et du 30 décembre 1974* (Lubumbashi: Editeur Mwanga-Hebdo, n.d.), pp. 131–142.

33. *Salongo*, 4 December 1973, p. 2.

34. Ibid., 7 January 1974, p. 5; *Mambenga*, 30 March 1974, p. 20.

35. *Salongo*, 8 and 9 December 1973, p. 2.

36. See chapter 6 above.

37. Interviews, Lisala, 1 February 1975, no. 2, p. 6; and 10 January 1975, no. 6, p. 4.

38. Administrative correspondence, 25 January 1974.

39. Interview, Lisala, 17 August 1975, no. 70; Field Log, 5 May 1975, pp. 73–74; interview, Lisala, 22 June 1975, no. 66, p. 6; interview, Lisala, 3 June 1975, no. 64, p. 4.

40. Interview, Lisala, 26 June 1975, no. 67; and interview, Kinshasa, 8 October 1975, no. 71.

41. Interview, Lisala, 26 May 1975, no. 61.

42. The first documentary indication I have is the previously cited "Compte rendu de la séance du travail" of 23 March 1974. I suspect, however, that this decision was made earlier.

43. Interview, Lisala, 4 July 1975, no. 68, pp. 2–3.

44. Interview, Lisala, 11 August 1975, no. 69, pp. 2–3; administrative correspondence, 27 February 1974, 28 March 1974.

45. Interviews, Lisala, 22 June 1975, no. 67, p. 6; and 27 May 1975, no. 62, p. 4.

46. Archives, Equateur Region, Economic Affairs Department, Mbandaka. Administrative correspondence, 3 September 1974; Région de l'Equateur, Division Régionale de l'Agriculture, *Rapport annuel 1974*, pp. 132–138.

47. In official documents such as those cited immediately above, the president's name is

not listed. Instead, these items are attributed to the "presidency." High-level managers at the plantations have informed me that President Mobutu himself is the acquirer.

48. Willame, *Patrimonialism and Political Change in the Congo.*

49. Bailey, *Stratagems and Spoils.* See chapter 4 above, note 15.

50. At that time the legal minimum wage for unskilled labor in that part of Equateur was Z0.27 (or $0.54) per day. The monthly rate would be Z7.02 plus a family allowance.

51. "Chronologie," *Etudes zairoises* 2 (June–July 1974): 163; administrative correspondence, 24 June 1974.

52. *Salongo,* 18 April 1974, p. 2.

53. Marx, *The Eighteenth Brumaire of Louis Bonaparte,* pp. 248–249.

54. Interview, Lisala, 26 May 1975, no. 61, p. 4; Field Log, 3 August 1975, pp. 105–106.

55. Administrative correspondence, 19 November 1974, 20 November 1974, and 20 November 1974.

56. Ibid., 4 July 1974.

57. Ibid., 17 June 1974.

58. Ibid., 18 June 1974.

59. Ibid., 30 August 1974.

60. Interview, Lisala, 28 January 1975, no. 8, p. 5. The tax problem was by no means restricted to Lisala. An article in *Elima* (Kinshasa) on 30 April 1974 noted that "since the acquirers have been managing their new establishments none of them has had, at present, the frankness, the honesty to declare officially to the tax service the figure realized during the course of the year 1972–1973 by the former owner." *Elima,* 30 April 1974. Parenthetically, I am grateful to Crawford Young for providing me with access to his *Elima* clipping file.

61. Région de l'Equateur, Division Régionale des Affaires Economiques, *Rapport annuel économique: Année 1973,* p. 2.

62. *Salongo,* 26 November 1974, p. 12; ibid., 14 March 1974, pp. 1–2.

63. Administrative correspondence, 6 September 1974, citing telegram of 19 August 1974; "Rapport succint du 3è trimestre de l'année 1974 sur l'evolution des prix et des approvisionnements des maisons zairianisées de la Zone de Lisala," 29 November 1974.

64. *Elima,* 23 May 1974.

65. Interview, Lisala, 3 June 1975, no. 64, p. 4.

66. "Rapport succint du 3è trimestre," and interview, Lisala, 10 January 1975, no. 6, p. 4.

67. Région de l'Equateur, Division Régionale de l'Agriculture, *Rapport annuel 1974,* p. 107.

68. Administrative correspondence, 26 March 1974.

69. Ibid., 28 June 1974.

70. Ibid. 2 August 1974.

71. Ibid., 23 December 1974.

72. Ibid., ? February 1973; "Rapport semestriel: Sur la marche de l'administration de la Zone de Bongandanga et des collectivités la composant," 15 December 1974.

73. "Rapport sur les activités de la scierie à Bosu-Wanga," 20 March 1975.

74. "Rapport sur la situation économique dans la Sous-région de l'Equateur," Basankusu, 25 may 1975. Archives, Equateur Region, Economic Affairs Department, Mbandaka.

75. Interview, Lisala, 3 June 1975, no. 64, p. 4.

CHAPTER 8

1. Walt Whitman, "Song of Myself," lines 1314–1316, in *Leaves of Grass: The First (1855) Edition,* ed. Malcolm Cowley (New York: Viking, 1959), p. 85.

2. Peter C. W. Gutkind, "The Emergent African Urban Proletariat," *Occasional Paper Series*, no. 8 (Montreal: McGill Universiy, 1974), p. 37.

3. Jewsiewicki, "La Contestation sociale et la naissance du prolétariat," p. 66.

4. Anstey, "Belgian Rule in the Congo and the Aspirations of the 'Evolué' Class," pp. 196–201; see chapter 2 above for a discussion of the *évolué* group with a slightly different emphasis.

5. This discussion is heavily indebted to Jewsiewicki's stimulating article, "La Contestation sociale et la naissance du prolétariat," pp. 47–70.

6. Weiss, *Political Protest in the Congo*, pp. 291–292.

7. On the situation in Bas-Zaire, see Monnier, *Ethnie et intégration régionale au Congo*, pp. 357–358; and Demunter, *Luttes politiques au Zaire*, pp. 294–295.

8. The consciousness of the village farmers is dealt with by Mulambu, "Cultures obligatoires et colonisation dans l'ex-Congo belge," p. 97. Kanyinda Lusanga relates another interesting example of this. In Kasai the villagers were required to sell their produce to the Europeans, and it was "the European buyer who set the price of the merchandise. The obligatory aspect of the requisitions determined the minimum quantity that had to be brought to the sale. Furthermore, the terms, 'buy' or 'sell' were almost never used to indicate this type of transaction. It was the verb 'Kuela' (to throw away, dispose of) which was used." Kanyinda Lusanga, "Le Phénomène de la colonisation et l'émancipation des institutions socio-politiques traditionnelles au Zaire," *Cahiers du CEDAF*, no. 1 (1975), p. 33.

9. CRISP, *Les Cahiers de Gamboma: Instructions politiques et militaires des partisans congolais (1964–1965)*, Travaux Africains du CRISP, Dossier Documentaire no. 3 (Brussels: CRISP, 1965).

10. Renée C. Fox, Willy de Craemer, and Jean-Marie de Ribeaucourt, " 'The Second Independence': A Case Study of the Kwilu Rebellion in the Congo," *Comparative Studies in Society and History* 8 (1965–66): 103. Emphasis in original. See, too, M. Crawford Young, "Rebellion and the Congo," in *Rebellion in Black Africa*, ed. Robert I. Rotberg (London, Oxford, New York: Oxford University Press, 1971), pp. 209–245; and Verhaegen, *Rébellions au Congo*.

11. Interview, Lisala, 25 June 1975, no. 56, p. 4.

12. Interview, Lisala, 27 March 1975, no. 54, p. 4.

13. Interview, Lisala, 6 July 1975, no. 57, pp. 6–7.

14. Interview, Lisala, 14 November 1974, no. 1 p. 6.

15. Interview, Lisala, 23 April 1975, no. 47, p. 2.

16. Interview, Lisala, 16 June 1975, no. 23, p. 2.

17. Interview, Lisala, 15 January 1975, no. 20, p. 2.

18. Interview, Lisala, 4 June 1975, no. 22, p. 2; and Field Log, 7 January 1975, p. 22.

19. "Discours du chef de l'état Mobutu Sese Soko Kuku Ngbendu Wa Za Banga à la tribune des Nations Unies à New York, jeudi 4 octobre 1973," *Cultures au Zaire et en Afrique*, no. 2 (1973), pp. 246–247.

20. Monseigneur Kabanga, "Je suis un homme: Lettre pastorale de Carême 1976," (Lubumbashi: Archéveché de Lubumbashi, March 1976), p. 6.

21. Interviews, Lisala, 21 February 1975, no. 8, p. 7; 27 February 1975, no. 12, p. 4; 24 January 1975, no. 6 p. 9; 6 March 1974, no. 14, p. 6; and 22 March 1975, no. 21, p. 8.

22. Field Log, 14 February 1975, pp. 40–41; and Field Log, 24 February 1975, pp. 45–46.

23. Administrative correspondence, 11 July 1973, 13 April 1975.

24. Ibid., 19 January 1972, 3 July 1973. Emphasis in original.

25. Ibid., 6 March 1973.

26. Interview, Lisala, 11 April 1975, no. 19, p. 5.

27. Administrative correspondence, 27 November 1973; and Field Log, 20 July 1975, p. 102.

28. Administrative correspondence, 6 June 1973; and Field Log, 4 July 1975, p. 93.

29. "Rapport administratif concernant les agissements du citoyen de Binga," n.d. [May–June 1973]. It is not clear how this was recorded verbatim. Nonetheless, I have reproduced it as it appeared in the report.

30. Administrative correspondence, 19 February 1975.

31. Field Log, 22 December 1974, pp. 19–20; ibid., 2 January 1975, p. 21; ibid., 17 January 1975, p. 27; administrative correspondence, 11 July 1975; and Field Log, 27 October 1975, p. 122.

32. Houyoux, *Budgets ménagers, nutrition et môde de vie à Kinshasa*, p. 275.

33. Interview, Lisala, 15 January 1975, no. 20, p. 5.

34. Interview, Lisala, 22 November 1974, no. 25. p. 4.

35. Interviews, Lisala, 27 November 1974, no. 26, p. 4; 9 January 1975, no. 53, p. 5; and 22 May 1975, no. 60, p. 3.

36. This point is suggested by Geoff Lamb, *Peasant Politics* (Sussex: Julian Friedman Publishers, 1974), p. 149.

37. Field Log, 1 March 1975, p. 50; interviews, Lisala, 20 February 1975, no. 11, p. 5; and 29 April 1975, no. 48, p. 5.

38. Interview, Lisala, 11 April 1975, no. 19, p. 4.

39. It should be borne in mind that the behavior of the acquirer group was not the only cause of the inflation at that time. Copper prices had fallen on the international market, while the cost of petroleum products had risen rapidly. Financial mismanagement undoubtedly played a role as well.

40. Field Log, 5 August 1975, p. 107.

41. Nzongola, "The Bourgeoisie and Revolution in the Congo," pp. 518–520.

42. This argument was suggested to me by Crawford Young.

43. Murray Edelman, "The Political Language of the Helping Professions," *Politics and Society* 4 (May 1974): 299.

44. Ludwig Wittgenstein, *Philosophical Investigations*, trans. G. E. M. Anscombe (Oxford: Basil Blackwell, 1968), p. 42. Emphasis in original.

45. Giddens, *The Class Structure of the Advanced Societies*, pp. 112–113; and Ralph Miliband, "Barnave: A Case of Bourgeois Class Consciousness," in *Aspects of History and Class Consciousness*, ed. István Meszáros (London: Routledge and Kegan Paul, 1971), pp. 22–23.

46. P. C. Lloyd's earlier views on the subject may be found in his "Class Consciousness Among the Yoruba," in *The New Elites of Tropical Africa*, ed. P. C. Lloyd (London: Oxford University Press, 1966), p. 331 et passim. A more recent statement of his essentially unchanged views is in his *Power and Independence: Urban Africans' Perception of Social Inequality* (London and Boston: Routledge and Kegan Paul, 1974), p. 4. For Gutkind's views, see his "The View from Below: Political Consciousness of the Urban Poor in Ibadan," *Cahiers d'études africaines* 15 (1975): 32.

47. Miliband, "Barnave: A Case of Bourgeois Class Consciousness," pp. 22–48; and Wittfogel, *Oriental Despotism*, p. 320.

48. Balandier, *Sens et puissance*, p. 271.

49. Interview, Lisala, 12 March 1975, no. 16, p. 7.

50. Field Log, 28 February 1975, pp. 48–49; Field Log, 23 July 1975, p. 103; and William F. Buckley, Jr., "On the Right: General Mobutu at the UN," *National Review*, 26 October 1973, p. 1199.

51. Interview, Lisala, 22 April 1975, no. 35, p. 3.

52. Administrative correspondence, 17 July 1974.

53. Scott, *The Moral Economy of the Peasant*, p. 173.

54. Young, *The Politics of Cultural Pluralism*, pp. 11–13.

CHAPTER 9

1. Lewis Carroll, *Alice's Adventures in Wonderland*, chap. 6. Emphasis in original.

2. On this point see Joan Vincent, "Room for Manoeuvre: The Political Role of Small

Towns in East Africa," in *Colonialism and Change: Essays Presented to Lucy Mair*, ed. Maxwell Owusu (The Hague, Paris: Mouton, 1975), pp. 115–144.

3. Included in this category are administrators as well. "Politico-administrative-commercial" would be too unwieldy.

4. Interview, Lisala, 12 August 1975, no. 45, p. 4.

5. Interview, Kinshasa, 8 October 1975, no. 71, p. 3.

6. John S. Saul, "The Unsteady State: Uganda, Obote and General Amin," *Review of African Political Economy*, no. 5. (January–April 1976), p. 17.

7. Ralph Miliband, *The State in Capitalist Society: The Analysis of the Western System of Power* (London: Quartet Books, 1969), p. 113.

8. The seminal work in this field is still Young, *Politics in the Congo,* p. 5. Also of great importance and interest are Jules Gérard-Libois and Benoît Verhaegen, eds., *Congo 1960*, 3 vols. (Brussels: CRISP, 1961), as well as the entire CRISP series; Hoskyns, *The Congo since Independence*; Lemarchand, *Political Awakening in the Belgian Congo*; and Willame, *Patrimonialism and Political Change in the Congo*.

9. Marx, *The Eighteenth Brumaire of Louis Bonaparte*, p. 146.

10. Administrative correspondence, 27 March 1975.

11. Election results may be found in *Elima*, 14 October 1975.

12. Cohen, *Urban Policy and Political Conflict in Africa*, p. 57.

13. Warren F. Ilchman and Norman Thomas Uphoff, *The Political Economy of Change* (Berkeley, Los Angeles, London: Univesity of California Press, 1971), p. 33.

14. Michael F. Lofchie, "Observations on Social and Institutional Change in Independent Africa," in *The State of the Nations: Constraints on Development in Independent Africa*, ed. Michael F. Lofchie (Berkeley, Los Angeles, London: University of California Press, 1971), p. 264.

15. On the so-called classless societies, see Grundy, "The 'Class Struggle' in Africa," pp. 379–393. The classic statement on the West African single parties remains Aristide R. Zolberg, *Creating Political Order* (Chicago: Rand McNally, 1966). I have also drawn on Colin Leys's review of Lofchie's *The State of the Nations,* in *Journal of Modern African Studies* 11 (June 1973): 315–317.

16. Abner Cohen, *Custom and Politics in Urban Africa: A Study of Hausa Migrants in Yoruba Towns* (Berkeley and Los Angeles: University of California Press, 1971).

17. Monseigneur Kabanga, "Je suis un homme," p. 10.

18. Scott, *The Moral Economy of the Peasant*.

19. Monseigneur Kabanga, "Je suis un homme," p. 9.

Bibliography

Unpublished Materials and Government Documents

Archives, Equateur Region, Economic Affairs Department, Mbandaka.

Archives, Equateur Region, Political Affairs Department, Mbandaka. Dossiers, Zone of Lisala, 1908–75.

Archives, Mongala Subregion, Political Affairs Department, Lisala.

Belgique. Ministère des affaires africaines. *Rapport sur l'administration de la Colonie du Congo belge présenté aux Chambres législatifs*, 1908–60.

Cité de Lisala. *Comptes des recettes et des dépenses*, 1968–74.

————. *Prévisions budgétaires*, 1968–75.

Collectivité de Boso-Simba. *Comptes des recettes et des dépenses, 1974.*

Collectivité de Mongala-Motima. *Prévisions budgétaires, 1975.*

Collectivité de Ngombe-Mombangi. *Comptes des recettes et des dépenses, 1974.*

Congo belge. *Bulletin Officiel, 1908–59.*

————. *Conseils de Province, Compte rendus analytiques des séances: Equateur,* 1929–59.

Engulu Baangampongo Bakokele Lokunga. "Vigilance et engagement révolutionnaire." Exposé aux cadres de la JMPR en session spéciale de l'Institut Makanda Kabobi, N'Sélé, 1 March 1975.

Etat Indépendant du Congo. *Bulletin Officiel*, 1885–1908.

Interviews. Lisala, Mbandaka, Kinshasa. Nos. 1–73. 1974–75.

Région de l'Equateur. Division Régionale de l'Agriculture. *Rapport annuel 1974.*

Région de l'Equateur. Division Régionale des Affaires Economiques. *Rapport annuel économique: Année 1973.*

Région du Haut-Zaire, Division Régionale de l'Agriculture. *Rapport annuel 1974.*

Région du Shaba, Division Régionale de l'Agriculture. *Rapport annuel 1974.*

République Démocratique du Congo, Assemblée Nationale. *Compte rendu analytique,* no. 34/72 (5 May 1972).

————. *Compte rendu analytique*, no. 14/71 (4 October 1971).

Schatzberg, Michael G. Field Log, 5 October 1974–27 October 1975.

"Zaire Colonial Documents: De Ryck Collection of General Administration, Equateur, Kivu, and Ruanda-Urundi [1885–1954]."

Zone de Bumba. *Rapport annuel des affaires politiques, 1974.*

Zone de Lisala. *Rapport annuel des affaires politiques*, 1969–74.

Zone de Mobayi-Mbongo. *Rapport annuel des affaires politiques, 1974.*

Books and Dissertations

Achebe, Chinua. *A Man of the People*. London, Ibadan, Nairobi: Heinemann Educational Books, 1966.

Anderson, Charles W.; von der Mehden, Fred R.; and Young, Crawford. *Issues of Political Development*. Englewood Cliffs, N. J.: Prentice-Hall, 1967.

Anstey, Roger. *King Leopold's Legacy: The Congo under Belgian Rule 1908–1960.* London: Oxford University Press, 1966.

Bailey, F. G. *Stratagems and Spoils: A Social Anthropology of Politics*. New York: Schocken Books, 1969.

Balandier, Georges. *Sens et puissance: Les Dynamiques sociales*. Paris: Presses Universitaires de France, 1971.

Barbé, Raymond. *Les Classes sociales en Afrique noire.* Paris: Economie et Politique, 1964.

Baumer, Guy. *Les Centres indigènes extracoutumiers au Congo belge.* Paris: Dormat-Monchréstien, 1939.

Bertrand, Hugues. *Le Congo: Formation sociale et mòde de développement économique.* Paris: François Maspero, 1975.

Bloch, Marc. *The Historian's Craft.* Translated by Peter Putnam. Manchester: Manchester University Press, 1954.

Bouvier, Paule. *L'Accession du Congo belge à l'indépendance: Essai d'analyse sociologique.* Brussels: Editions de l'Institut de Sociologie, Université Libre de Bruxelles, 1965.

Braekman, E. M. *Histoire du Protestantisme au Congo.* Brussels: Editions de la Librairie des Eclaireurs Unionistes, 1961.

Brokensha, David. *Social Change at Larteh, Ghana.* Oxford: Clarendon Press, 1966.

Burssens, H. *Les Peuplades de l'entre Congo-Ubangi.* Tervuren: Annales du Musée Royal du Congo Belge, 1958.

Bustin, Edouard. *Lunda under Belgian Rule: The Politics of Ethnicity.* Cambridge, Mass., and London: Harvard University Press, 1975.

Carroll, Lewis. *Alice's Adventures in Wonderland* and *Through the Looking-Glass: And What Alice Found There.*

Centers, Richard. *The Psychology of Social Classes: A Study of Class Consciousness.* Princeton: Princeton University Press, 1949.

Christie, Agatha. *The Mysterious Affair at Styles.* New York: Bantam, 1974.

Codère, Helen. *The Biography of an African Society, Rwanda 1900–1960: Based on Forty-eight Rwandan Autobiographies.* Tervuren: Musée Royal de l'Afrique Centrale, 1973.

Cohen, Abner. *Custom and Politics in Urban Africa: A Study of Hausa Migrants in Yoruba Towns.* Berkeley and Los Angeles: University of California Press, 1971.

Cohen, Michael A. *Urban Policy and Political Conflict in Africa: A Study of the Ivory Coast.* Chicago and London: University of Chicago Press, 1974.

Cohen Saul B., ed. *Oxford World Atlas.* New York: Oxford University Press, 1973.

Comeliau, Christian. *Fonctions économiques et pouvoir politique: La Province de l'Uélé en 1963–1964.* Léopoldville: Institut de Recherches Economiques et Sociales, n.d. [1965].

Coquilhat, Camille. *Sur le haut Congo.* Paris: J. Lebègue, 1888.

CRISP. *Les Cahiers de Gamboma: Instructions politiques et militaires des partisans congolais (1964–1965).* Travaux Africains du CRISP, Dossier Documentaire no. 3. Brussels: CRISP, 1965.

Dahrendorf, Ralf. *Class and Class Conflict in Industrial Society.* Stanford: Stanford University Press, 1959.

Demunter, Paul. *Luttes politiques au Zaire: Le Processus de politisation des masses rurales du Bas-Zaire.* Paris: Editions Anthropos, 1975.

Derman, William. *Serfs, Peasants, and Socialists: A Former Serf Village in the Republic of Guinea.* Berkeley and Los Angeles: University of California Press, 1973.

De Thier, Franz M. *Le Centre extra-coutumier de Coquilhatville.* Brussels: Université Libre, Institut de Sociologie Solvay, 1956.

Dhanis, Francis. *Le District d'Upoto et la foundation du camp de l'Aruwimi.* Publications de l'Etat Indépendant du Congo, no. 3. Brussels: Imprimerie Typo-Lithographique J. Vanderauwera, n.d.

Diop, Majhemout. *Histoire des classes sociales dans l'Afrique de l'ouest.* 2 vols. Vol. 2: *Le Sénégal.* Paris: François Maspero, 1972.

Fanon, Frantz. *Les Damnés de la terre.* Paris: François Maspero, 1968.

Gérard-Libois, Jules, ed. *Congo 1967.* Brussels and Kinshasa: CRISP and INEP, 1969.

———. *Katanga Secession.* Translated by Rebecca Young. Madison: University of Wisconsin Press, 1966.

——— and Verhaegen, Benoît, eds. *Congo 1960.* 3 vols. Brussels: CRISP, 1961.

———. *Congo 1962.* Brussels and Léopoldville: CRISP and INEP, 1963.

Giddens, Anthony. *The Class Structure of the Advanced Societies.* London: Hutchinson University Library, 1973.

Goldmann, Lucien. *Marxisme et sciences humaines.* Paris: Gallimard, 1970.

Gurvitch, Georges. *Etudes sur les classes sociales.* Paris: Editions Gonthier, 1966.

———. *The Spectrum of Social Time.* Translated by Myrtle Korenbaum. Dordrecht, Holland: D. Reidel, 1964.

Hopkins, Nicholas S. *Popular Government in an African Town: Kita, Mali.* Chicago: University of Chicago Press, 1970.

Hoskyns, Catherine. *The Congo since Independence: January 1960–December 1961.* London: Oxford University Press for the Royal Institute of International Affairs, 1965.

Houyoux, Joseph. *Budget ménagers, nutrition et mòde de vie à Kinshasa.* Kinshasa: Presses Universitaires du Zaire, 1973.

Hulstaert, Gustave. *Les Mongo: Aperçu général.* Archives d'ethnographie 5. Tervuren: Musée Royal de l'Afrique Centrale, 1961.

Ilchman, Warren F., and Uphoff, Norman Thomas. *The Political Economy of Change.* Berkeley, Los Angeles, London: University of California Press, 1971.

Kamitatu, Cléophas. *La Grande Mystification du Congo-Kinshasa: Les Crimes de Mobutu.* Paris: François Maspero, 1971.

Kazadi wa Dile, Jacques S. *Politiques salariales et développement en République démocratique du Congo.* Paris: Editions Universitaires, 1970.

Lacroix, Jean-Louis. *Industrialisation au Congo: La Transformation des structures économiques.* Paris and The Hague: Mouton, 1967.

Lamb, Geoff. *Peasant Politics.* Sussex: Julian Friedman Publishers, 1974.

Le Maire, Charles. *La Région de l'Equateur.* Brussels: Imprimerie et Lithographie A. Lesigne, 1895.

Lemarchand, René. *Political Awakening in the Belgian Congo: The Politics of Fragmentation.* Berkeley and Los Angeles: University of California Press, 1964.

Lenski, Gerhard E. *Power and Privilege: A Theory of Social Stratification.* New York: McGraw-Hill, 1966.

Leys, Colin. *Underdevelopment in Kenya: The Political Economy of Neo-Colonialism 1964–1971.* Berkeley and Los Angeles: University of California Press, 1974.

———. *Politicians and Policies: An Essay on Politics in Acholi, Uganda 1962–1965.* Nairobi: East Africa Publishing House, 1967.

Lloyd, P. C. *Power and Independence: Urban Africans' Perception of Social Inequality.* London and Boston: Routledge & Kegan Paul, 1974.

Lumumba, Patrice. *Congo, My Country.* With a foreword by Colin Legum. New York: Praeger, 1962.

Magotte, J. *Les centres extra-coutumiers: Commentaires des décrets des 23 novembre*

1931, 6 et 22 juin 1934 coordonnés par l'arrêté royal du 6 juillet 1934. Dison-Verviers: Imprimerie Disonaise, 1938.

Mamdani, Mahmood. *Politics and Class Formation in Uganda.* New York and London: Monthly Review Press, 1976.

Markakis, John. *Ethiopia: Anatomy of a Traditional Polity.* Oxford: Clarendon Press, 1974.

Marshall, T. H. *Citizenship and Social Class and Other Essays.* Cambridge: Cambridge University Press, 1950.

Marx, Karl. *The Eighteenth Brumaire of Louis Bonaparte.* In *Surveys from Exile,* pp. 143–249. Edited and with an introduction by David Fernbach. Translated by Ben Fowkes. New York: Vintage Books, 1974.

Marx, Karl, and Engels, Frederick. *The German Ideology.* Edited and with an introduction by C. J. Arthur. New York: International Publishers, 1970.

Merlier, Michel. *Le Congo de la colonisation belge à l'indépendence.* Paris: François Maspero, 1962.

Miliband, Ralph. *The State in Capitalist Society: The Analysis of the Western System of Power.* London: Quartet Books, 1969.

Mokolo wa Mpombo, Edouard. "Structure et évolution des institutions politiques et administratives de la Province de l'Equateur." Mémoire de licence, Université Lovanium, Kinshasa, July 1968.

Monnier, Laurent. *Ethnie et intégration régionale au Congo: Le Kongo Central 1962–1965.* Paris: Edicef, 1971.

Mpase Nselenge Mpeti. *L'Evolution de la solidarité traditionnelle en milieu rural et urbain au Zaire: Le Cas des Ntomba et des Basengele du Lac Mai-Ndombe.* Kinshasa: Presses Universitaires du Zaire, 1974.

Mukenge Tshilemalema. "Businessmen of Zaire: Limited Possibilities for Capital Accumulation under Dependence." Ph.D. dissertation, McGill University, 1974.

Nkrumah, Kwame. *Class Struggle in Africa.* New York: International Publishers, 1970.

Nzongola-Ntalaja. "Urban Administration in Zaire: A Study of Kananga, 1971–1973." Ph.D. dissertation, University of Wisconsin–Madison, 1975.

Office National de la Recherche et du Développement (ONRD). *Année politique au Congo 1968.* Kinshasa: ONRD, 1970.

Ossowski, Stanislaw. *Class Structure in the Social Consciousness.* Translated by Sheila Patterson. New York: Free Press, 1963.

Owusu, Maxwell. *Uses and Abuses of Political Power: A Case Study of Continuity and Change in the Politics of Ghana.* Chicago: University of Chicago Press, 1970.

Parkin, Frank. *Class Inequality and Political Order: Social Stratification in Capitalist and Communist Societies.* London: MacGibbon & Kee, 1971.

Peemans, Jean-Philippe. *Diffusion de progrès économique et convergence des prix; le cas Congo-Belgique, 1900–1960: La Formation du système des prix et salaires dans une économie dualiste.* Louvain: Editions Nauwelaerts, 1968.

République du Zaire. Département de l'Economie Nationale. *Conjoncture économique: Année 1973 et 1e trimestre 1974* 14 (December 1974).

Riggs, Fred W. *Administration in Developing Countries: The Theory of Prismatic Society.* Boston: Houghton Mifflin, 1964.

Royaume de Belgique, Ministère des Colonies. *Recueil à l'usage des fonctionnaires et des agents du service territorial au Congo belge.* 4th ed. Brussels: Société Anonyme M. Weissenbruch, 1925.

Samoff, Joel. *Tanzania: Local Politics and the Structure of Power.* Madison: University of Wisconsin Press, 1974.

Sartre, Jean-Paul. *Questions de méthode.* Paris: Gallimard, 1960.

Schatzberg, Michael G. "Bureaucracy, Business, Beer: The Political Dynamics of Class Formation in Lisala, Zaire." Ph.D. dissertation, University of Wisconsin—Madison, 1977.

Scott, James C. *The Moral Economy of the Peasant: Rebellion and Subsistence in Southeast Asia.* New Haven and London: Yale University Press, 1976.

Shivji, Issa G. *Class Struggles in Tanzania.* New York and London: Monthly Review Press, 1976.

Sklar, Richard L. *Corporate Power in an African State: The Political Impact of Multinational Mining Companies in Zambia.* Berkeley, Los Angeles, London: University of California Press, 1975.

———. *Nigerian Political Parties: Power in an Emergent African Nation.* Princeton: Princeton University Press, 1963.

Slade, Ruth M. *English-Speaking Missions in the Congo-Independent State (1878–1908).* Brussels: Académie Royale des Sciences d'Outre Mer, Classe des Sciences Morales et Politiques, 16, fasc. 2, 1959.

United Nations. *Demographic Yearbook 1976.*

———. *Statistical Yearbook*, 1959–65, 1976.

Van Der Kerken, Georges. *L'Ethnie Mongo.* 2 vols. Brussels: Institut Royal Colonial Belge, Section des Sciences Morales et Politiques, 13, fasc. 1 and 2, 1944.

Van Overbergh, Cyrille. *Les Bangala.* Brussels: Institut International de Bibliographie, 1907.

Vansina, Jan. *The Tio Kingdom of the Middle Congo 1880–1892.* London, New York, Toronto: Oxford University Press for the International African Institute, 1973.

———. *Introduction à l'ethnographie du Congo.* Kinshasa: Editions Universitaires du Congo, 1966.

———. *Kingdoms of the Savanna.* Madison: University of Wisconsin Press, 1966.

Vellut, J. L. *Guide de l'étudiant en histoire du Zaire.* Kinshasa and Lubumbashi: Editions du Mont Noir, 1974.

Verhaegen, Benoît. *Introduction à l'histoire immédiate: Essai de méthodologie qualitative.* Gembloux: Duculot, 1974.

———. *Rébellions au Congo.* 2 vols. Brussels: CRISP, 1966 and 1969.

———; Beys, Jorge; and Gendebien, Paul Henri, eds. *Congo 1963.* Brussels and Léopoldville: CRISP and INEP, 1964.

Weber, Max. *From Max Weber: Essays in Sociology.* Translated, edited, and with an introduction by H. H. Gerth and C. Wright Mills. New York: Oxford University Press, 1946.

Weiss, Herbert F. *Political Protest in the Congo: The Parti Solidaire Africain during the Independence Struggle.* Princeton: Princeton University Press, 1967.

Whitman, Walt. *Leaves of Grass: The First (1855) Edition.* Edited with an introduction by Malcolm Cowley. New York: Viking, 1959.

Wildavsky, Aaron. *Budgeting: A Comparative Theory of the Budgetary Process.* Boston, Toronto: Little, Brown, 1975.

———. *The Politics of the Budgetary Process.* Boston: Little, Brown, 1964.

Willame, Jean-Claude. *Patrimonialism and Political Change in the Congo.* Stanford: Stanford University Press, 1972.

———. *Les Provinces du Congo: Structure et fonctionnement.* 5 vols. Cahiers Economiques et Sociaux, Collection d'Etudes Politiques. Kinshasa: Université Lovanium, 1964–65.

Wittfogel Karl A. *Oriental Despotism: A Comparative Study of Total Power.* New Haven and London: Yale University Press, 1957.

Wittgenstein, Ludwig. *Philosophical Investigations.* Translated by G. E. M. Anscombe. Oxford: Basil Blackwell, 1968.

Wolf, Eric. *Peasants.* Englewood Cliffs, N.J.: Prentice-Hall, 1966.

———. *Sons of the Shaking Earth.* Chicago and London: University of Chicago Press, 1959.

Wolfe, Alvin W. *In the Ngombe Tradition: Continuity and Change in the Congo.* Evanston: Northwestern University Press, 1961.

Yabili Yalala Asani. *Code de la zairianisation: Receuil de textes et règlements des décisions du 30 november 1973 et du 30 décembre 1974.* Lubumbashi: Editeur Mwanga-Hedbo, n.d.

Young, Crawford. *The Politics of Cultural Pluralism.* Madison: University of Wisconsin Press, 1976.

———. *Politics in the Congo: Decolonization and Independence.* Princeton: Princeton University Press, 1965.

Zolberg, Aristide R. *Creating Political Order: The Party States of West Africa.* Chicago: Rand McNally, 1966.

Articles, Chapters, and Miscellaneous Documents

Allen, V. L. "The Meaning of the Working Class in Africa." *Journal of Modern African Studies* 10 (July 1972): 169–189.

Anselin, M. "La Classe moyenne indigène à Elisabethville." *Problèmes sociaux congolais*, no. 53 (June 1961), pp. 99–110.

Anstey, Roger. "Belgian Rule in the Congo and the Aspirations of the 'Evolué' Class." In *Colonialism in Africa 1870–1960.* 5 vols. Vol. 2: *The History and Politics of Colonialism 1914–1960*, pp. 194–225. Edited by L. H. Gann and Peter Duignan. Cambridge: Cambridge University Press, 1970.

Baeck, L. "An Expenditure Study of the Congolese Evolués of Leopoldville, Belgian Congo." In *Social Change in Modern Africa,* pp. 159–181. Edited by Aidan Southall. London: Oxford University Press for the International African Institute, 1961.

Bernier, G. and Lambrechts, A. "Etude sur les boissons fermentées du Katanga." *Problèmes sociaux congolais,* no. 48 (March 1960), pp. 5–41.

Birnbaum, Norman. "La Crise de la sociologie marxiste." *L'Homme et la société,* no. 23 (January–March 1972), pp. 23–39.

Buckley, William F., Jr. "On the Right: General Mobutu at the UN." *National Review,* 26 October 1973, p. 1199.

Callaghy, Thomas M. "State Formation and Centralization of Power in Zaire: Mobutu's Pre-eminent Public Policy." Paper presented at the African Studies Association meeting. Boston, 3–6 November 1976.

Champaud, Jacques. "L'Utilisation des équipements tertiaires dans l'ouest du Cameroun." In *La Croissance urbaine en Afrique noire et à Madagascar,* vol.

1, pp. 401–413. Paris: Centre Nationale de la Recherche Scientifique, 1972.

"Chronologie (février à mai 1974)." *Etudes zairoises* 2 (June–July 1974): 129–195.

Cohen, Robin. "Class in Africa: Analytical Problems and Perspectives." In *The Socialist Register 1972*, pp. 231–255. Edited by Ralph Miliband and John Savile. London: Merlin Press, 1972.

Collins, Paul. "The Political Economy of Indigenization: The Case of the Nigerian Enterprises Promotion Decree." *African Review* 4 (1975): 491–508.

Dalton, George. "How Exactly Are Peasants 'Exploited'?" *American Anthropologist* 76 (September 1974): 553–561.

Demunter, Paul. "Structure de classes et lutte de classes dans le Congo colonial." *Contradictions*, no. 1 (January–June 1973), pp. 67–109.

Denis, Jacques. "Coquilhatville: Eléments pour une étude de géographie sociale." *Aequatoria* 19 (1956): 137–148.

Derman, William. "Peasants: The African Exception? Reply to Goldschmidt and Kunkel." *American Anthropologist* 74 (June 1972): 779–782.

"Discours du chef de l'état Mobutu Sese Soko Kuku Ngbendu Wa Za Banga à la tribune des Nations Unies à New York, jeudi le 4 octobre 1973." *Cultures au Zaire et en Afrique*, no. 2 (1973), pp. 235–251.

"Le Discours du Président-Fondateur du Mouvement Populaire de la Révolution à l'occasion de l'ouverture de l'Institut *Makanda Kabobi* à la Cité du Parti le 15 Août 1974." *Etudes zairoises* 2 (June–July 1974): 197–207.

"Discours présidentiel de politique générale prononcé le 30 novembre 1973 devant le Conseil Législatif National." *Jiwe*, no. 3 (June 1974), pp. 107–139.

"Documents." *Etudes zairoises*, no. 2 (June–July 1974), pp. 209–230.

Dos Santos, Theontonio. "The Concept of Social Classes." *Science and Society* 24 (Spring 1970): 166–193.

Edelman, Murray. "The Political Language of the Helping Professions." *Politics and Society* 4 (May 1974): 295–310.

Fallers, Lloyd A. "Are African Cultivators to Be Called 'Peasants'?" *Current Anthropology* 2 (1961): 108–110.

Fox, Renée C.; de Craemer, Willy; and de Ribeaucourt, Jean-Marie. " 'The Second Independence': A Case Study of the Kwilu Rebellion in the Congo." *Comparative Studies in Society and History* 8 (1965–66): 78–109.

Gatarayiha Majinya; Kangafu Gudumbagana; and De Lannoy, Didier. "Aspects de la réforme administrative au Zaire: l'Administration publique et le politique de 1965 à 1975." *Cahiers du CEDAF*, nos. 4–5 (1976).

Goldschmidt, Walter, and Jacobson-Kunkel, Evalyn. "The Structure of the Peasant Family." *American Anthropologist* 73 (October 1971): 1058–1076.

Gould, David J. "Local Administration in Zaire and Underdevelopment." *Journal of Modern African Studies* 15 (September 1977): 349–378.

Gran, Guy. "Policy Making and Historic Process: Zaire's Permanent Development Crisis." Paper presented at the African Studies Association meeting. Boston, 3–6 November 1976.

Grundy, Kenneth W. "The 'Class Struggle' in Africa: An Examination of Conflicting Theories." *Journal of Modern African Studies* 2 (November 1964): 379–393.

Gutkind, Peter C. W. "The View From Below: Political Consciousness of the Urban Poor in Ibadan." *Cahiers d'etudes africaines* 15 (1975): 5–35.

———. "The Emergent African Urban Proletariat." *Occasional Paper Series*, no. 8. Montreal: McGill University, 1974.

Heijboer, B. M. "Esquisse d'histoire des migrations ngombe depuis le début du XVIIIè siècle." *Aequatoria* 10 (1947): 63–69.

Henrard, L. "Note sur la situation du commerce et de l'artisanat pratiqués par les indigènes au Centre Extra-Coutumier d'Elisabethville." *Problèmes sociaux congolais*, no. 7 (1948), pp. 100–118.

Hulstaert, Gustave. "La Société politique nkundo." *Etudes zairoises* 2 (June–July 1974): 85–107.

———. "A propos des Bangala." *Zaire-Afrique*, no. 83 (March 1974), pp. 173–185.

———. "Une Lecture critique de l'*Ethnie Mongo* de G. Van Der Kerken." *Etudes d'histoire africaine* 3 (1972): 27–60.

Jackson, R. H. "Political Stratification in Tropical Africa." *Canadian Journal of African Studies* 7 (1973): 381–400.

Jewsiewicki, Bogumil. "La Contestation sociale et la naissance du prolétariat au Zaire au cours de la première moitié du XXᵉ siècle." *Canadian Journal of African Studies* 10 (1976): 47–70.

Kabanga, Monseigneur. "Je suis un homme: Lettre pastorale de Carême 1976." Lubumbashi: Archéveché de Lubumbashi, March 1976.

Kanyinda Lusanga. "Le Phénomène de la colonisation et l'émancipation des institutions socio-politiques traditionnelles au Zaire." *Cahiers du CEDAF*, no. 1 (1975).

Kasongo Ngoyi Makita Makita et al. "Les Etudiants et les élèves de Kisangani (1974–1975): Aspirations, opinions et conditions de vie." *Cahiers du CEDAF*, nos. 7–8 (1977).

Kilson, Martin L., Jr. "Nationalism and Social Classes in British West Africa." *Journal of Politics* 20 (May 1958): 368–387.

LaPalombara, Joseph. "Penetration: A Crisis of Government Capacity." In *Crises and Sequences in Political Development,* pp. 205–232. Edited by Leonard Binder et al. Princeton: Princeton University Press, 1971.

Leclercq, Hugues. "L'inflation, sa cause: Le Désordre des finances publiques." In *Indépendance, inflation, développement: L'Économie congolaise de 1960 à 1965,* pp. 51–178. Edited by Institut de Recherches Economiques et Sociales [IRES]. Paris and The Hague: IRES and Editions Mouton, 1968.

Leys, Colin. Review of *The State of the Nations: Constraints on Development in Independent Africa,* edited by Michael F. Lofchie. *Journal of Modern African Studies* 11 (June 1973): 315–317.

———. "Politics in Kenya: The Development of Peasant Society." *British Journal of Political Science* 1 (July 1971): 307–337.

Lindblom, Charles E. "The Science of 'Muddling Through.'" *Public Administration Review* 19 (1959): 79–88.

Lloyd, P. C. "Class Consciousness among the Yoruba." In *The New Elites of Tropical Africa,* pp. 328–341. Edited by P. C. Lloyd. London: Oxford University Press, 1966.

Lofchie, Michael F. "Observations on Social and Institutional Change in Independent Africa." In *The State of the Nations: Constraints on Development in Independent Africa,* pp. 261–283. Edited by Michael F. Lofchie. Berkeley, Los Angeles, London: University of California Press, 1971.

Lokomba Baruti. "Structure et fonctionnement des institutions politiques traditionnelles chez les Lokele (Haut Zaire)." *Cahiers du CEDAF*, no. 8 (1972).

Lovens, Maurice. "La R.D.C., du Congrès de la N'Sélé au nouveau mandat présidentiel (mai–décembre 1970) II." *Etudes africaines du CRISP*, no. 125 (20 March 1971).

————. "La R.D.C., du Congrès de la N'Sélé au nouveau mandat présidentiel (mai–deécembre 1970) I." *Etudes africaines du CRISP*, no. 124 (30 January 1971).

[————.] "Le Régime présidentiel au Zaire." *Etudes africaines du CRISP*, no. 144 (20 December 1972).

MacGaffey, Wyatt, "Revolution or Repression?: The View From Matadi." *Africa Report* 16 (January 1971): 18–20.

Mambenga [Mbandaka], (newspaper), 1972–1975.

Mazrui, Ali A. "The English Language and Political Consciousness in British Colonial Africa." *Journal of Modern African Studies* 4 (November 1966): 295–311.

Mercier, Paul. "Remarques sur la signification du 'trialisme' actuel en Afrique noire." *Cahiers internationaux de sociologie* 31 (1961): 61–80.

Merriam, Alan P. "Politics and Change in a Zairian Village." *Africa-Tervuren* 26 (1975): 18–22.

Miliband, Ralph. "Barnave: A Case of Bourgeois Class Consciousness." In *Aspects of History and Class Consciousness,* pp. 22–48. Edited by István Meszáros. London: Routledge and Kegan Paul, 1971.

[Mokolo wa Mpombo, Edouard.] "Poids socio-politique des ressortissants de l'Equateur à Kinshasa." *Courrier africain*, no. 84 (8 November 1968).

[————.] "La Province de l'Equateur: Présentation morphologique des institutions politiques 1960–1967." *Courrier africain*, no. 82–83 (30 October 1968).

Mudimbe, V. Y. "Les Intellectuels zairois." *Zaire-Afrique*, no. 88 (October 1974), pp. 451–463.

Mulambu Mvuluya. "Cultures obligatoires et colonisation dans l'ex-Congo belge." *Cahiers du CEDAF*, no. 6–7 (1974).

Mumbanza mwa Bawele. "Les Bangala du fleuve sont-ils apparentés aux Mongo?" *Zaire-Afrique*, no. 90 (December 1974), pp. 625–632.

————. "Y a-t-il des Bangala?: Origine et extension du terme." *Zaire-Afrique*, no. 78 (October 1973), pp. 471–483.

Nesson, C. "Ecole et promotion sociale au Sahara algérien: Les Elèves de première du lycée de Touggourt (1964–1970)." In *Maghreb & Sahara: Etudes géographiques offertes à Jean Despois*, pp. 289–306. Paris: Société de Géographie, 1973.

Nzongola-Ntalaja. "The Authenticity of Neocolonialism: Ideology and Class Struggles in Zaire." Paper presented at the African Studies Association meeting. Boston, 3–6 November 1976.

Nzongola, Georges N. "The Bourgeoisie and Revolution in the Congo." *Journal of Modern African Studies* 8 (December 1970): 511–530.

Parkin, Frank. "Strategies of Social Closure in Class Formation." In *The Social Analysis of Class Structure*, pp. 1–18. Edited by Frank Parkin. London: Tavistock Publications, 1974.

Peemans, Jean-Philippe. "The Social and Economic Development of Zaire since Independence: An Historical Outline." *African Affairs* 74 (April 1975): 148–179.

————. "Capital Accumulation in the Congo under Colonialism: The Role of the

State." In *Colonialism in Africa 1870–1960.* 5 vols. Vol. 4: *The Economics of Colonialism*, pp. 165–212. Edited by Peter Duignan and L. H. Gann. Cambridge: Cambridge University Press, 1975.

Poulantzas, Nicos. "Les Classes sociales." *L'Homme et la société,* no. 24–25 (April–September 1972), pp. 23–55.

Rivière, Claude, "Classes et stratifications sociales en Afrique noire." *Cahiers internationaux de sociologie* 59 (1975): 285–314.

Rosenau, James N. "Toward the Study of National-International Linkages." In *Linkage Politics: Essays on the Convergence of National and International Systems*, pp. 44–63. Edited by James N. Rosenau. New York: Free Press, 1969.

Saint Moulin, Léon de. "Histoire des villes du Zaire: Notions et perspectives fondamentales." *Etudes d'histoire africaine* 6 (1974): 137–167.

Salongo [Kinshasa], (newspaper), *1972–1975.*

Saul, John S. "The Unsteady State: Uganda, Obote and General Amin." *Review of African Political Economy*, no. 5 (January–April 1976), pp. 12–38.

Saul, John S., and Woods, Roger. "African Peasantries." In *Essays on the Political Economy of Africa*, pp. 406–416. Edited by Giovanni Arrighi and John S. Saul. New York and London: Monthly Review Press, 1973.

Schatzberg, Michael G. "Islands of Privilege: Small Cities in Africa and the Dynamics of Class Formation." Paper presented at the Conference on the Small City and Regional Community. Stevens Point, Wisconsin, 30–31 March 1978.

————. "The Chiefs of Upoto: Political Encapsulation and the Transformation of Tradition in Northwestern Zaire." Paper presented at the African Studies Association meeting. Houston, 2–5 November 1977.

Scott, James C. "Exploitation in Rurual Class Relations: A Victim's Perspective." *Comparative Politics* 7 (July 1975): 489–532.

Sklar, Richard L. "Political Science and National Integration—A Radical Approach." *Journal of Modern African Studies* 5 (May 1967): 1–11.

Southall, Aidan W. "Stratification in Africa." In *Essays in Comparative Social Stratification*, pp. 231–272. Edited by Leonard Plotnicov and Arthur Tuden. Pittsburgh: University of Pittsburgh Press, 1970.

Stone, Lawrence. "Prosopography." *Daedalus* 100 (Winter 1971): 46–79.

Stryker, Richard E. "Political and Administrative Linkages in the Ivory Coast." In *Ghana and the Ivory Coast: Perspectives on Modernization*, pp. 73–102. Edited by Philip Foster and Aristide R. Zolberg. Chicago: University of Chicago Press, 1971.

Tutashinda, N. "Les Mystifications de l' 'authenticité.' " *La Pensée*, no. 175 (June 1974), pp. 68–81.

Van Cauwenbergh, A. "Le Développement du commerce et de l'artisanat indigènes à Léopoldville." *Zaire* 10 (June 1956): 637–664.

Vansina, Jan. "Les Kuba et l'administration territoriale de 1919 à 1960." *Cultures et développement* 2 (1972): 275–325.

Verhaegen, Benoît. "Les Associations congolaises à Léopoldville et dans le Bas-Congo de 1944 à 1958." *Etudes africaines du CRISP*, no. 112–113 (1970).

————. "Présentation morphologique des nouvelles provinces." *Etudes congolaises* 4 (April 1963): 1–25.

Verheust, Thérèse. "L'Enseignement en République du Zaire." *Cahiers du CEDAF*, no. 1 (1974).

Vincent, Joan. "Room for Manoeuvre: The Political Role of Small Towns in East Africa." In *Colonialism and Change: Essays Presented to Lucy Mair*, pp. 115–144. Edited by Maxwell Owusu. The Hague, Paris: Mouton, 1975.

Wallerstein, Immanuel. "Class and Class Conflict in Contemporary Africa." *Canadian Journal of African Studies* 7 (1973): 375–380.

Willame, Jean-Claude. "Patriarchical Structures and Factional Politics: Toward an Understanding of the Dualist Society." *Cahiers d'études africaines* 12 (1973): 326–355.

———. "La Réunification des provinces du Congo." *Etudes congolaises* 9 (July–August 1966): 68–86.

Williams, M. L. "The Extent and Significance of the Nationalization of Foreign-Owned Assets in Developing Countries, 1956–1972." *Oxford Economic Papers, N.S.* 27 (July 1975): 260–273.

Wolfe, Alvin W. "The Dynamics of the Ngombe Segmentary System." In *Continuity and Change in African Cultures*, pp. 168–186. Edited by William R. Bascom and Melville J. Herskovits. Chicago and London: University of Chicago Press, 1959.

———. "The Institution of Demba Among the Ngonje Ngombe." *Zaire* 8 (October 1954): 843–856.

Young, M. Crawford. "Rebellion and the Congo." In *Rebellion in Black Africa*, pp. 209–245. Edited by Robert I. Rotberg. London, Oxford, New York: Oxford University Press, 1971.

———. "Congo and Uganda: A Comparative Assessment." *Cahiers économiques et sociaux* 5 (Ocotber 1967): 379–400.

Index

ABAKO, 41, 154
Abidjan, 181
Abumobazi, 112
Achebe, Chinua, 121
Acholi, 1
adultery, 69
"agents of order," 66. *See also* collectivity personnel
agriculture: acquisition process in, 136–40; obligatory cultivation, 75; and social mobility, 81; and tax payments, 75–81
Agriculture Ministry, 149
airports, checkpoints at, 124
Air Zaire, 9, 124
alcoholism: and administrative performance, 68–69; and crop evacuation, 77
allied actors, defined, 28
ANEZA. *See* Association Nationale des Entreprises Zairoises
Angolans, and bar trade, 90, 91
Anselin, M., 31
Anstey, Roger, 17
anthropology: and immediate history, 15; micropolitics in, 1
Arabs, security against, 4
Association Nationale des Entreprises Zairoises (ANEZA), 131, 132
Association of Women Merchants, Lisala, 91, 132
automobiles: and inspections, 102; as symbols of wealth, 50, 51, 129, 147
Azikiwe paradox, 13, 14, 32, 153, 161

Bailey, F. G., 64
Bakongo, and beer, 90
Balandier, George, 22, 25, 171
Bamania, 42
Bandundu Region, 90, 132, 150
Bangala District, 4, 9, 136
Bank of Zaire, 119
Banque du Peuple, 177
Bapoto, chieftaincies of, 4
Baptist Missionary Society, 4

barge transportation, 9
bars, owners of, wealth, 90. *See also* beer, political economy of
Basankusu, 35, 43
Bas-Zaire, 40, 41; colonial system in, 154; Negeba Sector, 21; and trade, 90, 91. *See also* Zaire, as a whole
beer, political economy of, 83ff., 146–47; consumption, 84–85, 87, 180; and decolonization, 182; development, 93–97; distribution, 86–91; funded projects, 96; management, 142–43; national/local perspectives, 83–86; price control, 91–93; and taxation, 83, 93–97, 184; trade, 142–44, 146; wholesaling, 133
Befale, 137
Belgians, 136, 176; and beer, 83; departure of, 14, 17; early settlements by, 4; and occupational status, 53; and personnel vacuum, 39; Scheutists, 9; and staffs, appreciation of, 35, 37, 38
Belgo-Congolaise community, 16
Bikoro, 137
Binga, 132; mercenaries in, 124; plantations of, 136, 137, 140; rally in, 164
Bisengimana, 140
Bloch, Marc, 33
Bo-Boliko, 119
Boende, 35, 36, 124, 137
Bokungu, 137
Bolikango, Jean, 105, 118
Bongandanga, Zone of, 38, 72, 102, 124, 133, 149, 150
Bosondjo, plantations, 137
bourgeoisie, 182; and administration, 17; and decolonization, 178–80; emergence of, 176, 177; and intellectuals, 19. *See also* class, socioeconomic
"Bourgeoisie and Revolution in the Congo, The" (Nzongola), 19
Bouvier, Paule, 16
Bralima brewery, 87, 88, 89, 92, 95
breweries. *See* beer, political economy of